T0360638

GARLAND STUDIES IN

ENTREPRENEURSHIP

edited by
STUART BRUCHEY
ALLAN NEVINS PROFESSOR EMERITUS
COLUMBIA UNIVERSITY

DOING BUSINESS IN MINORITY MARKETS

Black and Korean Entrepreneurs in Chicago's Ethnic Beauty Aids Industry

Robert Mark Silverman

Routledge
Taylor & Francis Group

NEW YORK AND LONDON

First published 2000 by Garland Publishing, Inc.

Published 2017 by Routledge
605 Third Avenue, New York, NY 10017
2 Park Square, Milton Park, Abingdon, Oxon OX14 4RN

Routledge is an imprint of the Taylor & Francis Group, an informa busines

Copyright © 2000 by Robert Mark Silverman

*Library of Congress Cataloging-in-Publication Data is available
from the Library of Congress.*

ISBN 13: 978-0-8153-3798-0 (hbk)

Contents

Acknowledgments

In the film *Zero Effect*, Daryl Zero's sidekick Steve Arlo tells us that there are no good guys in the world and there are no bad guys in the world, there are just guys. In the context of this study, art certainly imitates life. No definitive normative judgements can be made about the business people examined in the pages that follow. Mainly, they are people who confront their environment in very human ways while making decisions from a business perspective. In fact, one of the unique characteristics of this study is that beneath its theoretical blanket one just finds people. One of the oddities of the social sciences is that we often lose site of a study's focus, the lived world, and instead represent people as extreme characters who inhabit a fantasy world. Although there is less adventure in an examination of regular guys and gals in a regular world, there is much to be gained from an in-depth analysis of the complexities and contradictions of their social existence. From that premise, this study both began and ended.

It is only fitting that at this juncture I extend my gratitude to the people who influenced the writing of this book. In particular, I must express appreciation to the merchants, distributors and manufacturers on the South Side of Chicago who participated in this study, since it would not have been completed without their assistance. Special thanks also goes to Joan Moore, Greg Squires, Victor Greene, Joe Rodriguez and Kwang Chung Kim for their comments and critiques of early drafts of this study. Additional gratitude goes to Garland Publishing for providing the opportunity to publish this work. Of course, I must thank my parents for their contribution to this venture, the adoption of an Australian Shepherd named Mel. Finally, I give extensive credit to my wife, Kelly Patterson, for all the intangibles she brought to this project which ultimately led to its completion.

Robert Mark Silverman

Doing Business In Minority Markets

CHAPTER 1:

Introduction

THE INTERNAL COLONIAL PARADIGM

The invisible hand of the market cannot conceal color. This study contends that the economy is an extension of society's system of racial and ethnic stratification. The central argument of this study is that the internal colonial paradigm should be used as a guiding principle in the analysis of minority business development in minority markets. Through the use of this paradigm, the institutional constraints of doing business in a minority market can be identified. Elevating the analysis of minority business development to an institutional level serves academic and practical ends. It allows for a more holistic understanding of the relationship between institutional forces and individual economic action, and it allows public officials to draw from these insights in a way that informs sound public policy. Although many issues are discussed in this study, its focus is on forwarding an argument for the internal colonial framework to public discourse. To build support for this argument, a case study is presented that focuses on the role of race and ethnicity in a specific sector of the economy, the ethnic beauty aids industry in Chicago. Through this case study, issues that affect the structure of minority businesses and their relative competitiveness will be examined. This goal of this analysis is to highlight the economic mechanisms responsible for the maintenance and reproduction of internal colonialism within the context of minority markets.

The ethnic beauty aids industry was selected as the subject of this case study because it is embedded in the context of minority

1

markets, which entail high concentrations of minority entrepreneurs and consumers. Minority entrepreneurs enter minority markets to avoid racial barriers they perceive in the mainstream economy, and minority consumers find minority markets more accessible and responsive to their consumption needs. It should be kept in mind that minority markets are not separate and equal to those found in the mainstream economy. They exist in poor communities, where physical and economic conditions deteriorate due to a lack of investment by mainstream institutions. In addition, minority markets are not naturally occurring markets, since they form in response to racial discrimination found in mainstream society. For these reasons, this study goes beyond a simple discussion of black and Korean entrepreneurs in the ethnic beauty aids industry. It focuses on the institutional environment that these entrepreneurs are embedded in, and how they respond to it through agency.

The actions of black and Korean entrepreneurs in minority markets are shaped by racial and ethnic stratification in society. Because of this, several distinctions are made. For instance, Korean entrepreneurs fill a middleman role in minority markets, while black entrepreneurs do not. This distinction, concerning the economic role of blacks and Koreans in minority markets, is intimately linked to issues of racial and ethnic stratification in mainstream society. Discernable economic roles stem from institutional arrangements in a society, and in contemporary America the acute subordination of blacks limits the scope of minority entrepreneurship. Several distinct economic roles have emerged within the parameters of the system of racial and ethnic stratification in America. This type of segmentation in the economy is illustrated in this case study of the ethnic beauty aids industry. The characteristics of this industry present a unique opportunity to examine minority entrepreneurship and to better understand the mechanism that produce racial and ethnic inequality in contemporary America.

In order to grasp the role of racial and ethnic stratification in the economy, several theoretical constructs need to be introduced. The following theoretical overview identifies a number of concepts central to this study. Five themes will be outlined in this discussion. First, the concept of internal colonialism is developed to illustrate how minority markets are shaped by racial imperatives in mainstream society. Second, the role of middleman minorities in internal colonial settings is discussed to highlight their social control function. Third, sojourning is identified as a defining characteristic of middleman minorities, and the relevance of sojourning in contemporary minority markets is discussed. Fourth, the role of class and ethnic resources in shaping minority entrepreneurship is examined. Fifth, several distinctions are made concerning the unique characteristics of black entrepreneurship in minority markets.

THEORETICAL OVERVIEW

Internal Colonialism and Minority Markets

To obtain an understanding of how minority markets operate we must begin with a discussion of internal colonialism. This study suggests that minority markets emerge in a neo-colonial context which forms the basis of racial and ethnic stratification in American society. This argument is an extension of early writings on colonialism highlighting the effect of dominant groups on subordinate groups.[1] Arguments concerning internal colonialism borrow from Shibutani and Kwan's discussion of colonialism and their conceptualization of "color lines."[2] According to these scholars, cleavages that emerge during periods of colonization are institutionalized in a society's system of ethnic stratification. This results in the establishment of racial and ethnic distinctions, or "color lines," which facilitate the maintenance of colonial relations. Shibutani and Kwan discuss a number of outcomes that can emerge from colonialism. However the process by which the colonization of one society by another results in the institutionalization of colonial relations through the development of color lines is seen as a constant.

Racial and ethnic stratification function to stabilize social relations to some degree in all societies. However, in societies with a history of colonialism, where dominant and subordinate roles have been closely associated with race and ethnicity, such stratification becomes more determinant. In such societies, elaborate systems of social relations develop that are sensitive to racial and ethnic cues. For instance, Memmi enters into an extensive discussion of how social relations are shaped by colonial conditions, and the consequences that these conditions have for the interpretation of race and ethnicity.[3] In a similar vein, Fanon describes the psychological ramifications that colonization has on racial and ethnic groups in terms of self-image and identity.[4] The effects of colonialism on colonized groups are far- reaching. Members of colonized groups are socialized by dominant institutions, causing them to internalize many of the stereotypes which rationalize their subordination. When the psychological effects of colonialism are combined with the economic and political subordination that it entails, the subordination of colonized groups becomes complete. For a colonized group, the scope of agency within a colonial setting is severely limited by outside institutions, and the scope of agency beyond a colonial setting is virtually nonexistent.

These ideas are central to the concept of internal colonialism that developed in reference to America's minority communities. European colonialism shaped social relations in America, and the contemporary system of racial and ethnic stratification developed in response to this colonial heritage. However, scholars have been hesitant to apply arguments centering on colonialism to issues of race and ethnicity in the United States. The discussion of the role of colonialism in shaping racial and ethnic stratification in American has been a controversial issue among scholars, despite the fact that the social experiences of Native Americans, Latinos, blacks and other groups have been shaped by a variant form of colonialism. A concerted effort to discuss the conditions of minority groups in America with reference to colonialism emerged briefly during the contemporary period, before it dissipated in the early 1970's. However, a number of important adaptations of earlier colonial arguments were applied to the American context in the discussion of internal colonialism.

Some of the most important theoretical adaptations of arguments concerning colonialism were made in reference to American blacks. Together this material defines the concept of internal colonialism in the United States.[5] In the broadest sense, these arguments focus on how blacks were forced to enter America as slaves, and how once in America they were stripped of their culture and identity while being forced to adopt mainstream values that proscribed their subordination. It is argued that these historically based conditions facilitated continued political and bureaucratic intervention in the black community, and that this intervention was affected by persistent racism and racial discrimination in the dominant society. The result of these pressures, which emanate from the mainstream society, was that blacks remained segregated in internal colonies. Blauner argued that these conditions were reflected in the nature of social relations between dominant institutions and subordinate groups in society, illustrating this with case studies focusing on police-community relations in minority neighborhoods, the institutional sources of "ghetto revolts," and racial conflict in the university.[6]

Other scholars applied the concept of internal colonialism to the political economy of the black community, which in many respects is synonymous with the concept of minority markets employed in this study. Tabb stressed that:

> The economic relations of the ghetto to white America closely parallel those between third-world nations and the industrially advanced countries. The ghetto also has a relatively low per-capita income and a high birth rate. Its residents are for the most part unskilled. Businesses lack capital and managerial know-how. Local markets are limited. The incidence of credit default is high. Little saving takes place and what is saved is usually not invested locally. Goods and services tend to be "imported" for the most part, only the simplest and most labor intensive being produced locally. The ghetto is dependent on one basic export - its unskilled labor power. Aggregate demand for this export does not increase to match the growth of the ghetto labor force, and unemployment is prevalent. As consumer goods are advertised twenty-four hours a day on radio and television, ghetto residents are constantly reminded of the availability of goods and services which they cannot afford to buy. Welfare payments and other transfers are needed to help pay for the ghetto's requirements. Local businesses are owned in large numbers, by non residents, many of whom are white. Important jobs in the local public economy (teachers, policemen, and postmen) are held by white outsiders. The black ghetto, then, is in many ways in a position similar to that of the typical underdeveloped nation.[7]

Many of these issues were rearticulated by others during the 1970's, and in more contemporary critiques of economic conditions in the black community.[8] In fact, with the exception of an increasingly visible presence of non-white immigrant entrepreneurs and modest gains in public sector employment among blacks, the conditions described above persist in minority markets.

Tabb points out that the ghetto is heavily dependent on resources from outside of the black community in the form of goods, services, jobs and public aid. But, he also recognizes that, "in the absence of intergovernmental transfers, things may still be worse for the residents of these areas."[9] In a real sense, the issue of welfare dependence in the context of internal colonialism is parallel to that of economic dependence in the context of colonialism. This is the case since welfare payments preserve the social order. Bonacich and Light make this point when they explain how "welfare curbs the reserve army of the unemployed," reducing the chances that wages in the mainstream economy would decline if job seekers flooded in from internal colonies.[10] Welfare also reduces the chances of mass uprisings, since it brings temporary economic relief to communities that suffer from a dearth of capital. Despite the efficiency of welfare and other forms of dependence in maintaining social order in poor communities, there are areas where dominant institutions are unable to maintain social equilibrium.

The Role of Middleman Minorities in Internal Colonies

Many of the commercial functions necessary for the maintenance of internal colonialism cannot be met by mainstream institutions. Because of this, there is a need for third parties to assume an economic role in minority markets. This role is often referred to as a middleman minority role. A number of authors have discussed middleman groups and the role they fill in the economy.[11] However, the general characteristics associated with middleman minorities have their foundation in Weber's analysis of "pariah people" and "pariah capitalism," and in Simmel's examination of "the stranger."[12] As the terms imply, middleman minorities are perceived as outsiders who serve as go-betweens for dominant and subordinate groups in society. The middleman role is facilitated by outsider status, which initially makes middleman minorities appear impartial to the dominant-subordinate relationship that exists in society. However, the initial perception of impartiality gives middleman minorities a false sense of security, since the material benefits that they accrue from their economic role makes dominant and subordinate groups in society resent them.

Because of the existence of resentment, middleman minorities function as mediators in the economy and they fill an additional role. They buffer mainstream institutions from the criticisms of subordinated groups. Blalock and Zenner attributes this social outcome to two characteristics of middleman minorities: they tend to be concentrated in peripheral areas of the economy where they have a relatively high degree of economic influence, and they are politically detached from mainstream institutions because of their outsider status.[13] These conditions contribute to the stigmatization of middleman minorities in both mainstream and internal colonial settings. Blalock stresses that the existence of an economic role for middleman groups grows out of social polarization, and it remains intact as long as mainstream institutions continue to benefit from existing social inequalities.[14] Because of this role, Blalock identifies middleman minorities as "natural scapegoats" serving "as a buffer which can often absorb any major strains the system may undergo short of complete rebellion by the subordinate group.[15]

These points are central to understanding the role of middleman minorities in internal colonies. First, their economic role is an outgrowth of institutional structures in mainstream society that generate inequality. Second, their role as natural scapegoats buffers mainstream institutions from social conflict. Together, these two roles serve an important social control function, which allows economic and social conflict to transpire an alteration in the system of ethnic stratification. In addition, the middleman minority role can be conceptualized as a somewhat permanent fixture of internal colonialism, since it is generated by forces in mainstream society. The precarious situation that the economic role of middleman minorities entails virtually ensures that middleman minorities will remain alienated in society. Middleman minorities maintain an outsider status in internal colonies, they are the target of resentment in both mainstream and internal colonial settings, and they periodically become scapegoats for inequality in society. Because they are embedded in an institutional context that they find foreign, middleman minorities have a limited ability to control the environmental constraints that they face. One of their few forms of agency is expressed in their attempt to minimize their exposure to polarized groups in society through sojourning.

Sojourning and Middleman Minorities

Sojourning is characteristic of middleman minorities. Recently, this point has been disputed by scholars, particularly in the case of contemporary Korean middleman minorities.[16] However, the following discussion offers clarification on this point. In order to understand why sojourning is intimately linked to the economic role of middleman minorities, it is useful to review the literature on sojourning behavior. Siu undertook the first significant analysis of sojourning behavior.[17] He offers the following description of the sojourner:

> The "sojourner" is treated as a deviant type of the sociological form of the "stranger," one who clings to the cultural heritage of his own ethnic group and tends to live in isolation, hindering his assimilation to the society in which he resides, often for many years. The sojourn is conceived by the sojourner as a "job" which is to be finished in the shortest possible time.[18]

This definition describes an adaptive strategy where an individual enters an economic setting with the intention of accumulating capital and exiting in the shortest possible time. It also reflects the perception that a given economic setting is not considered a desirable place for permanent settlement, but rather it is seen as a means to ultimately settling in the location where the sojourner strives to be.

These characteristics of sojourning are elaborated upon by Lee.[19] She enters into an extensive discussion of sojourning behavior among the Chinese in America, illustrating Siu's points and stressing that, "Chinese sojourners maintain a psychological and social separateness from the larger society and insulate themselves against the full impact of the dominant society's values, norms, attitudes, and behavior patterns."[20] From this perspective sojourning can be viewed not simply as economic opportunism, but as a defensive form of agency exercised by individuals or groups who fill an economic role in a volatile social environment. The most important characteristic of sojourning is the intention of the sojourner to remain in a given economic setting temporarily, and the resistance to establish any roots to that setting. In fact, it is not necessary for a sojourner to have any realistic intention to return to his or her nation of origin; the minimum requirement is the intention to leave the place of sojourning, and not to settle there permanently.

Sway illustrates this point well in her discussion of sojourning by both Jews and Gypsies.[21] She points out that although Jews practice sojourning behavior, they have demonstrated ambivalence towards a return to their homeland. In the case of Gypsies, the practice of sojourning is well documented, despite their status as a wandering people with no definitive homeland. Sway's perspective concerning sojourning is closely aligned with Bonacich's.[22] She points out that sojourners maintain a mental image of their ancestral homeland as, "somewhere to go if things get too bad in the host country."[23] In this light, references made to ones homeland are actually a defensive reaction to host hostility experienced by middleman groups, and not a true desire to return to their country of origin. This is a reflection of a sojourner's perception of a given location as a place for transitional economic activity. Which leads one to conclude that a sojourner's final resting place, upon the completion of a particular economic endeavor, is not of primary importance. The only element critical to sojourning is the initial intention to leave.

Bonacich makes another important point about sojourning. She identifies it as a practice that takes place among middleman minorities in a colonial setting.[24] The wedding of sojourning behavior, the middleman minority role, and a colonial setting is critical to this study. It is this conceptualization of sojourning that illuminates an important characteristic of Korean entrepreneurship in minority markets. Minority markets are embedded in internal colonies, and Korean merchants enter these markets as sojourners. Kim and Hurh illuminate this point when they discuss the manner in which Korean entrepreneurs envision their businesses on the South Side of Chicago as stepping stones to entry in the mainstream economy.[25] Because minority markets are part of internal colonies, the possibility for sojourning among Korean middlemen emerges. The intention among Korean merchants to eventually cease doing business in minority markets is further evidence of their sojourning behavior, regardless of whether they plan to eventually move into the mainstream American economy or back to Korea.

The Role of Class and Ethnic Resources in Minority Markets

In addition to sojourning, there are other aspects of middleman entrepreneurship that have been widely discussed in the literature. Perhaps the most important involves the role of class and ethnic resources. Unfortunately, there are almost as many definitions of class and ethnic resources as there are theorists. Without going into an elaborate taxonomy, some of the more focused discussions of class and ethnic resources will be identified in order to operationalized these concepts in a manner relevant to this study. Yoon's discussion of the distinction between class and ethnic resources is one of the more succinct in contemporary scholarship.[26] He clearly conceptualizes ethnic resources as those resources and forms of aid coming from co-ethnics. According to Yoon, "Ethnic resources may be material (e.g. financial aid), informational (e.g. business advice), or experiential (e.g. job training)."[27] In addition, ethnic resources entail support from ethnic customers, ethnic employees, ethnic suppliers, the ethnic media and ethnic organizations. With this definition, Yoon is able to draw a clear distinction between ethnic and class resources. Yoon describes class resources as those that are derived from private property, wealth, and investments in human capital. He points out that, "Class resources are available only to a segment of an ethnic group whose social and economic position in society enabled them to invest in human capital or to be endowed with these resources through their parents."[28]

Yoon acknowledges that in some respects class and ethnic resources seem to overlap, however he stresses that the theoretical distinction is important for an analysis of entrepreneurship. Light and Bonacich addressed this issues as well, pointing out that, "Although hard to differentiate at the margins, class and ethnic resources are different phenomena, each of which is capable of promoting entrepreneurship."[29] In the case of middleman entrepreneurs, there is evidence of both class and ethnic resources influencing entrepreneurship. For instance, Light points out that both types of resources have played a role in the development of Korean entrepreneurship in the contemporary period.[30] He identifies a litany of ethnic resources that have promoted Korean entrepreneurship: "rotating credit associations," "nepotistic trade guilds," "family firms," "ethnic homogeneity of business sales," and other ethnically linked factors such as "immigrant motivation and values."[31] However, Light acknowledges that class resources influence entrepreneurship.

Light is well known for his argument in *Ethnic Enterprise in America*, where he attributes differential levels of ethnic solidarity to account for higher rates of entrepreneurship among Asians than blacks.[32] However in a later work, Light points out that in addition to ethnic resources, class resources effect the rate of Korean entrepreneurship. This point is expressed clearly in the following comment:

> The contrast of Korean and Mexican or Black in Los Angeles is misleading. The displaced peasantry of Mexico and the American South are also disadvantaged in the labor force, but these rural migrants brought with them no class resources of capital or higher education to offset the disadvantage. Hence, it is no surprise that Mexican and Black people in Los Angeles have not established in proportion to their numbers as many businesses as have college-educated Koreans.[33]

The dual effect of ethnic and class resources raises important questions concerning the relative significance of each to entrepreneurship, as well as questions concerning the conditions under which one type of resources would be more important to successful entrepreneurship than the other.

Under certain conditions minority entrepreneurs may desire to mobilize ethnic resources, while under others they may mobilize class resources. This decision might bear on the size of a particular enterprise, or the characteristics of the market and the nature of competition. The point is, since both class and ethnic resources affect economic outcomes for middleman minorities, situations will arise where the mobilization of one type of resource is more advantageous than the mobilization of another. Yoon attempts to address these issues in the following comment:

> Two theoretical positions are taken on the utilization patterns of ethnic and class resources. The first position is that ethnic resources and class resources are in a substitutive relationship in the sense that, at a point in time, the more class resources one possesses, the less likely he or she is to depend on ethnic resources. The second position is that ethnic resources and class resources are in a substitutive relationship in the sense that as one's business grows, ethnic resources become irrelevant or insufficient and that class resources become more important.[34]

These points are important to this study for several reasons. They illustrate that the decision to mobilize class and ethnic resources can be influenced by a variety of social and economic factors. In the case of Korean middlemen, although the mobilization of ethnic resources is considered important to their entrepreneurial success, intensified competition from co-ethnics may elevate the importance of class resource for successful entrepreneurship. In fact, the conditions under which class and ethnic resources are substituted for one and other among Korean middlemen is a focus of this study.

This issue is also important when black entrepreneurs are discussed in this study. Black entrepreneurs have fewer class resources at their disposal that other entrepreneurial groups in society.[35] Although this disadvantage is well established, there is disagreement concerning the ability of black entrepreneurs to mobilize ethnic resources. For instance, Light makes several references to the lack of ethnic solidarity among blacks, identifying it as a factor contributing to failed entrepreneurship.[36] However, this is contradicted by Butler, who identifies a tradition of mutual aid and self-help in the black community which facilitates entrepreneurship.[37] His study indicates that black entrepreneurs have a history of mobilizing ethnic resources in response to their limited access to class resources. From this perspective, limited class resources available to black entrepreneurs leads to the cultivation of ethnic resources and a group economy. In fact, the unique role of ethnic resources in the black community can be viewed as a byproduct of internal colonialism.

This is the case since middleman entrepreneurs enter the black community with relatively higher levels of class resources than black entrepreneurs possess. This puts middleman minorities in a position where they can substitute class and ethnic resources to optimize the economic efficiency of their businesses, while black entrepreneurs must rely more heavily on ethnic resources. The inequality in class resources that exists between middleman and black entrepreneurs is exaggerated by the dependent relationship existing between minority markets and mainstream institutions. This relationship curtails the development of class resources in the black community. This institutional context creates a situation where better capitalized middleman minorities can enter minority markets for the purposes of sojourning, while the accumulation of wealth among blacks remains stagnant.

Black Entrepreneurs and the Economic Detour

In order to understand why black entrepreneurs find it difficult to accumulate capital and wealth, it is necessary to examine the institutional constraints that they confront. Black entrepreneurs rarely have full access to mainstream markets. In part, this results from capital constraints; however, at a more fundamental level the economic barriers they face are an outgrowth of racial discrimination in society. In fact, a number of scholars have discussed the plight of black entrepreneurship over the years.[38] General issues such as the limited access to capital, racism, and resulting constraints on the ability to compete with large scale business in the mainstream economy have truncated black entrepreneurship, and confined it to minority markets.

This process is discussed by Stuart, and later by Butler, with the concept of "an economic detour."[39] Stuart argues that during de jure legal segregation, black entrepreneurs followed an economic detour .[40] Blacks built businesses in minority markets, since white customers were hesitant to buy from black-owner businesses. Stuart stresses that since the average black business owner is undercapitalized and faces racism, "he must choose those lines of commerce and personal services that white competitors have either not elected to invade and nearly monopolize, or the very nature of which tend to make less effective the force of white competition and peculiar racial restrictions."[41] The concept of an economic detour is further developed by Butler, who points out that an economic detour entails government action, or inaction, that allows segregation to interfere with the normal operation of the marketplace.[42] In this discussion, Butler emphasizes that although other entrepreneurial groups have faced discrimination, black Americans have been the targets of racism in an institutional context, and this has placed them at a greater disadvantage in the economy.[43] Because the black experience with racism is unique in American society, black entrepreneurship has taken its own form.

Butler draws a clear distinction between the character of black entrepreneurship and immigrant entrepreneurship.[44] While other ethnic groups are free to operate in the larger economy, he stresses that blacks are not. In fact, he points out that the classic middleman minority serves more than its own community, while black entrepreneurs experience discrimination in the marketplace that prevents them from attracting a non-black clientele to their businesses. Although de jure legal segregation is no longer in place, black entrepreneurs are still stigmatized in society and their economic opportunities continue to be limited due to racism. For these reasons, black entrepreneurs do not fill a middleman role in minority markets. Instead, they have become an intricate component of a group economy in the black community. However, this group economy is not the same as the "ethnic enclave economies" identified by Portes, Manning and Zhou.[45]

The group economy in the black community differs from ethnic enclave economies along several important dimensions. Portes, Manning and Zhou describe ethnic enclave economies as settings where immigrants can obtain higher levels of social and economic mobility than in the mainstream economy.[46] As a result, ethnic enclave economies entail dual benefits, they offer immigrants higher levels of economic mobility than the mainstream economy, and they serve a social function as ethnic havens. Unlike an ethnic enclave economy, which has a dual economic and social function, the group economy in the black community serves primarily a social function. The group economy in the black community also creates a safe haven for blacks, buffering them from racism in mainstream institutions. However, blacks accrue few economic benefits from participation in the group economy that exists in minority markets.Wong makes this point clear, stating that black entrepreneurs see business ownership as "an end in itself," since the black entrepreneur's "principal motive is the desire to be his own boss - not profit making. Indeed, after overhead, his 'profits' are typically no more than prior working wages in the secondary labor market."[47]

Despite limited economic benefits, blacks receive important social benefits from the group economy in the black community. Entrepreneurship is a source of social autonomy from mainstream institutions for blacks. Wong points out that for black entrepreneurs, "small business enterprises were alternatives to the caste-like dual labor market in America which separates white and non-white."[48] Although minority markets entail the constraints of an internal colonial setting, black entrepreneurship in these markets represents a form of agency. In fact, the social meaning of black entrepreneurship has become an important rallying point for social change in the black community. For instance, the "doctrine of the double-duty dollar," which instructs black consumers to buy from black businesses has been articulated by black leaders since the early 1900's.[49] Black entrepreneurship is an institution in the black community that facilitates the mobilization and development of ethnic resources.

In this light, this examination of black and Korean entrepreneurship in minority markets is more expansive than previous research, which has focused on discussing how Koreans succeed in business and why blacks do not. Often, these explanations lead to a discussion of assumed cultural deficiencies of black entrepreneurs, without any coherent examination of black business. This study focuses on the role of class and ethnic resources for black and Korean entrepreneurs, without losing sight of the internal colonial structure in which they do business. By doing this, many of the pitfalls of prior studies are avoided. The result is a truer representation of constraints and agency in minority markets. However, in order to undertake this study a number of issues concerning research design had to be addressed and developed to ensure that its findings reflect general social processes. A great deal of care and reflection was applied to each step of the research process with this issue in mind. The next section of this chapter will be dedicated to a detailed discussion of the natural history of the methodology developed for this study, in order to identify the techniques and controls applied during the research process.

NATURAL HISTORY OF THE METHODOLOGY

Origins of the Research Question

In retrospect, this study began on April 29, 1992. On that date, I turned on the television in a my apartment in Tallahassee, Florida to get information about what was happening at home in Los Angeles. This was the day that the police were found "not guilty" for the beating of Rodney King, and subsequent rioting took place in several communities in Los Angeles. What I found most alarming about that day was the disparity that existed between the reporting of these events on television, and the interpretation of the same events conveyed to me over the telephone by my friends and relatives in Los Angeles. In fact, the concerns and impressions of many of the blacks, Koreans and whites who I spoke to in Los Angeles on that day, and in the days following the riots, seemed to escape the pundits. The basic issues and questions that grew out of that experience stayed with me, and in many ways influenced what would later become my dissertation.

In the summer of 1994, I found myself in an equally unsettling dilemma. I had just passed my preliminary examination for my doctoral degree in the Urban Studies Program at the University of Wisconsin - Milwaukee, but had no idea what my dissertation topic would be. One Saturday afternoon, in an act of sheer avoidance, I decided to drive my future wife to a beauty supply store in Milwaukee's black community. This trip was necessary since she needed to purchase some specialized beauty supplies that larger chain stores in our neighborhood did not carry. When we got there, I noticed that aside from myself there were no white faces in the store. The clientele was black, and the people who ran the store were Korean. This was a very familiar environment to me, since I had grown up with Korean friends whose parents had owned similar stores in Los Angeles. After looking around the store, another thing caught my attention. A large proportion of the merchandise that was for sale in this store appeared to be made by black-owned companies. So, I left that store with a number of new questions concerning the relationship between black and Korean businesses, and a few weeks later I decided to turn these questions into a dissertation.

Of course, that was only the beginning of a long process of conceptualizing this research and developing a methodology. In essence, this dissertation has always been a community study, although the actual research site was selected after the basic research questions had been identified. The research site for this study was established in the fall of 1994, after a number of theoretical and empirical issues had been considered, although many of the decisions about the research site were pragmatic ones. In some respects, Whyte's experience in selecting a research site for his community study, *Street Corner Society*, was similar to my own.[50] Whyte pointed out that his selection of a research site was not entirely informed by scholarship, "I made my choice on very unscientific grounds: Cornerville best fitted my picture of what a slum district should look like."[51] In fact, the balancing of methodological and pragmatic considerations is something that all ethnographers struggle with, and resolve. Yet, the end result of this exercise is a heightened sensitivity to research design.

A number of issues surrounded the decision to implement this study on the South Side of Chicago. The most important issues was sample size. One of the main reasons that the South Side of

Chicago was selected as the site for this research was because it contained the largest accessible concentration of black and Korean businesses in the ethnic beauty aids industry. This study called for a research site where both black and Korean entrepreneurs participate in the ethnic beauty aids industry, and a sizable population of each group was found in Chicago. Other locations were considered for this study, but they were not deemed appropriate since they either lacked an agglomeration of black and Korean businesses comparable to Chicago's, or they were inaccessible due to their geographic location. For example, Milwaukee was initially considered as a research site for this study, but its population of black and Korean businesses was not large enough for a detailed study of inter-ethnic business networks. There were sites outside of Chicago that met this criteria, but, they were located in regions of the country that were logistically inaccessible.

The South Side of Chicago had additional characteristics that made it an appropriate research site for this study. The site is historically significant. For example, Chicago has a rich history of black business development, particularly in the ethnic beauty aids industry, and a number of ethnic groups have pursued entrepreneurship in Chicago's minority markets over the years. In fact, the historical significance of the city added additional dimension to this study that would have been lacking in other locations. This facilitated the collection of archival data that is used to establish a historical foundation for some of this study's arguments and conclusions. Of course, there were also pragmatic issues that made the South Side of Chicago an appropriate setting for this study. The issue of proximity has been identified. This was an important consideration in the selection of the research site, since Chicago was close to the University of Wisconsin-Milwaukee, where my doctoral program and faculty are housed. The issue of proximity was also inherently linked to the availability of financial resources for this study, since there was no external source of funding for this research. This had a substantial effect on decisions concerning the scope of this study, and the rationing of my personal resources.

Nevertheless, the lack of financial support was not a hinderance to the development of grounded theory along the lines discussed by Glaser and Strauss.[52] Since this was essentially a one person project, I had intimate knowledge of all aspects of the research process. As a result, a holistic view of the research questions was developed through some of the more mundane aspects of the study, such as developing the research instruments, planning the field work, transcribing the interviews, and the initial coding and analysis of the data. In a larger study, where some of these functions would have been delegated to assistants, the ability to develop a holistic view, and as a result generate grounded theory, might have been somewhat hampered.

With that said, there were also a number of opportunities available to receive feedback on the data as it was being collected. For instance, transcripts from the interviews were circulated to members of my dissertation committee at regular intervals, and a great deal of discussion of emergent themes took place with them during the research process. One of the more useful tools during this process was electronic mail, since it allowed for ideas to be exchanged and recorded throughout the research. In fact, correspondences via electronic mail became important additions to my field notes and methodological notes as the study progressed. Although some of these tools and collaborations emerged naturally during the research process, the bulk of the research was the product of careful planning and implementation. One of the critical stages of this study involved the design of research instruments, where several methodological consideration were addressed.

Instrument Design and Pretests

The primary issue that affected decisions concerning instrumentation in this study was sample size. In fact, this matter was the topic of discussion throughout the research process. Sample size was an issue from the inception of this study, since the industry being studied is small and there were concerns about gaining access to the research site. In addition to sample size, there were concerns about the impact of time constraints on data collection. This was the case since the informants in this study were business owners who are unable to commit substantial blocks of time to an interview. For these reasons, instrumentation focused on developing mechanisms that would incorporate as many informants as possible into the study, and that would minimize the requisite time commitment for participants. To this end, dual research instruments were adopted. The primary research instrument was a formal interview guide. This was complemented by the secondary research instrument, a drop-off survey.[53]

The research instruments focused on a core set of questions which related to the theoretical issues under examination. In particular, the research instruments focused on examining issues concerning the business goals of middleman and black entrepreneurs, the business networks they had access to, the role of race in their businesses, and the attitudes that middleman and black entrepreneurs held about black consumers and the black community. Examples of these instruments are found in the appendices of this study. The sampling strategies used in conjunction with the research instruments, and the characteristics of the middleman and black entrepreneurs who were interviewed and surveyed, are discussed in later sections of this methodology. However, before moving on to these topics, further discussion of the role of using both the interview guide as a primary research instrument and the drop-off survey as a secondary research instrument is necessary.

The adoption of an ethnographic data collection strategy based on dual instrumentation served many purposes. First, if an informant refused to commit to a formal interview, the option of completing a brief survey was available. Second, upon the completion of an interview, informants were given surveys to return at a later date. The survey was used to check for consistency in the interview, and as a mechanism to maintain contact with the informant in the event that additional information was desired. Interestingly, although the survey and interview were designed to protect the anonymity of informants, many circulated business cards at the completion of an interview, or attached them to the survey with invitations to contact them with future questions. In many ways, research instruments were developed to accommodate the informants, and create opportunities the maximize data collection within the constraints of the research setting. Dual instrumentation allowed for data to be collected immediately during an interview, and incrementally through the survey and the informal contact that it generated.

The nature of this study also demanded that the research instruments be concise and flexible. I anticipated that informants would only be available for short periods of time, since they were involved in the operation of businesses. As a result, the interview was designed to be administered in less than one hour, and the survey was designed to take five minutes. Of course, in some instances interviews went beyond one hour, but the placement of questions and themes in the text of the interview guides allowed for the acceleration of interviews when informants became anxious to resume their work. This emphasis on remaining nonintrusive helped facilitate rapport with informants, since they were reassured that the interview would not interfere with their daily routine. The ability to administer the interview within the general time frame that was promised also made informants more willing to offer additional information informally, and to supply me with the names of other business owners to contact for interviews.

In addition to being concise, the research instruments were flexible. From their inception, the research instruments included a general set of questions about the nature of doing business in the ethnic beauty aids industry that could easily be adapted for different groups of informants. For example, the research instruments had to be malleable with respect to the informants' race or ethnicity. They also had to be adjustable to the relative position an informant held in the ethnic beauty aids industry, for instance, retailer, distributor or manufacturer. So a core set of questions was maintained throughout the study, with slight adaptations depending on the characteristics of the informants. This flexibility was an important attribute of the research instruments, since it allowed for additional types of informants to be added to the study as they emerged during the course of the research. For example, this study began as an examination of black manufacturers and Korean retailers, but other important groups such as ethnic beauty aids distributors and black retailers became more relevant to the research during the course of the study. The planned flexibility of the research instruments allowed for these groups to be incorporated into the study.

A great deal of care went into the development of the research instruments in order to address as many contingencies as possible before the actual field work began. Several drafts of the interview guide and survey were generated in collaboration with my dissertation committee. However, this was only the first step in the development of the research instruments. In response to concerns about sample size, the prototypes of the interview guides and surveys were tested outside of the research setting. The interview guide was pretested with a Korean store owner in Milwaukee, and the survey was pretested with both a Korean store owner in Milwaukee and a black manufacturer in North Carolina. The pretests of the prototypes for the interview guide and survey were valuable for a number of reasons. They exposed areas of the research instruments that needed modification, and they also spurred the development of several techniques that would improve my chances of identifying informants and gaining access to the research setting.

Identifying Informants and Gaining Access

The validity of this study is strongly influenced by how well I was able to locate informants. This step in the research process required that I address several pitfalls. One of the obstacles that was overcome during this step of the research was the absence of a comprehensive list of businesses in the ethnic beauty aids industry. The lack of a comprehensive list of businesses was further complicated by the rate of business failure and changes in ownership in this industry. Because of these issues, numerous sources were used to identify businesses. One of the more important sources were local business organizations, particularly organizations in the black and Korean communities. These organizations were extremely helpful in supplying the names of businesses, and in allowing me to use them as references to gain access to the research site. Another source were businesses directories published by ethnic organizations, such as the *Chicago Black Pages* and the *Chicago Korean Business Directory*. Through discussions with other scholars, I found that these two types of sources were the most widely used in studies of this nature. However, a number of other sources were also used, which helped to ensure that a wide range of businesses were identified for this study.

In some instances, discussions with other scholars working in Chicago led to the identification of informants. However, some less conventional techniques were also employed. One of these was archival material. On occasion, the names of business owners and individuals to contact were found in old newspaper clippings. These sources often led to interviews or other referrals. A number of businesses were also identified through respondents, who not only recommended that I interview some of their acquaintances, but in some cases personally introduced me. In other instances, informants identified the names of their competitors inadvertently during interviews. In fact, some of the sources of business names were truly unique. Religious organizations serve as one example. I received several names of business owners while sitting in the cafeteria of a Buddhist temple in Chicago. However, one of the most important ways in which businesses were identified for this study was by simply walking through the various minority markets in Chicago.

This particular strategy, although valuable, entailed several pitfalls. Identifying stores by walking through business districts on the South Side of Chicago led to a number of questions concerning how to initiate contact with business owners. A small number of attempts were made early in the research process to walk into stores and solicit interviews from the owners. However, this proved to be a very ineffective technique. In some cases there were language barriers, in others the store owners were concerned about my motives and identity. As a result, two strategies emerged that established a certain degree of legitimacy for me as a researcher in the eyes of business owners. The first strategy involved the preparation of an advance letter that briefly identified the purpose of my research. The most important aspect of the advance letter was that it was written on stationery from the Urban Studies Program at the University of Wisconsin - Milwaukee. In fact, close to 90 percent of the businesses that were contacted for interviews received advance letters, and they produced roughly 75 percent of the informants who were interviewed in this study.

The other strategy that emerged involved the aid of gatekeepers. In one case, this assistance came from a member of my dissertation committee, Professor Kwang Chung Kim. In some instances, walking into Korean businesses and speaking to the owner was impeded by language barriers. In this respect, Professor Kim served as a translator. However, he had also interviewed some of the Korean merchants on the South Side of Chicago in the past, and he was able to facilitate introductions with these individuals. In this respect, Professor Kim became an important gatekeeper in the Korean community. Gatekeepers played an important role in the black community as well. Interestingly, a Jewish distributor of ethnic beauty aids provided me with one of my initial contacts with a black business owners. Because the black business community is considerably smaller than the Korean business community, acknowledging that I had spoken to this black entrepreneur helped to establish my credibility among others. In fact, towards the end of the study, I began to suspect that black informants had some knowledge of my research through informal networks. Regardless, the assistance of gatekeepers was important for gaining access to

Korean businesses due to language barriers, while it was less consequential in accessing black businesses since language barriers did not exist.

Another issue that has been raised concerning access to informants involves racial diversity. A general question that has been raised by some scholars, and members of my dissertation committee, is whether a white researcher can gain access to a racially diverse group of informants. This question focuses on the likelihood that such a researcher might obtain candid responses from informants of a different race, and it inquires into the degree to which rapport can be developed among the interviewer and the informant when race becomes a variable. Although no response to questions of this nature can satisfy all parties, it is initially important to recognize that the success of such research is conditioned by the degree to which trust can be developed between the researcher and informants. In this particular research setting, a number of factors helped to facilitate the development of such trust. For instance, many of the informants had some rudimentary understanding of the purpose of academic research, so I was not perceived as a threat in the way that a journalist might have been. In some respects, fitting the stereotype of an academic drew attention away from my race, so assuming this persona resulted in benefits from the positive aspects of that stereotype.

However, the issue of how informants perceived my race during the course of this study is also somewhat ambiguous. For example, many of the respondents identified me as a Jew, because of my last name and appearance. This could have made them more forthcoming with information than if I were perceived as Anglo Saxon. In some instance, the opposite could have occurred. In fact, during some interviews with Korean informants, there were discussions of their affinity with "Jewish people" as opposed to "white people." In a similar vein, some of the black informants had a tendency to classify blacks, Jews and Koreans separately from whites. So, although it is difficult to say exactly what effect my race had on this study, it remained a highly salient issue to me during the course of the study. In addition, it should be noted that the racial dimension of the study was articulated to respondents in the advance letter they received, and the focus of the research encouraged informants to candidly discuss race. In fact, black, Jewish and Korean informants initiated discussions about race spontaneously in the interview process, since it was a highly salient issue to them. They had a genuine interest in explaining their perceptions about areas where race was important, and inconsequential, to their businesses. In this way, the nature of this study openly acknowledged many issues that remain unaddressed in other studies. In fact, the open discussion of race facilitated the development of rapport.

On telling point was that the only consistent opposition I faced to discussions about race came from the owners and representatives of white-owned companies. For instance, one white-owned company that was contacted during the course of this study sent a letter indicating that the owner was "reluctant to answer" questions on my survey because of their racial content, and requested that I eliminate such questions. In fact, all of the white-owned companies declined to participate in the study. This was in sharp contrast to the black, Jewish and Korean businesses that were contacted. They expressed a higher degree of interest in participating in a study about their business experiences. Of course, these are just examples of some observations about the nature of gaining access to a research site that is multiracial in nature. There are many other issues that grew out of this type of research that arose during field work and data analysis.

Issues in the Field

A number of issues emerged during the field work for this study that shaped the methodology. Some of these related to the multiracial nature of the research setting. Although many of these issues are touched upon in the previous section, the more common issues concerning race that arose during the field work should be described in some detail. The informants were comfortable discussing race, and this was clearly articulated during interviews. For instance, one black informant expressed his interest in having a candid discussion about race at the beginning of an interview stating, "Don't mind me, you can call colors and all of that." My general perception was that the black and Korean informants wanted to avoid a clinical discussion of race, and felt more comfortable discussing racial issues in a more concrete manner.

This issue is best exemplified by a conscious decision I made early in the field work to change some of the terminology adopted for the study. For example, during interviews it became apparent that formalized terms like "Korean American" and "African American" were not part of daily conversational English. This was true for both myself and my informants. However, these terms had been written into the interview guide initially, and were not altered until after some of the early interviews in the study. The problem that emerged was that I would ask a question using the term "Korean American" or "African American" and when an informant was responding to the question he or she would hesitate at the point where the terms "black" or "Korean" was normally used, and insert the term "African American" or "Korean American" in its place. At this point, it seemed that the informant would become less spontaneous, and more conscious of the formal structure of the interview. In fact, the quality of informants' responses improved as clinical terminology was dropped.

Another issue that emerged involved language barriers that I faced with Korean business owners. In some instances, it was impossible for me to interview a business owner because we spoke different languages. In a few cases, this barrier was overcome when a friend or relative of a store owner offered to interpret. Although the use of an interpreter has its limitations, since verbatim quotes are not always provided. A more common problem related to language barriers involved the heavy accents that some of the Korean informants spoke with. This was an issue because many of the Korean informants spoke quietly, and there was a great deal of noise in their stores where the interviews took place. It became important to transcribe these interviews quickly, due to the combination of strong accents, soft speech and background noise on the tape recordings. As a result, some data were lost. However, a simple technique was developed to control for this. After an interview of this nature, I would review the tape recording and augment my field notes in areas where responses were drowned out by background noise. In that way, the data could be partially restored.

The issue of background noise points to a more general issue about the field work. All of the interviews were conducted at the businesses of the informants. Because of this, there were often times when an informant was called away from an interview to attend to business. So, there was a constant need to keep the interview focused and on track. However, these breaks in the interviews created a unique opportunity to take field notes and make field observations inside of the businesses. This was particularly valu-

able, since I inadvertently observed interactions between employers and employees, and between customers and store owners. In
fact, many of the findings of this study were influenced by these
observations. There were instances when an informant would stop
the interview to deal with a customer or employee, and then return
to the interview to informally discuss the dynamics of a particular
issue he or she had just dealt with in the store. These experiences
sensitized me to the importance of the location of an interview to
research methodology, since the location has a direct effect on the
nature of the data that are collected. In fact, there was a direct relationship between these elements in the field work and the point in
the study where data saturation had been reached.

Deciding to Leave the Field

The point of data saturation is always determined on subjective
grounds. In some studies this point is reached relatively quickly,
and in others, many years of observation and study can transpire.
Towards the end of the field work for this study it became apparent that the point of data saturation was reached. This conclusion
was arrived at after a number of emergent themes had been discovered in the research, and these avenues had been explored.
However, an extensive discussion of the data for this study is
required in order to understand when the point of saturation had
been reached. This discussion is also necessary because this study
entailed a relatively small population. It focused on a group of
minority business owners in Chicago's ethnic beauty aids industry,
specifically, individuals who own retail, distribution, and manufacturing businesses in this industry. Sampling from this population was demanding. The ability to identify informants was hampered by the lack of information on the universe of interest, so
techniques had to be developed to overcome this obstacle. There
were issues of legitimacy and access to the field to be addressed.
And, the racial and ethnic characteristics of the population
required methodological adjustments. However, all of these issues
were compounded by the relatively small size of the population of
interest.

From the early stages of the research, measures were taken to
address concerns about the size of the population. Several months
were spent before the field work began conducting archival
research and preparing research instruments. From December

1994 to June 1995, archival research was done in preparation for the field work. This archival research was critical, since it added information about the ethnic beauty aids industry in Chicago which established a historical foundation for later conclusions. Much of this archival material was used in the early chapters of this study. An extensive effort was also focused on the refinement of the research instruments. From December 1994 to March 1995, the prototypes of the research instruments were tested and refined. This was an important aspect of the research process. In fact, a great deal of data had already been collected before field work had formally begun.

After a firm foundation had been established for the research, field work was initiated in June of 1995. The early stages of the field work were spent making observations, identifying businesses, and contacting community organizations involved on the South Side of Chicago. In fact, no efforts were made to interview or survey informants until a clear picture of the population and research site was pieced together. This entire process of discovery lasted from June of 1995 to January of 1996, when the interviewing phase of this study began. The interviewing process was intensive; it lasted from January of 1996 to August of 1996. The preparation that preceded the interviewing process was critical, since it allowed me to become acclimated to the research setting. This also improved the efficiency of the interviewing process. However, a number of decisions about the interviewing process continued to be influenced by the size of the population.

At first I planned to interview Korean merchants and black manufacturers, in order to better understand the minority business networks in the ethnic beauty aids industry. Early in the research process, I decided to begin the interviewing with Korean merchants selling ethnic beauty supplies, and once I had interviewed these individuals black business owners would be contacted. This strategy was adopted because the total number of Korean businesses was larger than the total number of black businesses. By interviewing the Korean merchants first, the research instruments could be further refined before the smaller group of black business owners were interviewed. This also allowed me to have a greater understanding of the structure of the industry before interviewing the black manufacturers, who are at the top of its hierarchy. In hindsight, this was a wise decision, since a number of emergent groups were identified in the interviews with Korean merchants. These groups were critical to understanding the networks in the ethnic beauty aids industry. For instance, the role of black merchants in the industry was unclear early in the study. More importantly, the role of black, Korean and Jewish distributors was unknown when the study began. The addition of each of these groups to the population of business owners was critical to the study.

By the end of the field work, data had been collected from a sizable proportion of the known population of business owners in Chicago's ethnic beauty aids industry. In total, the owners of forty Korean-owned beauty supply stores on the South Side of Chicago were identified, and ten of these individuals agreed to be interviewed. In addition to these ten merchants, one Korean merchant arranged for an interview with a black employee, and another Korean merchant arranged for an interview with a Korean employee. Three other Korean merchants were not interviewed, but responded to the survey. The remaining Korean merchants identified in the population decline to be interviewed and did not respond to the drop-off survey. However, the Korean merchants who were interviewed and surveyed represented a diverse cross-section of the population. They captured the breath of characteristics found among Korean-owned beauty supply stores throughout the South Side of Chicago. For instance, their stores varied in size. Two of the Korean merchants ran small stores with no employees. Six of the Korean merchants ran medium sized stores with three to five employees. Five of the Korean merchants ran large stores with six or more employees. The composition of the workers in the Korean-owned stores also varied along several dimensions. Family members worked in nine of the Korean-owned stores; however, this was usually limited to the spouse of a given Korean merchant, and in three cases an extended family member. In contrast, black workers were highly visible in Korean-owned stores. Eleven of the Korean owned stores had black employees, and seven of these store had at least three or more black employees. In addition, seven of the Korean merchants who were interviewed reported that they owned more than one beauty supply store on the South Side of Chicago.

The Korean merchants varied in several additional respects. Eleven of the Korean merchants were men and two were women.

In terms of age, two of the Korean merchants were in their thirties, five were in their forties, four were in their fifties, and two were over sixty. With regard to education, all of the Korean merchants had high levels of educational attainment. One of the Korean store owners had a high school degree, four had some college education, seven had completed their bachelors degrees, and one had earned a masters degree. Also, although all of the Korean merchants were immigrants, they had immigrated to the United States at different times. Two had been in the United States for less than ten years, six for less than twenty years, and five for twenty or more years. In addition, the Korean merchants had businesses in the black community for different periods of time. Two of them had been in business for less than three years, one operated a business for four to six years, and ten were in business for seven or more years.

Korean merchants represented the largest group of entrepreneurs in the population. In contrast, the owners of twelve black-owned beauty supply stores were identified. Three of these agreed to be interviewed. The others declined to be interviewed and did not respond to the drop-off survey. Despite the small size of this sample, the three black merchants who were interviewed were comparable to the black merchants who declined to be interviewed. The similarities between those who participated in the study, and those who did not became apparent after visiting all of the black-owned stores in the population, identifying their owners, and through informal discussions about them with respondants in this study. As a consequence, the three black merchants who were interviewed covered the range of different types of black store owners in the industry. One was strictly involved in retailing, another combined retail and distribution functions in one store on a limited scale, and the third combined these two functions on a somewhat larger scale. Family members worked in each of the black owned stores. However, the presence of family members was limited to one or two immediate relatives of a given black merchant. The number of employees who were not relatives of the store owners varied. One black store owner had no unrelated employees, another had four unrelated employees, and another had fourteen unrelated employees. In terms of race, all of the workers in black-owned stores were black.

The owners of black stores also varied along gender lines. Two of the owners in the sample were men, and there was one female merchant. This was representative of the gender distribution found in the population of black owned stores. The black merchants also represented three age cohorts. One of the black store owners was between forty an fifty, one was between fifty and sixty, and another was over sixty. Also, all of the black merchants were well educated, each having earned a bachelors degree. In addition, two of the black store owners had been in business for eleven years, while the other had been in business for over thirty years. As mentioned, two of the black merchants were also involved in the distribution of ethnic beauty supplies. This merchant-distributor function allowed them to be interviewed with regard to this role in ethnic beauty aids the industry as well. Two other black merchant-distributors were identified, but they declined to be interviewed, and they did not respond to the drop-off survey.

Of course, there are other groups involved in the distribution of ethnic beauty aids on the South Side of Chicago, and efforts were made to identify them. The owners of six Korean-owned distributorships were identified. Three of these agreed to be interviewed. One other Korean distributor was not interviewed, but responded to the survey. The other Korean distributors in the population declined to be interviewed and did not respond to the drop-off survey. In addition, the owners of two Jewish-owned distributorship were identified. One of them agreed to be interviewed. The other was not interviewed, but responded to the survey. Again, the sample of distributors was not large, but it captured the core characteristics of the various types of distributors in the population.

The distributorships ranged in size. One of the black distributors had six employees, the other had fourteen. Two of the Korean distributors had fifteen employees, one had over sixteen employees, and the other two had over thirty-five employees. One of the Jewish distributors had less than five employees, and the other had more than sixteen. In terms of gender, all of the distributors were men, with the exception of one black woman who distributed ethnic beauty aids. Four age cohorts were represented among the distributors. Two of the distributors were in their thirties, three were in their forties, one was in his fifties, and two were over sixty. All of the distributors were also well educated. One of the distributors had finished two years of college, and the other seven had completed their bachelors degrees. In addition, all of the distributors had been in business for over ten years.

Similar to the distributors, the population of black manufacturers in the ethnic beauty aids industry was small. However, black manufacturers were the most critical group to this study. So efforts were made to understand the role of all of the actors in ethnic beauty aids industry before interviewing them. To this end, an attempt was made to interview white manufacturers of ethnic beauty aids. Five white manufacturers of ethnic beauty aids were identified, but none of them agreed to be interviewed, and none of them responded to the survey. Because of this limitation, all of the information about white manufacturers in the ethnic beauty aids industry is based on archival materials and secondary sources. In contrast, a great deal of data were made available by black manufacturers in the industry. Seven black manufacturers of ethnic beauty aids were identified on the South Side of Chicago. Four of them agreed to be interviewed. The other three black manufacturers declined to be interviewed, and they did not respond to the drop-off survey. However, a great deal of information about these three black-owned companies was gathered in interviews with the other black manufacturers. In fact, the four black manufacturers who were interviewed had detailed knowledge of the businesses of other companies in the ethnic beauty aids industry. For instance, some of the black manufacturers interviewed were former employees and business associates of other manufacturers in the industry. Because of such ties, they were familiar with the scope of manufacturing activities in the ethnic beauty aids industry. In addition, their businesses reflected the diversity of black-owned companies found in the industry.

These black-owned companies varied in size. One of the black-owned manufacturers had fewer than five employees, one had fifteen employees, and two had over twenty employees. All of the black manufacturers interviewed were men. They represented three age cohorts. One was in his thirties, two were in their forties, and another was in his fifties. Each of the black manufacturers was well educated. Three held bachelors degrees, and one had a masters degree. In addition, the black manufacturers had been in business for various periods of time. One of the black manufacturers had been in business for less than five years, one for seven years, another for fifteen years, and the other for over twenty years. Because the population was small, each of manufacturer had an intimate knowledge of the natural history of the industry. This same quality was found among the distributors and retailers who were interviewed. As a result, interviews with these individuals led to the development of a holistic view of the ethnic beauty aids industry.

There were two other potential groups of informants for this study, black consumers and black beauticians. However, they were not interviewed or surveyed, since their function in the ethnic beauty aids industry went beyond the scope of this study. The focus on businesses that manufacture, distribute and sell ethnic beauty aids excluded these two groups from this study, since they are primarily end users of such products. Although an examination of the attitudes of black consumers and beauticians would generate additional information concerning the relationship between internal colonialism and minority markets, its proper treatment would require a separate analysis. The distinction between end users of ethnic beauty aids and businesses that manufacture, distribute and sell such products in minority market became apparent as research and data collection for this study progressed. In fact, by the end of the field research, it became evident that an added examination of end users in the ethnic beauty aids industry would make this study overly cumbersome and complex.

For these reasons and others, a point of data saturation had been reached by the end of the interview process. New groups had emerged and were examined, a high degree of redundancy was found in the comments of informants, and a rudimentary conceptual framework was surfacing. At this stage in the research, the decision was made to leave the field and begin coding and analyzing the data. This transition occurred naturally, since the volume of archival information, field observations, and interview data had reached a critical mass. At the time of the final interview, I was anticipating many of the informants responses with accuracy. This was one of many signals that it was time to leave the field and begin coding and analyzing the data. In a similar manner to prior stages of the research process, the coding and analysis of the data involved a number of methodological decisions. The strategy adopted during this phase of the study was responsive to the unique characteristics of the population being studied.

Coding and Analysis

The conventional methods for coding and analyzing qualitative data were adopted for this study. These methods are the same as those identified by Glaser and Strauss in their discussion of the "constant comparative method of qualitative analysis."[54] In essence, these methods involve: coding qualitative data into categories, comparing the categories to one and other, integrating the categories and their properties, delimiting theory based this analysis, and writing the theory. In addition, the open coding, axial coding, and selective coding techniques for qualitative data analysis that have been introduced in the methodological literature since the formulation of the constant comparative were also applied.[55] Although these new techniques represent some of the refinements to qualitative analysis over the years, the governing principles of this type of analysis has essentially remained the same. One of the more attractive attributes of the methods adopted was their applicability to a wide range of data. This characteristic makes them appropriate for this study, given the integration of the various types of data that it entails.

The integrative nature of this study requires a certain degree of flexibility in the methodology if theory is to be derived. In fact, the generation of grounded theory was a goal of this research. To that end the data generated in this study will be present in a manner that addresses the general themes laid out in the literature review. This approach is used to highlight how these issues manifest themselves in various segments of the industry being studied. Illustrations are given using the data from the study to build a framework for the formation of a generalizable theory. Through this mode of organization, issues will be identified that relate back to the five themes discussed in the literature review: the effects of internal colonialism on minority markets, the role of middleman minorities in minority markets, the relationship between sojourning and middleman minority behavior, the effects of class and ethnic resources on minority entrepreneurship, and the concept of an economic detour as it relates to black entrepreneurship. In each of these discussions a case will be made for the utility of applying the internal colonial paradigm to the conceptualization of institutional effects on minority business development in minority markets.

OUTLINE OF THE STUDY

The remainder of this study is divided into eight chapters. Each focuses on institutional effects on black and Korean entrepreneurship on the South Side of Chicago. These effects are discussed in the context of the five main themes identified in the literature review. Chapters 2 and 3 look at the institutional forces that have shaped minority markets on the South Side of Chicago in a historical context. In chapter 2 the historical development of the ethnic beauty aids industry is examined from the perspective of black manufacturers. This chapter focuses on how the scope of manufacturing was limited in the ethnic beauty aids industry by institutional forces, particularly those driven by racism and racial discrimination in mainstream society. It is argued that the internal colonial context that many black manufacturers operated in during the formation of the ethnic beauty aids industry contributed to the economic instability of their companies, and this resulted in a unique pattern of business formation and dissolution. This argument is further developed in later chapters, where connections are made between the racial barriers minority entrepreneurs face and theoretical arguments concerning the internal colonial paradigm.

Chapter 3 outlines such a linkage broadly. In this chapter, the concept of internal colonialism is addressed in a more general manner, examining how racism and racial discrimination in mainstream society affected the historical development of minority entrepreneurship on the South Side of Chicago. In particular, this chapter discusses the genesis of minority markets on the South Side of Chicago, and the function of middleman and black entrepreneurs in the context of internal colonialism. It is argued that, in part, internal colonialism has been reproduced on the South Side of Chicago through the introduction of middleman minorities in its minority markets, and that this process has been driven by economic incentives produced in mainstream society. As an extension of this argument, a more central theme to the concept of internal colonialism is identified, the issue of economic dependence. This issue is addressed through a discussion of the welfare economy that has been created on the South Side of Chicago by mainstream institutions, and its social control function. The role of the welfare economy is discussed further in chapters 4.

Together, chapters 4 through 6 discuss the contemporary context of doing business on the South Side of Chicago from the perspective of the local merchant. Although each chapter addresses a different dimension of the merchants' experience, all of these dimensions are unified by one commonality, that they occur within the context of internal colonialism. Chapter 4 examines two issues that are critical to understanding the social and institutional forces that reproduce internal colonialism on the South Side of Chicago, sojourning on the part of middleman minorities, and the role of the welfare economy in producing economic dependence in the black community. Chapter 5 looks at how changes in the role of mainstream institutions on the South Side of Chicago affect the nature of ethnic solidarity among middleman and black merchants. The focus of this chapter is on how the perception of declining welfare spending affects ethnic cooperation among different entrepreneurial groups in an internal colonial setting. Finally, chapter 6 deals with another issues concerning the effects of internal colonialism on minority markets, the relationship between middleman merchants and black employees. It is argued that a symbiotic relationship has developed between these two groups in response to internal colonialism. In this arrangement Korean merchants bring class resources to minority markets, while black employees bring important ethnic resources to Korean-owned stores that help reduce conflicts with black customers.

The issue of class and ethnic resources is reexamined in chapter 7, through an examination of ethnic beauty supply distributors on the South Side of Chicago. This chapter discusses the role of these resources for middleman and black entrepreneurs in the context of internal colonialism. It is argued that as economic scarcity expanded on the South Side of Chicago, middleman minorities focused on the development of class resources. In contrast, growing scarcity has caused black entrepreneurs to focus on cultivating ethnic resources. In chapter 8, these issues are examined in the context of black manufacturers in the ethnic beauty aids industry. Again, the issue of ethnic resources comes to the forefront for this group, and it is tied to institutional barriers that black entrepreneurs face in gaining access to the mainstream economy. It is argued that by pursuing entrepreneurship via an economic detour based on the mobilization of ethnic resources, blacks are able to overcome these barriers to economic participation. However, their role in the economy is limited, since black entrepreneurs lack sufficient capital to compete with other groups in minority markets. Chapter 9, the conclusion to this study, summarizes its central findings and discusses the degree to which they can be generalized. It also examines the effects that racism and undercapitalization have on minority entrepreneurship, arguing that a public agenda should be adopted attacking institutional sources of these constraints.

NOTES

[1]Albert Memmi, *The Colonizer and The Colonized*, (New York: The Orion Press, 1965); Tammuz Shibutani and Kean M. Kwan, *Ethnic Stratification, A Comparative Approach*, (New York: The Macmillan Company, 1965); Frantz Fanon, *Black Skin, White Mask*, (New York: Grove Weidenfeld, 1968).

[2] Tammuz Shibutani and Kean M. Kwan, *Ethnic Stratification, A Comparative Approach*, (New York: The Macmillan Company, 1965).

[3] Albert Memmi, *The Colonizer and The Colonized*, (New York: The Orion Press, 1965).

[4] Frantz Fanon, *Black Skin, White Mask*, (New York: Grove Weidenfeld, 1968).

[5] William K. Tabb, *The Political Economy of the Black Ghetto*, (New York: W.W. Norton and Company, 1970); Robert Blauner, *Racial Oppression in America*, (New York: Harper and Row, 1972); Stokley Carmichael and Charles V. Hamilton, "White Power the Colonial Situation," in *The Black Ghetto: Promised Land or Colony*, ed. Richard J. Meister, (Lexington: D.C. Heath and Company, 1972): 173-183.

[6] Robert Blauner, *Racial Oppression in America*, (New York: Harper and Row, 1972).

[7]William K. Tabb, *The Political Economy of the Black Ghetto*, (New York: W.W. Norton and Company, 1970): 22-23.

[8] Daniel R. Fusfeld, "The Ghetto as an Economic Subsystem." in Harold G. Vatter and Thomas Palm, ed. *The Economics of Black America*, (New York: Harcourt Brace Jovanovich, Inc, 1972); Manning Marable, *How Capitalism Underdeveloped Black America*, (Boston: South End Press, 1983); Jawanza Kunjufu, *Black Economics, Solutions for Economic and Community Empowerment*, (Chicago: African American Images, 1991).

[9] William K. Tabb, *The Political Economy of the Black Ghetto*, (New York: W.W. Norton and Company, 1970): 22.

[10] Ivan Light and Edna Bonacich, *Immigrant Entrepreneurs, Koreans in Los Angeles, 1965-1982.*, (Berkeley: University of California Press, 1988): 344-347.

[11] Hubert Blalock, *Toward a Theory of Minority-Group Relations*, (New York: Capricorn Books, 1967); Edna Bonacich, Edna, "A Theory of Middleman Minorities," *American Sociological Review*, 38 (1973): 583-594.; Edna Bonacich, *The Economic Basis of Ethnic Solidarity, Small Business in the Japanese American Community*, (Berkeley: University of California Press, 1980); Pyong Gap Min, *Ethnic Business Enterprise, Korean Small Business in Atlanta*, (New York: Center for Migration Studies, 1988); Marlene Sway, *Familiar Strangers, Gypsy Life in America*, (Champaign: University of Illinois Press, 1988); Walter P. Zenner, *Minorities in the Middle, A Cross-Cultural Text*, (Albany: State University of New York Press, 1991); Pyong Gap Min and Andrew Kolody, "The Middleman Minority Characteristics of Korean Immigrants in the United States," *Korea Journal of Population and Development*, 23.2 (December 1994): 179-202.

[12] Max Weber, *Ancient Judaism*, Translated and Edited by Hans H. Gerth and Don Martindale, (Glencoe: The Free Press, 1952): 492-500; Georg Simmel, "The Stranger," In *Simmel, On Individuality and Social Forms*, Donald N. Levine, eds, (Chicago: The University of Chicago Press, 1971): 143-149; Max Weber, *Economy and Society*. 2 vols, Guenther Roth and Claus Wittich, eds, (Berkeley: University of California Press, 1978): 614-623.

[13] Hubert Blalock, *Toward a Theory of Minority-Group Relations*, (New York: Capricorn Books, 1967): 79-84; Walter P. Zenner, *Minorities in the Middle, A Cross-Cultural Text*, (Albany: State University of New York Press, 1991).

[14] Hubert Blalock, *Toward a Theory of Minority-Group Relations*, (New York: Capricorn Books, 1967): 79-84.

[15] Ibid, 81.

[16] Pyong Gap Min, *Caught in the Middle, Korean Communities in New York and Los Angeles*, (Berkeley: University of California Press, 1996): 20.

[17] Paul C. P. Siu, "The Sojourner." *The American Journal of Sociology*, 58 (1952): 33-44.

[18] Ibid, 34.

[19] Rose Hume Lee, *The Chinese in the United States of America*, (Oxford: Oxford University Press, 1960): 69-85.

[20] Ibid, 70.

[21] Marlene Sway, *Familiar Strangers, Gypsy Life in America,* (Champaign: University of Illinois Press, 1988): 21-23 and 125- 127.

[22] Edna Bonacich, "A Theory of Middleman Minorities," *American Sociological Review*, 38 (October 1973): 583-594.

[23] Ibid, 593.

[24] Ibid, 583-594.

[25] Kwang Chung Kim and Won Moo Hurh, "Ethnic Resources Utilization of Korean Immigrant Entrepreneurs in the Chicago Minority Area,"*International Migration Review* , 19.1 (1985): 82-109.

[26] In-Jin Yoon, "The Changing Significance of Ethnic and Class Resources in Immigrant Businesses: The Case of Korean Immigrant Businesses in Chicago," *IMR*, 25.2 (1991): 303-331; In-Jin Yoon, "The Growth of Korean Immigrant Entrepreneurship in Chicago," *Ethnic and Racial Studies*, 18.2 (1995): 315-335.

[27] In-Jin Yoon, "The Changing Significance of Ethnic and Class Resources in Immigrant Businesses: The Case of Korean Immigrant Businesses in Chicago," *IMR*, 25.2 (1991): 318.

[28] Ibid.

[29] Light, Ivan. and Edna Bonacich, *Immigrant Entrepreneurs, Koreans in Los Angeles, 1965-1982,* (Berkeley: University of California Press, 1988): 19.

[30] Ivan Light, "Asian Enterprise in America, Chinese, Japanese, and Koreans in Small Business," in Scott Cummings, ed. *Self- Help in Urban America, Patterns of Minority Business Enterprise,* (Port Washington: National University Publications, 1980), 33-57.

[31] Ibid.

[32] Ivan Light, *Ethnic Enterprise in America, Business and Welfare Among Chinese, Japanese, and Blacks,* (Berkeley: University of California Press, 1972).

[33] Ivan Light, "Asian Enterprise in America, Chinese, Japanese, and Koreans in Small Business," in Scott Cummings, ed. *Self- Help in Urban America, Patterns of Minority Business Enterprise,* (Port Washington: National University Publications, 1980): 41-42.

[34] In-Jin Yoon, "The Changing Significance of Ethnic and Class Resources in Immigrant Businesses: The Case of Korean Immigrant Businesses in Chicago," *IMR*, 25.2 (1991): 318-319.

[35] Robert L. Boyd, "Inequality in the earnings of Self-Employed African and Asian Americans." *Sociological Perspectives*, 34.4 (1991): 447-472; John Sibley Butler, *Entrepreneurship and Self-Help Among Black Americans, A Reconsideration of Race and Economics,* (Albany: State

University of New York Press, 1991); Timothy Bates, *Banking on Black Enterprise, The Potential of Emerging Firms for Revitalizing Urban Economies*, (Washington D.C.: Joint Center for Political and Economic Studies, 1993); Timothy Bates, "An Analysis of Korean-Immigrant-owned Small-Business Start-ups with Comparisons to African-American-and-Nonminority-Owned Firms," *Urban Affairs Quarterly*, 30.2 (1994): 227-248; Melvin L. Oliver and Thomas M. Shapiro, *Black Wealth, White Wealth, A New Perspective on Racial Inequality*, (New York: Routledge, 1995).

[36] Ivan Light, *Ethnic Enterprise in America, Business and Welfare Among Chinese, Japanese, and Blacks*, (Berkeley: University of California Press, 1972); Ivan Light, "Asian Enterprise in America, Chinese, Japanese, and Koreans in Small Business," in Scott Cummings, ed. *Self-Help in Urban America, Patterns of Minority Business Enterprise*, (Port Washington: National University Publications, 1980): 33-57.

[37] John Sibley Butler, *Entrepreneurship and Self-Help Among Black Americans, A Reconsideration of Race and Economics*, (Albany: State University of New York Press, 1991).

[38] E. Franklin. Frazier, *Black Bourgeoisie, The Rise of a New Middle Class in the United States*, (New York: Collier Books, 1962); Gunnar Myrdal, *An American Dilemma, The Negro Problem and Modern Democracy*, (New York: Harper and Row, 1962); Eugine P. Foley, "The Negro Businessman, In Search of a Tradition," *Daedalus*, 95, (Winter 1966): 107-144.; W.E. Burghardt DuBois, "Publication Number 4, 1899, The Negro In Business," In W.E. Burghardt DuBois, ed., *Atlanta University Publications, Volume 1*, (Octagon Books, Inc.: New York, 1968): 13-14.; Abram L. Harris, *The Negro as Capitalist, A Study of Banking and Business Among American Negroes*, (New York: Negro University Press, 1969); Joseph Pierce,*Negro Business and Business Education, Their Present and Prospective Development*, (Westport: Negro University Press, 1971); Booker T. Washington, *The Negro in Business*, (New York: AMS Press, 1971); Manning Marable, *How Capitalism Underdeveloped Black America*, (Boston: South End Press, 1983): 133-167; John Sibley Butler, *Entrepreneurship and Self-Help Among Black Americans, A Reconsideration of Race and Economics*, (Albany: State University of New York Press, 1991); Timothy Bates, *Banking on Black Enterprise, The Potential of Emerging Firms for Revitalizing Urban Economies*, (Washington D.C.: Joint Center for Political and Economic Studies, 1993); St. Clair Drake and Horace R. Cayton, *Black Metropolis, A study of*

Negro Life in a Northern City. (Chicago: University of Chicago Press, 1993).

[39] M.S. Stuart, *An Economic Detour, A History of Insurance in the Lives of American Negroes,* (College Park: McGrath Publishing Company, 1969); John Sibley Butler, *Entrepreneurship and Self-Help Among Black Americans, A Reconsideration of Race and Economics,* (Albany: State University of New York Press, 1991).

[40] M.S. Stuart, *An Economic Detour, A History of Insurance in the Lives of American Negroes,* (College Park: McGrath Publishing Company, 1969).

[41] Ibid, xxv.

[42] John Sibley Butler, *Entrepreneurship and Self-Help Among Black Americans, A Reconsideration of Race and Economics,* (Albany: State University of New York Press, 1991): 72-73.

[43] Ibid, 72-73.

[44] Ibid. 74-75.

[45] Alejandro Portes and L. Bach, *Latin Journey, Cuban and Mexican Immigrants in the United States,* (Berkeley: University of California Press, 1985); Alejandro Portes and Robert D. Manning, "The Immigrant Enclave, Theory and Empirical Examples," in Susan Olzak and Joane Nagel, eds, *Competitive Ethnic Relations,* (New York: Academic Press, Inc., 1986), 47-68.; Min Zhou, *Chinatown, The Socioeconomic Potential of an Urban Enclave,* (Philadelphia: Temple University Press, 1992).

[46] Ibid.

[47] Charles Choy Wong, "Black and Chinese Grocery Stores in Los Angeles' Black Ghetto," *Urban Life,* 5.4 (January 1977): 460.

[48] Ibid, 460.

[49] Booker T. Washington, *The Negro in Business,* (New York: AMS Press, 1971); Jawanza Kunjufu, *Black Economics, Solutions for Economic and Community Empowerment,* (Chicago: African American Images, 1991); St. Clair Drake and Horace R. Cayton, *Black Metropolis: A Study of Negro Life in a Northern City,* (Chicago: University of Chicago Press, 1993); Ivan Light, Hadas Har-Chvi and Kenneth Kan, "Black/Korean Conflict in Los Angeles," in Seamus Dunn, ed., *Managing Divided Cities,* (London: Kent University Press, 1994).

[50] William Foote Whyte, *Street Corner Society, The Social Structure of an Italian Slum, Fourth Edition,* (Chicago: University of Chicago Press, 1993).

[51] Ibid, 283.

[52] Barney G. Glaser and Anselm L. Strauss, *The Discovery of Grounded Theory, Strategies for Qualitative Research*, (New York: Aldine de Gruyter, 1967).

[53] For a discussion of techniques for developing questionnaires and interview guides see, Peter H. Rossi, James D. Right and Andy B. Anderson, *Handbook of Survey Research*, (New York, Academic Press, Inc., 1983); John Lofland and Lyn H. Lofland, *Analyzing Social Settings, A Guide to Qualitative Observation and Analysis, Second Edition*, (Belmont: Wadsworth Publishing Company, 1984); Michael Quinn Patton, *Qualitative Evaluation and Research Methods, Second Edition*, (Newbury Park: Sage Publications, 1990).

[54] Barney G. Glaser and Anselm L. Strauss, *The Discovery of Grounded Theory, Strategies for Qualitative Research*, (New York: Aldine de Gruyter, 1967): 101-115.

[55] see Anselm L. Strauss, *Qualitative Analysis for Social Scientists*, (New York: Cambridge University Press, 1987); Anselm Strauss and Juliet Corbin, *Basics of Qualitative Research, Grounded Theory Procedures and Techniques*, (Newbury Park: Sage Publications, 1990).

CHAPTER 2:

Race And The Ethnic Beauty Aids Industry

OVERVIEW

In this chapter, the historical development of Chicago's ethnic beauty aids industry is examined from the perspective of black manufacturers. The central argument of this chapter is that the business strategies of black manufacturers in Chicago's ethnic beauty aids industry have been shaped by racism and racial discrimination in mainstream society from the industry's inception to the contemporary period. This point is highlighted through an examination of three generations of black manufacturers in Chicago. The experiences of these black manufacturers are discussed in the context of three historical periods.

The first encompasses the years between the Great Migration and the Great Depression, when the ethnic beauty aids industry emerged as a black institution. This is a critical period in the development of the ethnic beauty aids industry, since it was when many of the business strategies used by past and current black manufacturers to overcome racial barriers to economic participation were developed.

The second period covers the years between the Great Depression and the civil right movement, when the ethnic beauty aids industry demonstrated its resilience to economic and social turmoil growing out of racial discord between blacks and whites in society. This was a critical period, since black manufacturers in the ethnic beauty aids industry managed to emerge from the Great Depression while other institutions in the black community disappeared. It was also a crucial period, since these manufacturers became the focus of public discourse during the civil rights movement, which compromised their leadership position in the black community.

Finally, The third period examined in this chapter entails the years from the civil right movement to 1990, when black manufacturers began to lose ground to white-owned conglomerates in corporate America. This period is important because it highlight how racism and racial discrimination have been reproduced in the contemporary period, causing black manufacturers of ethnic beauty aids to continue to face barriers to participation in the mainstream economy. In addition, it demonstrates how efforts aimed at removing these barriers have been complicated by the expanding role of large white-owned conglomerates and the growing influence of the global economy in black America.

The consideration of these three periods together is crucial, since they highlight how firmly the ethnic beauty aids industry was established as a black institution in Chicago, and how the instability of contemporary black manufacturers in this industry is tied to the historical experiences of black entrepreneurs with racism and racial discrimination in mainstream society. Consequently, it is argued that black manufacturers of ethnic beauty aids have continued to confront variant forms of racism and racial discrimination in each of these historical periods, despite changes in the social context in which they are embedded.

This argument is expanded upon in chapter 3, where the effects of racism and racial discrimination on the business activities of black, Jewish and Korean merchants on the South Side of Chicago are examined from a historical perspective. In a similar manner to this chapter's discussion of black manufacturers, chapter 3 argues that the historical development of black, Jewish and Korean small business on the South Side of Chicago has occurred in response to persistent racism and racial discrimination in white America. Together, the subject matter of this chapter and chapter 3 establish the historical foundation for the discussion of contemporary black, Jewish and Korean-owned businesses in Chicago's ethnic beauty aids industry.

Initially, this chapter's examination of black manufacturers and the next chapter's discussion of black, Jewish and Korean merchants on the South Side of Chicago are presented separately, in order to highlight the overarching effects that racism and racial discrimination have had on the development of the ethnic beauty aids industry in Chicago. As a result, the discussion of Jewish and Korean entrepreneurs will be limited in this chapter. These entrepreneurial groups will be identified mainly for contextual purposes, since this chapter's primary goal is to identify the historical effects of racism and racial discrimination in mainstream society on black manufacturers in Chicago's ethnic beauty aids industry. Once this foundation is established, a more detailed discussion of black and middleman entrepreneurs can be embarked upon in chapter 3. Consequently, this chapter serves as a reminder that racism and racial discrimination in mainstream society forms the backdrop for relations between blacks and other minority groups in America.

BLACK BEAUTY AIDS MANUFACTURERS IN BRONZEVILLE, FROM THE GREAT MIGRATION TO THE GREAT DEPRESSION

Race and the Development of Minority Markets in Black Chicago

Chicago has historically had one of the largest concentrations of ethnic beauty aids firms in America. This development was the result of a number of interrelated factors. Being national in focus, the ethnic beauty aids industry needed to be centrally located and in close proximity to major railroad lines. Geographically, Chicago was an ideal location. In the early 1900's, when the ethnic beauty aids industry emerged, Chicago was also a new city, teeming with industry, growth and opportunities. Most importantly, Chicago was a major destination for blacks during the Great Migration.[1] The Great Migration spurred the development of a sizable market composed of black consumers in Chicago.

Between 1890 and 1930, Chicago's black population grew dramatically. In 1890, Chicago's black population totaled 14,271; and it grew to 30,150 by 1900.[2] As the migration of blacks continued during the early and mid-1900's, Chicago's black population continued to grow in size. In 1910, Chicago's black population had reached 44,103; in 1920 it was 109,458; and in 1930 it was 233,903.[3] The emergence of a sizable black population in Chicago at the turn of the century, and the subsequent segregation of this community, allowed for the development of a minority markets on the South Side of Chicago. For example, Drake and Cayton commented that:

> The Great Migration created the "Negro market." Both white and Negro merchants, as well as the Negro consumer, became increasingly conscious of the purchasing power of several hundred thousand people solidly massed in one compact community.[4]

The Great Migration had such a strong influence on the development of a minority market on the South Side of Chicago that in 1938, *Time* identified it as America's "centre of Negro business."[5]

As Chicago's black population increased, opportunities for black and middleman entrepreneurs expanded.[6] For instance, Drake and Cayton identified over 2,600 business enterprises owned by blacks on the South Side of Chicago in 1938, and over 2,800 owned by Jews.[7] Despite the concentration of black and Jewish-owned businesses on the South Side of Chicago during this period, a number of inequalities existed between the two groups of entrepreneurs. For instance, most of the 2,600 business enterprises owned by blacks on the South Side of Chicago in 1938, "were small retail stores and service enterprises on side streets, or in the older, less desirable communities."[8] In contrast, the Jewish-owned businesses identified on the South Side of Chicago at this time were more likely to be located on main streets and in major shopping districts.[9] In fact, in 1938, *Time* reported that virtually all of the commercial property in the major shopping districts on the South Side of Chicago belonged, "to whites, most of them Jews, and they make it tough for Negroes to go into business in these prize areas."[10]

These distinctions, although existing at the parochial level, were a reflection of the relative disadvantages that many black businesses faced in the economy during this period. For instance, both black merchants and black manufacturers in the ethnic beauty aids industry were undercapitalized when compared to their Anglo Saxon and Jewish counterparts in the economy. In part, undercapitalization grew out of the greater levels of racism and racial discrimination experienced by blacks in society. In addition, it stemmed from relative inequalities in wealth between blacks and many other entrepreneurial groups. However, despite these inequalities, a sizable concentration of black manufacturers of ethnic beauty aids existed in Chicago during this period. For instance, Drake and Cayton identified over a dozen black manufacturers of ethnic beauty aids on the South Side of Chicago in 1938, constituting one-third of all manufacturing enterprises owned by blacks in Chicago.[11]

Chicago's black manufacturers ran businesses similar to those operated by blacks in other cities during this period. For instance, between 1906 and 1937 Annie Minerva Turnbo-Malone owned and operated a network of cosmetics factories and beauty-training schools under the name Poro College, which were headquartered in St. Louis, Missouri.[12] Similarly, Sarah Breedlove Walker ran the Madame C.J. Walker Manufacturing Company in Indianapolis, Indiana from 1911 until her death in 1919.[13] However, the business climate black manufacturers found in Chicago was different in several respects.

Although the presence of black manufacturers in the ethnic beauty aids industry was common in other cities during this period, the relatively large number of black manufacturers found in Chicago was unique. Black manufacturers in Chicago accrued many benefits from the agglomeration of black businesses and consumers on the South Side, allowing them to implement their business strategies on a relatively larger scale than black manufacturers in smaller cities. These characteristics allow for a more detailed analysis of the effects of racism and racial discrimination on the business strategies of black-owned firms in the ethnic beauty aids industry. For example, the experiences of an early black manufacturer in Chicago, Claude Albert Barnett, illustrate how the presence of racial barriers affected the business strategies adopted by black manufacturers during the early development of the ethnic beauty aids industry .

Claude A. Barnett: A Black Manufacturer's Response to Racism and Racial Discrimination

Using the Black Press to Overcome Racial Barriers. Barnett's accomplishments in business were tied to the city of Chicago and the opportunities it offered. He made his way to Chicago in the early 1900's, and like many of his peers, he found Chicago to be a good environment for the pursuit of entrepreneurship in the ethnic beauty aids industry. A number of forces brought Barnett to Chicago. He was born in Sanford, Florida, on September 16, 1889.[14] He was well educated, graduating from the Tuskegee Institute, (Tuskegee, Alabama) in 1906.[15] Barnett's experience at the Tuskegee Institute had a lasting impact on his life, and he maintained strong ties to his alma mater until his death in 1967.[16] Like other successful entrepreneurs, education was an important asset that Barnett possessed. However, his education extended beyond the academy. What he learned both formally and informally in daily life made the difference between success and failure. Barnett spent his early adult life working, learning, and networking. He brought these experiences with him to Chicago, and they influenced his later business decisions.

After college Barnett held various jobs, and upon hearing about growing opportunities for blacks in Chicago he moved to the North. Chicago was a place where Barnett could put down roots and build his business. In 1916 he formed the Associated Negro Press (ANP), the first major wire service for nationwide coverage of news in the black community.[17] To Barnett, the ANP was not just a news service, it was a resource for the development of other business ventures. Using the ANP as a negotiating tool, Barnett made several arrangements with black newspapers and magazines around the country, stipulating that the ANP would provide them with stories in exchange for advertising space. Through this mechanism Barnett became a key advertising figure in the black community. His clients included many of the larger black businesses of his time, such as Annie Minerva Turnbo-Malone's Poro Colleges.

Barnett's access to advertising space facilitated several additional business ventures. Most important was a small manufacturing company called the Kashmir Chemical Company, located at 312 S. Clark Street in Chicago. Kashmir was incorporated on February 18, 1918, as a manufacturer of cosmetics and haircare products for black consumers.[18] Under Barnett, Kashmir was incredibly innovative, both in its national focus and its positive advertising strategy. Unlike many of the small ethnic beauty aids companies that preceded it, Kashmir developed a national market. Three elements facilitated this development: the central location of Chicago as a staging ground for the firm, the ability to gain endorsements from black celebrities and entertainers in Chicago, and the extensive access the ANP had to various black newspapers for advertising purposes. These features allowed Barnett to make several important innovations in marketing.

Barnett was the first manufacturer of ethnic beauty aids to use positive advertisements to sell cosmetics. Prior to Kashmir, a typical advertisement would portray an unattractive woman with the message that to avoid looking like her, one should purchase a given manufacturer's goods. In contrast, Barnett used positive images. Kashmir's advertisements were known for the use of beautiful black models and celebrities, as well as positive messages about the physical attributes of black women. Kashmir adopted this strategy gradually. When one examines the company's advertisements over time an obvious trend develops, moving from older negative advertisements to more sophisticated positive advertisements. For instance, an example of the earlier format appeared in an advertisement for Kashmir around 1920.[19] The advertisement included a picture of a woman sitting alone in a ballroom, with the caption, "Why be a poor neglected wallflower, shunned by everybody, because your skin is ugly and your hair is not pretty? Why not let 'The Kashmir Way' and the Kashmir Preparations put you in the crowd with those who laugh and make merry and feel happy?"[20] At the same time that this advertisement was run, one could see the emergence of positive advertisements by Barnett. For example, a typical positive advertisement during this period featured sensuous photographs of black cabaret dancers and vaudeville stars like Coral Greene, Florence Mills, and Ada Smith.[21] The format of such advertisements was simple, photographs of local celebrities were juxtaposed with their endorsements of Kashmir Products.

Kashmir: Racial Identity and the Response to White Competition. Kashmir was successful promoting its products through the black press, and sales grew rapidly. However, the company did not have the necessary financial and legal resources to compete directly with larger white-owned firms. In fact, Kashmir's success attracted the attention of Procter and Gamble, maker of a similar line of products called *Cashmere*. Procter and Gamble accused the Kashmir Chemical Company of encroaching on its market by introducing a name brand similar to its own. A legal battle over copyright infringement ensued which eventually led to the reorganization of the Kashmir Chemical Company, and the reintroduction of Kashmir Products under a new name, Nile Queen. However, the Kashmir Chemical Company never fully

recovered from this confrontation. It survived for a few years with
the Nile Queen line of products, but eventually both companies
(The Kashmir Chemical Company and the Nile Queen
Corporation) were dissolved in December of 1926.[22] Although it
eventually failed, Nile Queen continued to promote its products
with positive messages in the black press. Following "The Kashmir
Way," Nile Queen incorporated photographs of beautiful black
women with positive statements about their natural attributes. The
following passage is representative of the messages that were conveyed to black consumers through Nile Queen advertisements:

> There is just as much real beauty in the colored race as in any
> people of the world if it is properly developed. Only by the
> most careful make-up can the Caucasian equal the creamy
> yellow, the matchless browns, and the satiny, glossy dark skin
> of the Colored Woman. But you must know how to take care
> of your hair and complexion. The climate of America and the
> northern countries is not ideal for colored people. Their skin
> was for centuries accustomed to the mild, balmy atmosphere
> of India, Africa, southern Italy, France and Morocco. To meet
> the changed conditions you must exercise extreme care in
> your selection of toilet articles. Nile Queen Preparations are
> manufactured in Kashmir Laboratories from the purest of oils
> and perfumes, after the famous Cleopatra formulas. The
> Kashmir Chemical Co. is one of the leading Race Business
> organizations.[23]

As time progressed, Kashmir and Nile Queen's message became
more positive and focused on black consumers. The advertisements emphasized positive aspects of being black, and the company increasingly identified itself as a "Race Business." Appeals were
made to black customers, asking them to support the company
because it was a black-owned business. This was apparent in the
letterhead of the Kashmir Chemical Company which stated,
"*KASHMIR IS A COLORED CONCERN.* We are looking out
for our Race. *YOU* must not fail us."[24]

When put into perspective, the emphasis on race in the advertising strategy used by Barnett and his contemporaries was rea-
sonable. Black companies were under a constant threat in the
business world, and they operated at an extreme disadvantage
when compared to larger white-owned companies. So, it was good
business to try to connect with consumers, and one of the main ties

that black businesses had with their customers was race. The "Race Business" theme was not simply a component of a company's advertising strategy, it also carried social meaning. It alerted consumers to the possibility that a company employed black Americans, and it invested in the black community.

Racial identity was an important resource to black businesses. This is indicated in a series of letters that were exchanged in 1920 between the Kashmir Chemical Company and F.B. Ransom, the attorney for the Madame C.J. Walker Manufacturing Company. This incident began when Ransom contacted Kashmir in order to address rumors that were circulating among salesmen about the Madame C.J. Walker Manufacturing Company. His message was clear:

> Frequently reports reach this office to the effect that representatives of your Company are spreading the report that the Madam C.J. Walker Manufacturing Company has sold an interest in its business to some white person or concern. .... There has been absolutely no change in the management of the Madam C.J. Walker Mfg. Company since its incorporation in 1911 and I wish you would at least instruct your representatives that they lay themselves liable to being called into court and make good their charges if they persist in making same.[25]

Barnett quickly responded to Ransom's letter, denying that the accusations were true, and agreeing to bring the matter to the attention of his employees. He also attempted to defuse this conflict with his competitor through a plea for racial solidarity. In this statement aspects of the isolation that black businesses felt was apparent:

> I am very sorry that you have thought it necessary to make a charge which seems to us unjust because it has been in my mind that these leaders in our line would find it of advantage to get closer together in a sort of mutual understanding with an idea of preserving in so far as possible, this particular business within our group. Any time you are in Chicago, we would be very glad to have you drop in and pay us a visit.[26]

Ransom grudgingly accepted Barnett's explanation, informing him that he had knowledge of a salesman from the Kashmir Chemical Company who had stated that the Madame C.J. Walker

Manufacturing Company had "sold out to a white man," but he indicated that the matter was resolved to his satisfaction.[27]

Ransom's reply to Barnett discussed the disadvantages that black businesses had when competing with larger white-owned companies. He addressed this issue directly in his reply to Barnett:

> I rather appreciate the tone of your letter, however, and nothing would please me greater than to see and have talk with you as I am entirely in accord with you in that organizations such as ours should co-operate fully with each other so as to force such as the Plough's Chemical Company and other unscrupulous white concerns off the market.[28]

The presence of larger mainstream companies tended to supersede competition among black entrepreneurs at the parochial level. However, race was only the most apparent distinction to be made between black and mainstream businesses involved in the manufacturing and distribution of ethnic beauty aids. At a more fundamental level, these firms did business differently. The sales approach adopted by black-owned firms was distinct from the approach adopted by white-owned firms.[29] For instance, black-owned firms were more active in the area of door-to-door sales. They were particularly effective at using this approach to sell direct to black-owned barber shops and beauty salons.

Sales Strategies Used in Overcoming Racial Barriers to the Mainstream Economy

Selling door-to-door was a necessity to black companies, since retailing underdeveloped in the black neighborhoods they served, and since access to the shelves of the few retailers in black neighborhoods was further limited due to racial discrimination by white and Jewish store owners. Even if racial barriers were overcome and black businesses gained access to white and Jewish-owned stores, the high cost of advertising and promoting products made it difficult for them to compete. In order to sell goods through stores, a manufacturer needed to invest capital in advertising to develop and maintain a market. However, black manufacturers were undercapitalized. Because of this, door-to-door sales to black barbers and beauticians were considered a more cost effective way for small and medium sized black manufacturers to distribute their products. Door-to-door sales allowed black firms to accomplish three things: they made it possible for manufacturers to avoid the racial barriers to market access encountered in white and Jewish-owned stores, they lowered the costs of advertising, and they increased the association of a company's products with "the race" through their affiliation with black barbers and beauty salon owners. In effect, this marketing strategy allowed black manufacturers to overcome racial barriers through the mobilization of ethnic resources.

This strategy can be contrasted with the marketing approach adopted by larger mainstream firms. Typically, a larger mainstream firm would market their products through drug stores owned by mainstream corporations and Jewish merchants in the black community, and the challenge would be to get black consumers into the drug stores to buy those products. Advertising was the principal mechanism used to facilitate this type of consumer behavior. Mainstream firms would target black consumers with advertising campaigns featuring black celebrities, who regularly endorsed their products. The products and the celebrities became synonymous. The association between products manufactured by whites and a black spokesperson was strong; however, these companies did not mobilize informal networks in the black community. Although many black-owned firms lacked extensive advertising budgets and found it difficult accessing the shelves of drug stores owned by mainstream corporations and Jewish merchants, they tended to compensate for these structural disadvantages with the direct sales approach. This approach was beneficial for a number of reasons. Its main benefit was that it allowed smaller black companies to access informal networks in the black community and get feedback from black customers. While the larger mainstream companies had limited information about the demand for ethnic beauty aids in the black community, black firms were privy to the pulse of the black consumer. As a result, most of the major innovations in the ethnic beauty aids industry came from these smaller black firms.

Direct contact with black customers was the key to getting information and tapping new markets. Murray's Superior Products Company is a perfect example of how these innovations occurred. Claude A. Barnett described how Murray's Superior Products Company got started in a letter he sent to A.L. Holsey, the Secretary of the National Negro Business League in 1933:

The reason I say that periodically a new product will succeed
is best illustrated by Murray's success. The preparations for
women had enjoyed a vogue for some years. Men disdained
them. Suddenly some ten or twelve years ago, men began to
show a desire to have their hair slicked. Murray, as an expert
barber in one of the shops frequented by these young fops
saw the virtue of a preparation which might do it better than
the alkali products then in use. He was not the first to make
a wax preparation but his was the best, and using barber
shops as a medium, the growth of his concern was rapid.[30]

Even as other companies followed suit, Murray's Superior
Products remained the top manufacturer of hair pomade for men.
Charles D. Murray founded the company and operated it until his
death in 1955.[31] The success of Murray's company resulted from
his ability to access informal networks in the black community,
and the ability to promote it as a "race business." In these ways,
Murray followed a business formula similar to that of his peers.

In addition to maintaining contact with black customers,
Murray developed a national market for his products through a
sophisticated advertising campaign in the black press. For example, Murray featured endorsements from Joe Louis, the World's
Heavyweight Champion, in advertisements for his products that
appeared in *The Crisis* .[32] Of course, this is a clear representation
of the positive style of advertising that Claude A. Barnett pio-
neered with Kashmir. However, Murray went a step further, featuring himself in an advertisement in *The Crisis*.[33] This type of
advertisement conveyed a more sophisticated set of messages than
found in the standard celebrity endorsement. Murray was the
focus of this advertisement. It portrayed him as a successful black
businessman. The advertisement included photographs of his factory, its executive suites, and the black executives and employees
who worked there. This advertisement was designed to alert black
consumers to the connection between purchasing Murray's products and supporting black-owned business. It was in sharp contrast
to white-owned companies that used black celebrities to promote
their products, since the black faces on Murray's billboard also
reflected the company's board room.

Anthony Overton: The Need for Autonomous Economic Institutions in Black America

Innovative products and good marketing strategies were only part of the formula for successful black entrepreneurship. Blacks had limited economic opportunities, since they faced racial animosity in daily interactions and through institutional discrimination. Black entrepreneurs knew that the success of their businesses was ultimately determined by the degree to which they developed independent resources to drive economic development and growth. One of the best examples of a black entrepreneur whose success was, in large part, attributed to the development of a vast conglomerate was Anthony Overton.

Overton epitomized the successful black entrepreneur of the early 1900's. Like many of his contemporaries, he had humble beginnings before migrating to Chicago. Overton was born in Monroe, Louisiana on June 24, 1864, the son of house slaves.[34] His childhood was a reflection of the hopes that many blacks held following the Civil War. Overton's parents encouraged him to pursue his education. After the family moved to Topeka, Kansas in 1877, he was enrolled in high school, and graduated in 1881.

Overton was exposed to business at a early age, and he took to it readily. He worked in a dry goods store, then ventured out on his own as a green grocer.[35] His business was profitable, and he eventually sold it, using the proceeds to attend the University of Kansas Law School, where he received his LL.B. degree in 1890. After a brief career as an attorney, Overton was appointed as a judge in the Topeka Municipal Court in 1892. This appointment was the result of Overton's qualifications and his political savvy, which he used to make connections in the local Republican Party. As a municipal judge Overton was effective, but it seemed that his opportunities for advancement were limited because of race. In 1909 he left the bench and entered into a business partnership with another black American, John Forbes, forming the Overton Hygienic Manufacturing Company.[36] In its early years, the company manufactured baking powder, flavor extracts, toiletries, cosmetics, and other household items. In 1910, Overton bought his partner out, and ran the company alone. In 1911, Overton moved his company to Chicago in order to take advantage of the city's strategic location and its growing business opportunities for blacks.

Overton was able to expand his company in Chicago, building it into a large conglomerate. At its height, Overton's business empire included: the Overton Hygienic Manufacturing Company, the Great Northern Reality Company, the *Chicago Bee*, the Victory Life Insurance Company, and the Douglas National Bank.[37] These concerns, along with the agglomeration of other black-owned businesses, comprised a potent force for economic development in Chicago's Black Belt during the early 1900's. The presence of large black-owned conglomerates and the agglomeration of many black businesses in Chicago helped black entrepreneurs cope with racial barriers in the early 1900's. Overton was conscious of the social context that his business was embedded in, and he made several efforts to address these conditions.

Overton's business policies were clearly influenced by the racial atmosphere in Chicago, and in the country in general. He stressed that his business had an integrated workforce, although he also recognized the need to hire black Americans.[38] This was a strategic issue since heavy scrutiny was placed upon black businesses by mainstream institutions, making it necessary for Overton to emphasize his company's openness to white Americans, particularly in the area of hiring. Overton was also aware of the symbolic meaning of his business to blacks, and the scrutiny he was under by those who viewed his company, and companies like it, as both tokens and icons. To be successful, black businesses had to treat black consumers with respect, while simultaneously proving to mainstream society that they did not favor blacks over whites. Because of this, Overton stressed the integrated nature of his workforce, and he made marketing decisions reflecting his feeling that his products should not degrade blacks. For example, he refused to manufacture items such as skin bleaches.[39]

Social stratification within the black community also influenced Overton's business decisions. The growth of the black community in Chicago during the early 1900's was accompanied by a growing black middle class. Many aspects of Overton's business expansion were focused on meeting the needs of a diversifying black community. Increased social stratification in the black community led to greater product diversification in the ethnic beauty aids industry. An early attempt of Overton's to tap into this changing market came with the introduction of the *Half-Century*, a magazine for middle class blacks; this magazine has been referred to as the precursor of *Ebony*.[40]

Overton's line of cosmetics was marketed to the black middle class through the *Half-Century*. The magazine was also used to deliver Overton's message on race pride, racial independence and self- help. Of course, these messages were geared toward the middle class readers of the *Half-Century*, reaffirming their ideological perspective and solidifying class distinctions in the black community. The political message of the *Half-Century* contrasted with other black newspapers and magazines of its time, such as the *Chicago Defender* which appealed to the interests of a black working class audience. In 1918, Overton phased out the *Half-Century*, replacing it with the *Chicago Bee*, which continued to voice the interests of middle-class blacks until the late-1940's. The importance of the *Half-Century*, and its offshoot the *Chicago Bee*, was both its ideological message and the benefits of conglomeration that it brought to Overton's emerging business empire.

Overton's early experiment in the black press with the *Half-Century* was followed with the creation of what would become other black institutions in Chicago, such as: the Douglas National Bank in 1922, the Great Northern Real Estate Company around the same time, and the Victory Life Insurance Company in 1923. These businesses were housed in the Overton Hygienic/Douglas National Bank Building located at 36th and State Street in Chicago.[41] By 1929 Overton's politics and business strategies were paying off, and the Overton Hygienics Manufacturing Company was assessed by Bradstreet and Dun with a net worth in excess of $1 million.[42]

BLACK MANUFACTURERS IN BLACK METROPOLIS, FROM THE GREAT DEPRESSION TO THE CIVIL RIGHTS MOVEMENT

The Great Depression Savaged Black America

Unfortunately, Overton's empire and other black institutions could not weather the Great Depression. Many of the assets of the Douglas National Bank, the Great Northern Real Estate Company, and the Victory Life Insurance Company were lost during the depression.[43] What survived was the core of Overton's business empire: the Overton Hygienics Manufacturing Company and the *Chicago Bee*. When Overton lost control of his other businesses, he consolidated the remaining two in the Chicago Bee Building, where they continued to operate until Overton's death on July 3, 1946.[44] The financial muscle that Overton had developed during the 1920's was gone. All that remained were the ideas, the medium, and the cosmetics that his earlier success was built upon. In fact, Overton's businesses never fully recovered from the depression. In a 1933 letter from Claude A. Barnett to A.L. Holsey, the absence of Overton's company from a list of major manufacturers of ethnic beauty aids is clearly identified, "Estimates furnished me today by one of the leaders in the field and of the Negro group lists the concerns colored and white in their importance as follows: Poro, Mme. Walker, Murray, and Apex. He does not include the Overton-Hygienic in this first four."[45] In four years the Overton Hygienic Manufacturing Company, a $1 million concern in 1929, effectively disappeared. Overton's experience helps demonstrate how black businesses can obtain some level of flexibility through conglomeration and agglomeration. His experience also demonstrates that despite these advantages, black businesses still run a high risk of falling victim to broader structural shifts in the mainstream economy.

At the parochial level these shifts led to elevated tension between black consumers and businesses owned by mainstream corporations and Jews in the black community.[46] In fact, a number of corporate and Jewish-owned stores were boycotted on the South Side of Chicago during this period. These boycotts emerged as black institutions were collapsing under the weight of the depression, while white and middleman entrepreneurs continued to remain economically viable in minority markets. Much of the resentment that fueled these boycotts was generated by the uncertainty the Great Depression generated in black America, and the piecemeal approach that the government had adopted to address the economic collapse of the black community. These conditions placed businesses that primarily served the black community at risk when structural factors caused the economy to contract.

Various issues during the Great Depression exaggerate these conditions on the South Side of Chicago. For instance, black consumers tended to draw their incomes from sectors of the economy that were at greater risk of contracting during periods of economic instability. As a result, the gap between unemployment in Chicago's white and black communities more than tripled during the course of the Great Depression.[47] The economic insecurity black consumers faced created long-term challenges for businesses in minority markets. In addition, black businesses tended to be undercapitalized, and they operated at low profit margins than large corporate and small Jewish-owned businesses in the black community. These problems were both generated and complicated by racial barriers that black entrepreneurs faced in mainstream society. In fact, when black entrepreneurs were able to overcome the economic barriers they faced, racial tension in mainstream society continued to hamper their ability to participate in the economy. The experience of one black entrepreneur, S.B. Fuller, illustrates how these issues affect black business.

S.B. Fuller: A Black Manufacturer Emerges from the Great Depression

Race and the Reproduction of the Ethnic Beauty Aids Industry. Fuller entered the ethnic beauty aids industry toward the end of the Great Depression, a time when many of his predecessors were facing insolvency. Yet, the vacuum the depression created in the ethnic beauty aids industry opened opportunities for young entrepreneurs like Fuller. Similar to the black entrepreneurs who preceded him, Fuller had humble beginnings. He was born on a Farm in Oauchita Parish, Louisiana on June 15, 1905.[48] Fuller had a limited formal education, leaving school after the sixth grade. However, he continued to learn about business through work. He had his first job in door-to-door sales when he was nine years old, and with the encouragement of his mother, he continued to develop his business skills with the ultimate goal of running his own firm in the future.[49] When he was fifteen his family moved to Memphis, Tennessee, and two years later his mother died leaving Fuller responsible for the care of his six brothers and sisters. Fuller continued to take odd jobs and pursue his business goals after his mother's death. However, the opportunity to realize this dream was not available to him until later when he moved to Chicago.

In 1928 Fuller hitchhiked to Chicago, and he found temporary work in a coal yard.[50] In 1930, he found a new job selling insurance for the Commonwealth Burial Association Insurance Company. He was successful, even during the early years of the depression, and in 1934 he was promoted to manager. However, Fuller was unsettled in this position and ultimately set out on his own. He came to this decision for a variety of reasons, but broad economic forces were the strongest. The depression was creating instability in the banking and insurance industry during this time, and a shrinking pool of banking and insurance customers, along with the daily uncertainty that the depression caused, made any additional income attractive. In this uncertain environment, Fuller discovered a new business to enter, selling soap door-to-door.

In 1935 Fuller acquired some capital, twenty-five dollars, and he used it to finance his new business. Fuller later reflected on the windfall that launched his business:

> "That $25 was really all the money I had to my name. Fuller said. "And I had that much because I went and had my car refinanced and they gave me $25 in what they said was some earned interest. I was happy to get it and I wanted to use the money to do something that could do me and my family some good."[51]

Fuller did just that, turning his initial investment in a relatively unknown stock of powders, face creams and lotions into a seemingly endless stream of profits. In just a year he had saved enough money to establish the Fuller Products Company at 3441 South Indiana Avenue, in the Chicago Defender Building.[52] In 1939 Fuller Products relocated to a larger facility, a factory at 2700 South Wabash Avenue in Chicago where the company remained for several years.[53] However, Fuller faced several obstacles to business success, many related to race. In fact, like other black Americans, Fuller found it difficult to obtain loans from mainstream banks to finance his business ventures, so he relied on monies that he could raise in the black community. This was a situation that repeatedly hampered the development of his company.

Fuller's success resulted from the adoption of some of the same business strategies as his predecessors. For instance, Fuller adopted a strategy of door-to-door sales, and it worked. Regular contact with black barbers and beauticians increased the visibility of Fuller's company in the black community. This strategy allowed him to minimize conflicts with white retailers over access to shelf space, and the door-to-door strategy allowed him to identify areas where there was demand for new product. Also, due to racial climate, efforts were made to integrate the workforce of Fuller Products. After acquiring his manufacturing facility on Wabash Avenue, Fuller retained the white employees who worked there.

This rare and delicate situation, whites working for a black man, was beneficial to Fuller. In part, this was true because the arrangement provided Fuller with a skilled staff of white workers who could transfer their knowledge to black employees that were later hired. However, the retention of white employees also served a public relations function, since some whites were suspicious of the business practices of black entrepreneurs.

The Limits of Leadership in a Racially Charged Environment. In fact, Fuller became a visible leader in the black community as his business expanded. From 1941 to 1946 he served as the president of the Chicago Negro Chamber of Commerce, and received several awards from black organizations.[54] Fuller's most notable stride in business came in 1947, when he acquired Boyer International Laboratories, a white cosmetics firm. With this acquisition, Fuller had achieved what many black entrepreneurs could not. He had established himself in the mainstream economy. Boyer International was the manufacturer of Jean Nadal Cosmetics and H.A. Hair Arrangers, product lines that were distributed widely to whites in the South. Nevertheless, this acquisition was not widely publicized, since a black man buying a white company in the South had the potential of generating controversy. So, Fuller made a business decision and purchased the company clandestinely. He later reflected on this take-over in an interview in the *Chicago Tribune*, "The sale was handled quietly and not many people knew the person who bought the company was a black man. The owner had some trouble and wanted to sell it. I wanted to grow, and I was able to buy Boyer."[55] As it grew, Fuller Products gained notoriety. Fuller's success gave him access to privileges that other black entrepreneurs had been denied. Shortly after the purchase of Boyer International, Fuller became the first black member of the National Association of Manufacturers, and he also maintained membership in a variety of small regional business organizations.

Fuller developed a firm belief in the boundless nature of opportunities available to black Americans. He was confident in the future and believed in the "American dream," and like many Americans he found the brewing social unrest in the country over civil rights to be disconcerting. After all, Fuller found the grievances of the emerging civil rights movement in sharp contrast to the future he saw unfolding for himself. In 1956, a year after Rosa

Parks sparked the Montgomery Bus Boycott, Fuller held a convention in Chicago to announce his plans to build his business into a $100 million concern within ten years. At the dinner for the convention Fuller was outspoken, his tone was vividly captured in a story that ran in the ANP.

The story described how Fuller openly opposed comments made by speakers on the after dinner program. He took issue with their calls for legislative remedies to racial discrimination. As the ANP reported:

> Fuller tossed aside his prepared speech and gave a description of his own controversial philosophy on race relations. It drew cheers and applause from some of his audience and groans from others. "I am opposed to this thing of passing laws to help colored people," said Fuller. "Colored people need to help themselves. I am not afraid of the people in Tennessee or Alabama. I would not permit any of them to dislike me because I would plunge right in and sell myself to them. That's what the Negro should do all over the South."[56]

Fuller went on to recommend that blacks who were denied the right to vote in the South should simply approach hostile whites and, "sell people on their right to vote."[57] He continued with this line of reasoning:

> "Colored People in America must stop assuming and start selling. Colored people can start any kind of corporation anyone else can start. Let them go into business." "No one can keep colored people from getting an education if they want it bad enough. I have often wondered just why we have to go to school with white children? I never had a chance. I did not go to the sixth grade." "The reason for this little misunderstanding down south is that the people down there are Christian. They have been engaged all these years on selling themselves on the idea that Negroes are inferior. If they ever stopped believing Negroes are inferior to them, they could not keep up their attitudes because it would violate the Golden Rule they are taught in their religion."[58]

Several elements of Fuller's personal background came together to form his ideology: he was an ordained minister, he grew up in the South during de jure legal segregation, and above all he was a businessman. These elements blended into a worldview that combined a strong sense of the entrepreneurial spirit with an equal amount of faith in the ability of whites to use reason when confronted with issues of race. Fuller's beliefs were based on an individualistic ideology which was in sharp contrast to the idea of group mobilization that was growing around the issue of civil rights.

White Racists, Black Businessmen and Black Power at Odds. Ironically, the downfall of Fuller Products can be attributed to confrontations between Fuller and large organized groups. In a strange way these confrontations tested his belief in selling both his products and himself. But, at the time Fuller could only see a bright future for his company and race relations. After all, in 1956 Fuller's company had sales in excess of $18 million, he employed over 5000 salesmen (one third of whom were white), and he sold over 300 products.[59] Amazingly, the company was still growing and diversifying. Fuller went on to acquire the Pittsburgh Courier Publishing Company, publisher of the *New York Age* and the *Pittsburgh Courier*, two of the nation's most prominent black newspapers.[60] He also invested heavily in real estate. He purchased the Regal Theater in Chicago, a center for black entertainment, and he owned several smaller businesses in the black community.

Fuller used his network of businesses and investments to promote his products, himself and his ideology. For example, the *Pittsburgh Courier* often ran stories about Fuller. In a typical article, Fuller was quoted boasting about the two issues he gained notoriety for, business and race relations:

> "Here I am, world; I can match you! I have a God-given gift.
> I employ more Negroes and know more about them than any
> Negro in the country. I feel I am here to protect and employ
> them. To this end have I dedicated my life, and herein lies
> both my happiness and my love."[61]

The article went on to elaborate on Fuller's business accomplishments, his home in suburban Chicago, and of course his ideology based on his belief in self-help. Increasingly, Fuller returned to the issue of civil rights:

> "I have always felt, and I still say, that the salvation of the
> Negro lies in the Negro himself," Fuller reminisced. "The sit-
> ins, stand-ins, move-ins...you name it," he continued, "all
> might be fine. But what do they accomplish? The important
> thing is for us to do, as Negroes, is to appraise ourselves;
> acknowledge the truth and improve ourselves." The promi-
> nent industrialist maintains that if half the money Negroes

> are now donating to what they call civil rights causes, were
> diverted into established Negro businesses...thereby provid-
> ing jobs for other Negroes, we would not only solve the relief
> problem but we would gain a maximum of respect.[62]

Ironically, Fuller made these statements after he had come under attack by the White Citizens' Council, a white supremacist group in the South.[63] The White Citizens' Council organized a boycott of Boyer International in retaliation for similar boycotts staged by blacks in the South. In response, southern store owners pulled Fuller's products off of their shelves, sales of Jean Nadal and H.A. Hair Arranger dropped, and Fuller was forced to sell off the Boyer lines. This was devastating, because at the time, 60 percent of Fuller's sales were to whites through the Boyer lines in the South. However, Fuller stuck to his values stating that he had, "always believed that black producers should sell to white customers, the same way whites sell to blacks."[64] He went on to say, "If there had-n't been racial problems, we would be well over the $100 million mark."[65]

The boycott by the White Citizens' Council heighten Fuller's sensitivity to some issues concerning race. His business decisions were influenced by the knowledge that whites scrutinized black businesses. This is illustrated in a comment made by Fuller in a 1963 interview in *U.S. News & World Reports* :

> Here, in our organization the white people are very sensitive
> about being treated as inferior in our organization. They are
> more concerned about discrimination than the Negroes are.
> One thing I find in my organization is this: If I don't watch
> very closely, the Negro bosses here will discriminate, and hire
> all Negroes and no whites. I'm constantly watching them to
> see that they hire people on their merit and not on the color
> of their skin.[66]

Fuller's experience with the boycott created a desire to be free of scrutiny from whites, and this compromised his credibility in the black community on issues concerning racial discrimination. Fuller made several efforts to distance himself from the civil rights move-ment. He articulated a position that the civil rights movement was misguided, and it reinforced the notion of blacks as second class citizens. Fuller's statements enraged many blacks who saw him as an apologist, or an "Uncle Tom." Fuller's response to these accu-sations was fiery, "No Negro Calls me an 'Uncle Tom.' He can't call me 'Uncle Tom' because I employ white people. And 'Uncle Tom' never employed any white people."[67]

Tensions between Fuller and civil rights advocates came to a head in late 1963, over a speech he delivered to the National Association of Manufacturers. In this speech he stated that, "a lack of understanding and not racial barriers was keeping blacks from making progress."[68] This was a reiteration of Fullers earlier comments, however he was increasingly reaching a mainstream audience. When Fuller was making these statements to a predominantly black audience it was perceived as a healthy dialogue in the black community, but the possibility that Fuller's statements would somehow undermine efforts to expand civil rights prompted a strong response from black organizations. Fuller Products was targeted for a consumer boycott, but this time it was organized by black Americans.

Fuller never understood why blacks chose to boycott his products. He believed his message had been misinterpreted. In all fairness, Fuller probably thought that his belief that the black community was suffering from economic deprivation, which could only be addressed through the development of internal resources, was the central concern of his people. This was the perspective of Fuller and other black entrepreneurs who preceded him. It reflected their experiences, their sense of the world, and the views of their upper-middle-class peers. Unfortunately, Fuller's opinions were not shared by blacks from other social strata. His inability to defer to these individuals, and to understand that they did not share his experience as an entrepreneur was instrumental in Fuller's undoing.

Fuller's clashes with the White Citizens' Council and civil rights advocates had devastating effects on his business, but his inability to weather these attacks was a reflection of deeper institutional forces that undermine all black-owned businesses in minority markets. In fact, the boycott of Fuller Products by black consumers took place during a period of growing tension between black and white America, and it signaled a general shift in the racial climate in mainstream society. This same atmosphere of racism and racial discrimination precipitated confrontations at the parochial level between black consumers and middleman merchants during the 1960's. For instance, the Watts Riot in Los Angeles occurred after the police killed a black motorist, although at the parochial level it resulted in conflicts between blacks and Jewish merchants. Similarly, the assassination of Martin Luther King Jr. in 1968 resulted in the looting of Jewish-owned stores in several black neighborhoods around the country. For instance, in Chicago Jewish-owned businesses were damaged due to extensive looting and arson where, "Several blocks on Madison and Roosevelt were completely flattened, resembling more of an open plain than the aftermath of a riot."[69]

Analogously, the downfall of Fuller Products was brought about by the same racial climate that generated opposition to the civil rights movement, although it was articulated in a more subtle manner. Regardless, the demise of Fuller Products was a result of the endemic problem that this racial climate had historically produced for black entrepreneurs, particularly when trying to gain access to credit and mainstream markets. In fact, this became apparent after the immediate effects of the boycotts had passed, and Fuller attempted to reorganize his company. Fuller structured a deal to sell Boyer International to a white buyer in New York City, and he used the proceeds of the sale and a bank loan that they attracted to leverage a new project, the Fuller Department Store in Chicago. With the acquisition of a Department Store, Fuller believed he could make his business more resilient and flexible. Door-to-door sales could be used strategically to expose the company to new customers, while established markets could be maintained by a single store in a fixed, centralized, location. Fuller would received an additional benefit from owning his own department store, he would reduce the risk of having sales damaged due to boycotts and white merchants pulling products from their shelves. But, financial constraints put the Fuller Department Store out of business.

Shortly after Fuller had used the proceeds from the sale of Boyer International to leverage the purchase of the Fuller Department Store, the buyer in New York pulled out of the deal, and Fuller was left in debt. To make matters worst, Fuller had been extending credit to welfare recipients. This created a confrontation with the Social Service Administration in Chicago.[70] The Fuller Department Store had established a policy where welfare recipients could purchase up to $100 worth of goods for $30 down. The Social Service Administration publicly urged their clients not to honor these debts with Fuller. As a result, these consumers stopped making payments. Fuller was left with over $1 million in uncollectible debts. Because of these setbacks Fuller Products declared bankruptcy in 1968, and sold off most of its real estate and newspaper holdings.[71] Fuller was left with his cosmetics and toiletries lines. Bankrupt, in debt and with little capital, Fuller refocused on the old formula, door-to-door sales. At this point, Fuller was relegated to a minor position in the business world. However, he remained active in Chicago's black business community until his death in 1988.[72]

FROM THE CIVIL RIGHTS MOVEMENT TO THE GLOBAL ECONOMY, CORPORATE AMERICA RAIDS THE SOUTH SIDE

The Growing Influence of Outsiders in Black America

Fuller was like many of the black entrepreneurs who preceded him. His company experienced a period of rapid growth due to its unique position in the minority market; however, it could never make the jump from being a medium sized firm to a corporate giant. Attempts to move into the mainstream economy were thwarted by social barriers, institutional barriers, and outright racism. Yet, the need for Fuller's company to grow was ever present, since larger mainstream competitors were encroaching on his market. In fact, black entrepreneurs found their ability to compete economically diminishing at all levels in minority markets during this period. For instance, in the area of retailing, black entrepreneurs faced stiff competition from better capitalized corporate and Jewish merchants historically, and in the early 1970's they also began to be crowded out of the market by Korean merchants in the black community.

Although Jewish merchants were beginning to retreat from the black community during this period, blacks were blocked from participating in ethnic succession by the growing presence of a better financed group of Korean merchants in the black community. However, these conditions at the parochial level simply mirrored growing inequalities between black manufacturers and larger white-owned conglomerates, where the true struggle for control of the ethnic beauty aids industry unfolded. However, black manufacturers were at a greater disadvantage as time passed, since the

costs of doing business were increasing as white-owned conglomerate invested more time and resources in marketing strategies in
minority markets. The problems that black manufacturers faces
were further compounded by the persistence of racial barriers to
capital and mainstream markets.

As a result, competition from larger white-owned conglomerates intensified in the ethnic beauty aids industry, and black manufacturers found few options open to them beyond the traditional
business strategies used by blacks to cope with racism and racial
discrimination in the economy. The experiences of another black
businessman, George Johnson, illustrate how the nexus between
racial discrimination in mainstream society and the growing
involvement of white-owned conglomerates in minority markets
affected the stability of black manufacturing in the ethnic beauty
aids industry.

George Johnson: A Black Manufacturer at the End of the Civil Rights Movement

Steering Black Manufacturers to Minority Markets. The most per-
vasive issues that George Johnson faced as an entrepreneur in the
ethnic beauty aids industry were racism and growing competition
from large white-owned companies. However, the two issues were
closely related, since the inability to compete with larger companies, in part, resulted from earlier capital constraints linked to
racial discrimination. Obtaining capital for entrepreneurship was
critical to Johnson, since he came from a working class background and had little personal wealth to start his business with initially. Johnson was born in Richton, Mississippi, on June 16,
1927.[73] Two years after his birth his mother relocated the family to
Chicago, where she planned to find work. Johnson grew up in the
city, and attended school until the eleventh grade. In 1944, he left
school and began to work at Fuller Products. He started as a door-
to-door salesman, and after a few months became a production
chemist. By the early 1950's, he had been promoted to production
manager at Fuller Products. However, Johnson had recently married, and he began to search for ways to increase his income. In
1954, he decided to resign from Fuller Products and go into business himself.

Johnson developed a new formula for hair-straightening, and
entered into a business partnership with a Chicago-based barber,

Orville Nelson, whose clientele included notable black celebrities such as Duke Elington and Nat King Cole. The partnership would take advantage of both Johnson and Nelson's strengths, "Nelson took charge of promotions and sales, given his built-in client base, and Johnson oversaw the manufacturing responsibilities."[74] The two men agreed to contribute $250 each to this business venture, and this was when Johnson faced his first racial barrier to obtaining venture capital for his business. He went to a local white-owned finance company to get a loan and, "An unimpressed loan officer called the idea 'ridiculous' and turned him down."[75] A few days later Johnson went to another branch of the same company and applied for a $250 loan for a fictitious vacation to California, and was approved. With this capital, Johnson established the Johnson Products Company, and launched its first product line, Ultra Wave Hair Culture.

After a short period of time, the partnership between Johnson and Nelson was dissolved, and Johnson retained control of his company. In 1955, Johnson's wife and brother had joined the company, and Johnson worked to develop a market for his products. He began developing this market in Chicago, and then branched out to other cities. Johnson, "hustled as a one-man sales force through the city's black barber shops, and soon his swings took him to Indianapolis, Detroit and beyond."[76] Johnson cultivated a market for his products in the black community. In his first year of operation, sales reached $18,000.[77] In his second year they rose to $75,000.[78] By 1958, the company had to move to a three story manufacturing facility to accommodate growing demand, as its sales reached $250,000.[79] At this time, Johnson Products was exclusively selling its products to black barbershops; however, their popularity eventually pushed Johnson to expand into the retail market. In 1966, Johnson Products marketed a low priced line of products to black consumers. The products were promoted through a marketing campaign in the black press, and sold through chain stores and discount stores owned by Jews and Koreans that Johnson could access in the black community.

Although confined to the black community, Johnson's experiment with the retail market was successful. In 1969, Johnson Products became the first black owned company to be listed on the American stock exchange. Johnson raised $8,400,000 in the public offering for expansion purposes. Although this allowed

Johnson to overcome barriers to capitalization that he had experienced in the past, it also made his company, and the ethnic beauty aids industry, more visible to potential competitors in the corporate world. Despite the large sum that Johnson raised, he was still limited to minority markets. In part, because he was not well enough capitalized to break out of this niche market and compete with larger conglomerates, but also since racial barriers were still constraining the growth of Johnson Products. So, Johnson focused on advertising and developing new products for the minority market. For instance, in 1970, it was pointed out that, "Almost all of his $2,000,000 advertising budget goes into black print media, radio and an occasional TV special aimed at nonwhites."[80] Faced with limited access to mainstream markets, Johnson expanded the scope of advertising in the black community, by utilizing the print media and through sponsoring television shows that targeted black Americans, such as the program "Soul Train."

Johnson Products grew rapidly in the 1970's, and it became the largest black manufacturing company in the country. Between 1968 and 1973, the company's sales quadrupled.[81] In 1971 gross sales were $14 million, they grew to $24 million in 1973, and reached $39.4 million in 1976.[82] However, racial barriers and growing competition began to weigh heavily on the company by the mid-1970's. The first indication that Johnson Products had reached its limits came in 1975 when Johnson attempted to introduce a product to white consumers. The product was Black Tie, a cologne for men. However, Johnson was unable to gain access to upscale department stores to market this product. In fact, the distributors who carried the product insisted on placing it in the ethnic section of chain stores, and on steering it toward Jewish and Korean-owned stores in the black community. This practice undermined Johnson's efforts to reach white consumers. Johnson's comments about the fate of Black Tie clearly identify how race became a barrier to market entry:

> It was clear that the hang up was the fact that this particular fragrance, specifically developed for the general consumer market, was produced by Johnson Products, a black manufacturer. When all the dust settled, the debacle cost our company around $8 million.[83]

The Black Tie affair was only the first in a number of events that led to the demise of Johnson Products.

The Role of Government and Corporate America. In 1976, Johnson Products was the target of selective regulation by the Federal Trade Commission (FTC). At that time, the FTC ordered Johnson Products to issue safety warnings on its products containing lye, while larger white-owned companies with similar products on the market were not required to issue such warnings. Johnson challenged the order, but the FTC claimed that, "it went after Johnson's company because it was the market leader."[84] Two years later, the FTC changed its policy and began to apply its regulations to white-owned conglomerates who manufactured products containing lye as well. However, by this time irreversible damage had been done to the reputation of Johnson Products. In the end the company lost market shares, since black consumers saw the FTC warnings as an indication that their products were unsafe. To protect his company, Johnson solicited support from leaders in the black community. In the late 1970's, Jesse Jackson launcher a campaign to urge retailers and consumers to buy ethnic products made by blacks. However, these efforts failed to stop the decline of Johnson Products.

In 1980, Johnson Products' market share in the ethnic beauty aids industry had declined from 60 percent to 40 percent.[85] By 1984, Johnson products had reported a net loss of $4.1 million, and this loss reached $4.5 million the next year.[86] This reflected an industry wide trend for black manufacturers. As the 1980's progressed, the market shares of black manufacturers in the ethnic beauty aids industry were declining, while those of white-owned conglomerates were increasing.[87] Many blacks in the industry suspected that larger white-owned companies aimed to control the ethnic beauty aids industry. In 1986, this suspicion was affirmed in comments made by the president of Revlon's professional products division in *Newsweek*, "In the next couple of years, the black-owned businesses will disappear. They'll all be sold to white companies."[88] This statement drew heated criticism in the black community. Jesse Jackson announced a national boycott of Revlon products, and the American Health and Beauty Aids Institute (AHBAI), an organization of black businesses in the ethnic beauty aids industry, added $3 million to its existing $2 million campaign designed to encourage black consumers to buy ethnic beauty aids manufactured by blacks.[89]

Johnson supported these efforts, and attempted to mobilize resources in the black community to rehabilitate his company. He also returned to marketing strategies used by earlier black entrepreneurs. In 1985, he launched a new line of products using a celebrity endorsement. This was the Team Jordan personal products line, a line of mens products endorsed by Michael Jordan of the Chicago Bulls. However, Johnson continued to face the same racial barriers to product development with Team Jordan as he did with Black Tie, which kept the products away from white consumers. The inability to enter the mainstream market, and growing competition from white-owned conglomerates in minority markets, forced Johnson to make a number of changes in his company. In the mid-1980's, Johnson Products downsized, making cuts in its workforce and salaries. Johnson also began to liquidate the companies assets to raise capital. In 1987, Johnson borrowed $10 million against his company, sold real estate near the company's headquarters for $1 million, and sold the company's beauty school and salons in order to raise capital.[90] However, these efforts had little effect, and Johnson Products continued to experience financial troubles. In 1988, the company reported a $2.3 million loss.[91]

Johnson eventually had to relinquish control of his company in 1989, after divorcing his wife. However, he remained involved at Johnson Products, acting as a consultant. As a result of the divorce, Johnson's son, Eric Johnson, became the president of Johnson Products. Eric Johnson continued to downsize Johnson Products in an attempt to lower the companies operating costs. By 1991, the strategy had resulted in a slight recovery for the company. Johnson Products earned $3.2 million in profits that year.[92] Despite this turn of events, Eric Johnson eventually left the company in 1992 due to internal conflict with its board of directors. The following year, Johnson Products was purchased by the Ivax Corporation, a large white-owned pharmaceutical company based in Miami, Florida.[93] By this time, Johnson had severed ties with Johnson Products, living off of other investments and real estate he had acquired over the years.

CONTINUITY AND CHANGE FOR BLACK MANUFACTURERS, 1890-1990

This chapter has examined the experiences of three generations of black manufacturers in Chicago's ethnic beauty aids industry. The first generation was active from the Great Migration to the Great Depression, a period when the many of the core business strategies adopted by black manufacturers were formulated in a systematic manner. The second generation was active from the Great Depression to the civil rights movement, a period when black manufacturers in the ethnic beauty aids industry demonstrated their resilience to both economic and political instability. The third generation was active from the civil rights movement to the early 1990's, a period when competition from corporate America increased as the global economy expanded.

Each of these historical periods has imprinted contemporary minority markets on the South Side of Chicago. For instance, many current themes related to ethnic solidarity and self-help in the black community can be traced to the first historical period examined in this chapter. Similarly, these themes have been rearticulated in a broader based message of group mobilization and equality that emerged in the black community during the civil rights movement. In addition, although isolated from white America, minority markets are increasingly being exposed to the global economy. For instance, at the parochial level, new waves of immigrants are taking on traditional middleman roles in the black community. While at the corporate level, large white-owned conglomerates are increasingly pursuing profits in the black community.

Many similarities are found in the experiences of black manufacturers in Chicago's ethnic beauty aids industry, as a result of imprinting from one historical period to the next. For instance, all of the black manufacturers discussed in this chapter coped with capital constraints, which limited the scope of their business activities. However, these constraints were compounded by racial barriers to business development. All of the black manufacturers also found it difficult gaining access to stores owned by whites and middleman groups. This limited their ability to reach black consumers, and to enter the mainstream market in order to sell their products to white consumers. In addition, the black manufacturers

reacted to the perception that their businesses were heavily scrutinized by whites. In some instances, this scrutiny resulted in consumer boycotts initiated by angry whites who opposed the
participation of blacks in the mainstream economy. In other
instances, this scrutiny took the form of legal action aimed at protecting white-owned companies from black-owned competitors. In
some instances, these conflicts between black and white Americans
aggravated tension at the parochial level between blacks and middleman entrepreneurs, such as Jews and Koreans. However, the
end result was that black manufacturers were unable to compete
on equal terms with white manufacturers. This was not simply an
issue of business size, but a more complex dynamic incorporating
racial cues.

A number of adaptations emerged in response to the racial and
economic barriers that black manufacturers faced. Hindered by
capital constraints and racial discrimination, black manufacturers
chose to mobilize ethnic resources in the black community. They
focused on developing the minority markets that they found themselves embedded in. By doing so, they benefitted from the knowledge gained through informal networks in black barber and beauty
shops. Black manufacturers also augmented their influence in the
black community by utilizing the black media. These were important resources for black entrepreneurs, who faced competition
from better capitalized white-owned conglomerates. The ability of
black manufacturers to cultivate ethnic solidarity in the black community was vital to their survival, despite the growing interest of
white-owned conglomerates in the ethnic beauty aids industry.

The issues raised in this chapter add dimension to the discussion
of black-owned businesses in the next chapter, since many of the
issues examined in relation to black manufacturers in the ethnic
beauty aids industry are also identified in more general discussions
of the underdevelopment of black business. This supports arguments which state that black businesses are shaped by economic
and social constraints in society, many of which grow out of the
experiences blacks have with racism and racial discrimination in
America. These social conditions have generated pressures in society, compelling black business to remain outside of the mainstream
economy and confined to minority markets.

In a similar manner, this chapter also adds credence to a general framework for the discussion of Jewish and Korean entrepre-

neurship in the black community, focusing on the influence of racism and racial discrimination on their economic activities. This is the case, since to some extent racial barriers also limit the degree to which these entrepreneurial groups can participate in the mainstream economy. These barriers create incentives for middleman entrepreneurs, like Jews and Koreans, to pursue economic activities in the black community, rather than in white America. In the next chapter, institutional factors in mainstream society which influence the scope of black, Jewish and Korean entrepreneurship on the South Side of Chicago will be discussed in more detail.

NOTES

[1] For a detailed discussion of the Great Migration see, St. Clair Drake and Horace R. Cayton, *Black Metropolis, A Study of Negro Life in a Northern City*, (Chicago: University of Chicago Press, 1993); James R. Grossman, *Land of Hope, Chicago, Black Southerners, and the Great Migration*, (Chicago: University of Chicago Press, 1989); Allan H. Spear, *Black Chicago, The Making of a Negro Ghetto*, (Chicago: University of Chicago Press, 1967).

[2] Allan H. Spear, *Black Chicago, The Making of a Negro Ghetto 1890-1920*, (Chicago: University of Chicago Press, 1967): 12.

[3] Ibid, 12.

[4] St. Clair Drake and Horace R. Cayton, *Black Metropolis, A Study of Negro Life in a Northern City*, (Chicago: University of Chicago Press, 1993): 434.

[5] "Business in Bronzeville," *Time*, (18 April 1938): 70.

[6] Lizabeth Cohen, *Making a New Deal, Industrial Workers in Chicago, 1919-1939*, (New York: Cambridge University Press, 1990): 147-158; St. Clair Drake and Horace R. Cayton, *Black Metropolis, A study of Negro Life in a Northern City* (Chicago: The University of Chicago Press, 1993): 433-437.

[7] St. Clair Drake and Horace R. Cayton, *Black Metropolis, A study of Negro Life in a Northern City*, (Chicago: The University of Chicago Press, 1993): 438.

[8] Ibid, 438.

[9] Ibid, 438.

[10]"Business in Bronzeville," *Time*, (18 April 1938): 70.

[11] St. Clair Drake and Horace R. Cayton, *Black Metropolis, A study of Negro Life in a Northern City*, (Chicago: The University of Chicago Press, 1993): 461.

[12] John N. Ingham and Lynne B. Feldman, *African-American Business Leaders, A Bibliographical Dictionary*, (Westport: Greenwood Press, 1994): 634-640.

[13] Ibid, 680-693.

[14] Barnett, Claude Albert, Biographical Sketch, n.d., Claude A. Barnett Collection, Chicago Historical Society, Chicago, IL, Box 405, Folder 6.

[15] Ibid.

[16] A variety of materials related to Claude A. Barnett's ties to the Tuskegee Institute are found in the Claude A. Barnett Collection at the Chicago Historical Society.

[17] "C.A. Barnett,77, Founder of Negro Wire Service, Dies," *Chicago Sun-Times*, (3 August 1967): 88.

[18] Letter to Claude A. Barnett from the Office of the Secretary of State of Illinois, 9 January 1947, Claude A. Barnett Collection, Chicago Historical Society, Chicago, IL, Box 263, Folder 3.

[19] Pamphlet for Kashmir Preparations, n.d. but pre-1921, Claude A. Barnett Collection, Chicago Historical Society, Chicago, IL, Box 262, Folder 3.

[20] Ibid.

[21] Ibid.

[22] Letter to Claude A. Barnett from the Office of the Secretary of State of Illinois, 9 January 1947, Claude A. Barnett Collection, Chicago Historical Society, Chicago, IL, Box 263, Folder 3.

[23] Pamphlet for Nile Queen Preparations, n.d. but post-1921, Claude A. Barnett Collection, Chicago Historical Society, Chicago, IL, Box 262, Folder 3.

[24] Letterhead for Kashmir Chemical Company, 1920, Claude A. Barnett Collection, Chicago Historical Society, Chicago, IL, Box 262, Folder 2.

[25] F.B. Ransom's letter to the Kashmir Chemical Company, 18 March 1920, Claude A. Barnett Collection, Chicago Historical Society, Chicago, IL, Box 262, Folder 2.

[26] Kashmir Chemical Company's reply to F.B. Ransom, 19 March 1920, Claude A. Barnett Collection, Chicago Historical Society, Chicago, IL, Box 262, Folder 2.

[27] F.B. Ransom's reply to the Kashmir Chemical Company, 20 March 1920, Claude A. Barnett Collection, Chicago Historical Society, Chicago, IL, Box 262, Folder 2.

[28] Ibid.

[29] Barnett discusses the details of these differences in a letter he sent to A.L. Holsey the Secretary of the National Negro Business League, 29 October 1930, Claude A. Barnett Collection, Chicago Historical Society, Chicago, IL, Box 261, Folder 6.

[30] Barnett discusses Murray's Supreme Products Company in a letter he sent to A.L. Holsey the Secretary of the National Negro Business League, 4 March 1933, Claude A. Barnett Collection, Chicago Historical Society, Chicago, IL, Box 261, Folder 6.

[31] "Charles D. Murray, Obit.," *Chicago Tribune*, (26 July 1955).

[32] Advertisement for Murray's Superior Products Featuring Joe Louis, *The Crisis*, 45.4 (April 1938).

[33] Advertisement for Murray's Superior Products Featuring Charles D. Murray, *The Crisis*, 45.4 (April 1938)

[34] James J. Flynn, *Negroes of Achievement in Modern America*, (New York: Dodd, Mead and Company, 1970): 109-120.

[35] Ibid.

[36] There is some dispute over the year that the Overton Hygienic Manufacturing Company was formed. A notation in *The Crisis* dates the company's inception back to 1898 in Kansas City, see *The Crisis*, (September 1915): 242. Also, Ingham dates the company back to the same date see John N. Ingham and Lynne B. Feldman. *African-American Business Leaders, A Bibliographical Dictionary,* (Westport: Greenwood Press, 1994): 492-499. However, the confusion seems to be the result of an earlier company operated by Overton going bankrupt and later being reorganized by Overton and Forbes in 1909.

[37] The genesis of this conglomerate is briefly described in "Chicago Claims Supremacy," *Opportunity*, (March 1929): 92-93.

[38] James J. Flynn, *Negroes of Achievement in Modern America*. (Dodd, Mead and Company: New York, 1970): 109-120.

[39] John N. Ingham and Lynne B. Feldman. *African-American Business Leaders, A Bibliographical Dictionary,* (Westport: Greenwood Press, 1994): 492-499.

[40] Ibid.

[41] Russell L. Adams, *Great Negroes Past and Present*, (Chicago: Afro-Am Publishing Company, 1964): 71.

[42] "Anthony Overton, Known As the 'Merchant Prince' of His Race, Heads the Overton Hygienic Manufacturing Company, Rated by Bradstreet and Dun At a Million Dollars," *Pittsburgh Courier*, (10 August 1929).

[43] St. Clair Drake and Horace R. Cayton, *Black Metropolis, A study of Negro Life in a Northern City*, (Chicago: The University of Chicago Press, 1993): 462-463; Allan H. Spear, *Black Chicago, The Making of a Negro Ghetto 1890-1920* (Chicago: The University of Chicago Press, 1967): 184.

[44] John N. Ingham and Lynne B. Feldman. *African-American Business Leaders, A Bibliographical Dictionary*, (Westport: Greenwood Press, 1994): 492-499; "Anthony Overton, Obit," *Chicago Tribune*, (4 July 1946).

[45] Barnett's letter to A.L. Holsey the Secretary of the National Negro Business League, 4 March 1933, Claude A. Barnett Collection, Chicago Historical Society, Chicago, IL., Box 261, Folder 6.

[46] Lizabeth Cohen, *Making a New Deal, Industrial Workers in Chicago, 1919-1939*, (New York: Cambridge University Press, 1990): 151-154; St. Clair Drake and Horace R. Cayton, *Black Metropolis, A Study of Negro Life in a Northern City*, (Chicago: University of Chicago Press, 1993): 439-453.

[47] St. Clair Drake and Horace R. Cayton, *Black Metropolis, A Study of Negro Life in a Northern City*, (Chicago: University of Chicago Press, 1993): 214-218.

[48] *Dudley's Haircare Fact Book*, (Greensboro: Dudley Products Inc., 1993): 24-27.

[49] John N. Ingham and Lynne B. Feldman. *African-American Business Leaders, A Bibliographical Dictionary*, (Westport: Greenwood Press, 1994): 244-249.

[50] *Dudley's Haircare Fact Book*, (Greensboro: Dudley Products Inc., 1993): 24-27.

[51] "The Dean of Black Entrepreneurs," *Chicago Tribune*, (9 June 1987): 3-1.

[52] "Fuller Brings It To Your Door, House-To-House Selling Pays Off," *The Chicago Defender*, (26 May 1951): 13.

[53] Ibid.

[54] Ibid.

[55] "The Dean of Black Entrepreneurs," *Chicago Tribune*, (9 June 1987): 3-1.

[56] ANP release titled "Largest Cosmetic Business Holds Annual Conference, Plan $100 Million Concern," 39 July 1956, Claude A. Barnett Collection, Chicago Historical Society, Chicago, IL, Box 261, Folder 7.

[57] Ibid.

[58] Ibid.

[59] "Aiming for $100-Million Sales," *Fortune*, (September 1957): 76.

[60] John N. Ingham and Lynne B. Feldman. *African-American Business Leaders, A Bibliographical Dictionary*, (Westport: Greenwood Press, 1994): 244-249.

[61] "Salvation of Negro in America Lies in Controlling Economy," *Pittsburgh Courier Centennial Edition*, (17 August 1963): 4- 1.

[62] Ibid.

[63] "S.B. Fuller, A Man and His Products," *Black Enterprise*, 6.1 (August 1975): 46.

[64] Ibid.

[65] Ibid.

[66] "A Negro Businessman Speaks His Mind," *U.S. News & World Reports*, (19 August 1963): 58.

[67] Ibid.

[68] "The Dean of Black Entrepreneurs," *Chicago Tribune*, (9 June 1987): 3-1.

[69] Howard Aldrich and Albert J. Reiss, Jr., "The Effects of Civil Disorder on Small Business in the Inner City," *Journal of Social Issues*, 26.1 (1970): 191.

[70] "S.B. Fuller, A Man and His Products," *Black Enterprise*, 6.1 (August 1975): 46.

[71] Ibid.

[72] "S.B. Fuller Dead, a Business Legend, Obit.," *Chicago Defender*, (25 October 1988); "S.B. Fuller, Black Entrepreneurs' Dean, Obit.," *Chicago Tribune*, (26 October 1988).

[73] John N. Ingham and Lynne B. Feldman. *African-American Business Leaders, A Bibliographical Dictionary*, (Westport: Greenwood Press, 1994): 357-366.

[74] Ibid, 358.

[75] "Making Black Beautiful," *Time*, (7 December 1970): 87.

[76] Ibid, 88.

[77] John N. Ingham and Lynne B. Feldman. *African-American Business Leaders, A Bibliographical Dictionary*, (Westport: Greenwood Press, 1994): 358.

[78] Ibid, 358.

[79] Ibid, 358.

[80] "Making Black Beautiful," *Time*, (7 December 1970): 88.

[81] John N. Ingham and Lynne B. Feldman. *African-American Business Leaders, A Bibliographical Dictionary*, (Westport: Greenwood Press, 1994): 360.

[82] Ibid, 360.

[83] Ibid, 361.

[84] Ibid, 361.

[85] Ibid, 362.

[86] "Big Marketers Move in on Ethnic Haircare," *Advertising Age*, (12 May 1986): 24.

[87] *Dudley's Haircare Fact Book*, (Greensboro: Dudley Products Inc., 1993): 35.

[88] Penelope Wang and Maggie Malone, "Targeting Black Dollars, White-Owned Companies Muscle Minority Firms Out of the Hair-Care Market," *Newsweek*, (13 October 1986): 54.

[89] Phyllis Furman, "Ethnic Haircare Marketers Battle for Shares," *Advertising Age*, (2 March 1997): 52.

[90] John N. Ingham and Lynne B. Feldman. *African-American Business Leaders, A Bibliographical Dictionary*, (Westport: Greenwood Press, 1994): 363.

[91] "Johnson Products Tries to Catch a New Wave," *Business Week*, (27 August 1990): 56.

[92] "Brawl in the Family at Johnson Products," *Business Week*, (23 March 1992): 34; "Johnson Products Co. Regrouping After Family Row," *Black Enterprise*, (May 1992): 17.

[93] "A Compulsive Buyer or a Master Builder," *Business Week*, (28 June 1993): 38.

CHAPTER 3:

The Context Of Minority Entrepreneurship On The South Side Of Chicago

OVERVIEW

The South Side of Chicago has been a minority market since the early 1900's. This status, and the inherent social constraints associated with it, have shaped entrepreneurship in the ethnic beauty aids industry on the South Side of Chicago historically. The central argument of this chapter is that minority markets are created and maintained by racism and racial discrimination in mainstream society. Several dimensions of minority markets on the South Side of Chicago are discussed in order to illustrate this point.

The first major section of this chapter outlines some of the theoretical issues associated with the development of underdevelopment on the South Side of Chicago. First, there is a discussion of how racism and racial discrimination have historically isolated minority markets on the South Side of Chicago. Then, the relationship between social isolation and consumer behavior in minority markets is examined. Finally, the relationship between the social isolation of minority markets and some of the similarities between black, Jewish and Korean merchants on the South Side of Chicago is identified.

The second major section of this chapter focuses on the historical development of black and Jewish entrepreneurship on the South Side of Chicago, from the Great Migration to the civil rights movement. First, the early development of separate economic niches for black and Jewish entrepreneurs on the South Side of Chicago is discussed. Then, the relationship between the underdevelopment of black business and internal colonialism on the South Side of Chicago is explored. Finally, the relationship between economic underdevelopment and black-Jewish conflict on the South Side of Chicago during this period is examined.

The third major section of this chapter focuses on the development of Korean entrepreneurship on the South Side of Chicago during the post-1970 period. First, there is a discussion of some of the factors that facilitated the succession of Jewish merchants by Korean merchants on the South Side of Chicago during the early 1970's. This discussion is followed by an examination of some of the incentives for Korean merchants to remain on the South Side of Chicago, and some of the racial barriers that impeded their ability to access the mainstream economy.

The material in this chapter is presented to frame the theoretical and historical issues identified in chapters 1 and 2. Most importantly, this chapter elaborates on the concept of a minority market, and it provides illustrations for arguments concerning internal colonialism. To this end, the discussion of black, Jewish and Korean entrepreneurs illuminates some of the nuances of doing business in a minority market.

THE DEVELOPMENT OF UNDERDEVELOPMENT ON THE SOUTH SIDE OF CHICAGO

Social Isolation and Economic Underdevelopment

The disadvantages that black and immigrant entrepreneurs faced in the economy, and the role of mainstream institutions in highlighting inequalities between them, should be considered as components of doing business in a minority market. These issues encompass some of the qualitative difference between mainstream and minority markets. An awareness of the structural constraints present in a minority market is required in order to understanding the disadvantages that individual minority-owned businesses experience. Entrepreneurship in a minority market occurs in an institutional setting that incorporates a unique set of environmental constraints and psychological adaptations. The principle environmental constraints of a minority market relate to William Julius Wilson's discussion of social isolation.[1] Using this concept, it can be argued that minority markets have become isolated from mainstream institutions as a result of the racial antagonism and capital constraints that blacks experience in mainstream society. Because of this, minority markets have remained underdeveloped and separate from the mainstream economy. The expectations of consumers and entrepreneurs in minority markets have developed in response to a history of neglect by mainstream institutions. Over time, the social isolation of minority market was compounded by geographic isolation, since minority markets grew in size. As minority markets became larger, they have also became more isolated from the mainstream economy. These concentration effects produced large areas of economic underdevelopment. This process is illustrated by examining the history of minority business development on the South Side of Chicago.

The growth of minority markets on the South Side of Chicago occurred over a period of decades. A pattern developed where minority markets grew as the black population became concentrated in South Side neighborhoods and suburbs. By the 1930's several minority shopping districts had emerged on the South Side of Chicago west of State Street along "43rd, 47th, 51st, and 57th Streets."[2] As the black population grew, other shopping districts took on the characteristics of minority markets. By the early 1970's the Madison-Pulaski shopping district west of Downtown Chicago, the Maxwell Street market at the intersection of Maxwell Street and Halsted Street, the Englewood mall at 63rd Street and Halsted Street, and the Roseland shopping district located between 110th and 113th Streets on Michigan Avenue functioned as minority markets. By 1990, Chicago's minority markets encompassed all of the predominantly black neighborhoods on the West Side of Chicago, the South Side of Chicago and in northwestern Indiana. Despite the combined size of these minority markets, the state of business on the South Side of Chicago has remained underdeveloped for decades. This is the result of the historical effects of racial discrimination, public sector neglect and economic exploitation by institutions in mainstream society.

Historically, economic underdevelopment on the South Side of Chicago is well documented.[3] Small undercapitalized businesses, a lack of public investment, and derelict commercial property were identified as characteristics of the business climate on the South Side of Chicago for decades. For example, in 1950, Claude A.

Barnett, who was the founder of the Associated Negro Press (ANP), posed these questions about economic conditions on the South Side of Chicago:

> What has happened right here on the South Side on nearly every cross street? Why do we have four or five times as many restaurants or eating places in a block as necessary, most of them dirty and unsanitary? Who ought to police that sort of thing and insist on limiting the number of each type of business in a given area, so we might have one successful business instead of a lot of half run establishments cutting each other's and the publics throats?. . .Who does it in the white neighborhoods? Why have 31st Street, 35th Street, 39th Street, 43rd and most of the cross streets on the South Side become infested with dives and saloons and storefront churches? There is enough money in these areas to support first class stores. Why do the high class merchants run away? Why is it that on 35th Street near where I office for example, there are three liquor dives, with wine heads and half stupefied people staggering in and out all day long, all owned by low type white people in full view of and right across from a police station?[4]

These statements were made nearly a half century ago. However, underdevelopment continues to characterize the South Side of Chicago, and this is reflected in the attitudes black consumers bring to minority markets.

Underdevelopment and Consumer Behavior

The environmental constraints of minority markets produce a number of psychological adaptations for consumers, and subsequently entrepreneurs. Several unique characteristics have been associated with black consumers in minority markets.[5] It has been argued that black consumers draw their incomes from sectors of the economy that are at risk of contracting during periods of economic instability.[6] As a result, black consumers try to stretch their dollars and have a tendency to set aside savings at higher rates than whites at comparable income levels.[7] Black consumers also face racial discrimination in the mainstream economy. In some cases, black consumers face discrimination when shopping for durable goods such as household appliances and automobiles. In others, they experience discrimination when trying to purchase less expensive consumer products and services. As a result, some black consumers prefer to make purchases in minority markets, in order to avoid the racial barriers that they find in the mainstream economy. In addition, black consumers find specialized products and services in minority markets that are not as accessible in the mainstream economy. One example are the products that are manufactured in the ethnic beauty aids industry. In fact, there are a number of incentives for black consumers to shop in minority markets.

Despite these incentives, minority markets offer a limited range of goods and services. In fact, the absence of many goods and services in minority markets, and the presence of racial barriers to economic activity in the mainstream economy affects the economic behavior of black consumers. As a result, black consumers in minority markets expend higher rates of their disposable income on nondurable goods like clothing and personal services. For instance, Marcus Alexis identified the link between racial barriers and the behavior of black consumers when he stated that, "The greater emphasis of blacks on clothing is explained by the inability of blacks to purchase some forms of recreation or shelter. Thus, clothing becomes a substitute for inaccessible alternatives."[8] This comment highlights how racial barriers shaped the economic behavior of black consumers, and subsequently the business environment in minority markets. However, black consumers remain autonomous within the structure of minority markets. For instance, some black consumers express agency through a high degree of price consciousness, which partly stems from their limited economic means. In addition, some black consumer adopt ethnocentric consumption patterns that reflect their sensitivity to racial discrimination in the mainstream economy, and their belief in the benefits of maintaining an ethnic economy in the black community.

Because black consumers are price conscious and sensitive to racial discrimination, business transactions in minority markets are potentially volatile. Tension in minority markets is magnified by the presence of blight in minority shopping districts, signaling to black consumers that local merchants extract capital but do not invest in their communities. These conditions created long-term challenges for immigrant-owned businesses in minority markets. Sometimes, immigrant-owned businesses are seen as a source of outside exploitation, and they become the focus of tension in the black community during periods of economic and social change in mainstream society. Although social conflict is often played out at the parochial level, it should be noted that minority markets emerge as a result of racial discrimination in mainstream society, which produces segregation and underdevelopment in the black community. Therefore, conflict at the parochial level is actually a reflection of structural inequalities that exist between the mainstream society and minority groups.

Similarities Among Black, Jewish and Korean Entrepreneurs

An examination of black, Jewish and Korean entrepreneurs must be sensitive to the degree to which each of these minority groups faces antagonism from mainstream institutions. When minority entrepreneurs are examined as actors within the context of the minority market, a number of common themes emerge. For instance, black, Jewish and Korean entrepreneurs in minority markets all experience capital constraints. They often start their businesses with personal savings, use informal community-based networks to raise capital, and have limited access to mainstream sources of capital. Black, Jewish and Korean entrepreneurs in minority markets also have limited contact with other mainstream institutions in both the public and private sectors. The inability to establish networks in mainstream society, coupled with the perception of racial discrimination in mainstream society, steers these entrepreneurs to minority markets where economic opportunities are limited.

Minority markets are reenforcing environments, since their social isolation allows people who participate in them to form common perceptions about mainstream society. In part, the formation of limited solidarity is furthered by daily interactions where Anglo members of society are absent. Since minority markets lack a noticeable presence of Anglo customers and merchants, their participants become more aware of the distinction between minority and mainstream markets. However, the level of solidarity among minority groups, generated by their mutual isolation from mainstream society, remains limited. This is the case, since relations between consumers and entrepreneurs in minority markets are strained by the persistence of acute economic scarcity. Black, Jewish and Korean entrepreneurs in minority markets are exposed to a number of complaints and criticisms from black consumers. Black customers in minority markets complain about the quality of merchandise that they are offered, the cleanliness of the stores where they shop, the in-store policies of immigrant and black entrepreneurs, and the quality of service that such business-es offer. In addition, black customers expect businesses in minori-ty markets to fill a social function in the black community. For instance, they are critical of businesses that do not generate jobs and invest in the black community.

Black, Jewish and Korean entrepreneurs are constrained in their ability to address the concerns of black customers. This is because they have limited access to mainstream institutions, and they have difficulty mobilize autonomous resources. Also, they operate in a highly competitive environment where they lack the ability to con-trol the price of the finished goods that enter minority markets. However, there are subtle differences in how black, Jewish and Korean entrepreneurs adapt to minority markets, and in how their actions are perceived by black consumers. An examination of these nuances illustrates how minority markets are maintained, and how they fit into the broader discussion of internal colonialism found chapter 1.

BLACK AND JEWISH ENTREPRENEURSHIP IN BRONZEVILLE, FROM THE GREAT MIGRATION TO THE CIVIL RIGHTS MOVEMENT

The Development of Separate Economic Niches for Blacks and Jews

Blacks and Jews began to do business in minority markets on the South Side of Chicago during the Great Migration years. Their experiences with minority markets set the foundation for later entrepreneurs. An examination of early black and Jewish entre-preneurship on the South Side of Chicago links the genesis of minority markets in Chicago to issues concerning Korean entre-preneurs in the contemporary context. The discussion of black manufacturers in chapter 2 identified some of the constraints affecting minority entrepreneurship historically, however this dis-cussion is more discrete. It focuses on the development of black and Jewish entrepreneurship during the pre-1970 period, empha-sizing how the institutional structure of minority markets affected the economic activities of each group.

In the early and mid-1900's, black and Jewish entrepreneurs competed for black dollars on the South Side of Chicago. However, black and Jewish entrepreneurs were not in direct competition, since each group occupied a specialized niche in the economy. The formation of these niches was visible in the early 1900's. For instance, a 1913 survey of State Street businesses revealed that black entrepreneurs clustered in service trades such as barber shops, beauty salons, saloons, restaurants, and pool rooms.[9] These remained the dominant black business clusters into the mid-1900's.[10] During the same period, the vast majority of the grocery, clothing, furniture, hardware and general merchandise stores on the South Side of Chicago were operated by Jews.[11] In 1938, it was estimated that about three-fourths of the merchants on the South Side of Chicago were Jewish.[12] The presence of a sizable cluster of Jewish merchants on the South Side of Chicago from the early to mid-1900's is well documented.[13] The formation of separate economic niches for black and Jewish entrepreneurs was driven by differences in each group's ability to mobilize capital, and by differences in how each group was perceived by black consumers.

Undercapitalization as a Component of Internal Colonialism

Capital constraints explain much of the disparity between black and Jewish entrepreneurs. In the early to mid-1900's, undercapitalization limited the scope of black business on the South Side of Chicago. Black entrepreneurs found it difficult to enter into direct competition with better financed Jewish merchants, and this situation led to a number of ramifications. For instance, the underdeveloped state of black business generated friction between black merchants and consumers on the South Side of Chicago.[14] In some cases, black elites and pundits discussed underdevelopment in the context of historical conditions that black entrepreneurs, and blacks as a group, faced.

An example of such a discussion is found in a speech presented by Claude A. Barnett to the Chicago Negro Chamber of Commerce in May of 1950, which discussed black business development in the city from 1900-1950.[15] The impression one gets from Barnett's comments is that it was difficult for blacks to pursue entrepreneurship during this period due to social constraints. Barnett made this clear in the following passage:

> Its amazing how little real, fundamental appreciation we as a group have for business. Talk to the average boy or girl. Ask them what they are planning to be. You will find them answering about every type of profession imaginable from teacher to social worker, from lawyer to doctor. But you seldom hear one plotting to be a grocer or a butcher or to open a plumbing or carpenter shop or a machine shop or to start a sales agency. They never think in terms of conducting a hardware store or a dry goods store. Perhaps there's a reason. Our youngsters imitate what they hear at home and in the streets. Certainly business is hardly what we hear discussed in the average Negro home.[16]

Barnett described how a lack of initial interest in business contributed to the underdevelopment of black entrepreneurship. However the thrust of his comments focused on how the lack of accumulated business knowledge in the black community was merely a symptom of the structural constraints that lay beneath the surface of the black experience in America.

Barnett pointed out that the structural constraints that black entrepreneurs faced stemmed from a legacy of historical relationships between minority markets and mainstream markets. He discussed how the limited role of black business in minority markets reflected this:

> Practically all of the big business institutions in Africa are controlled either by the British, the French, the Dutch or the Belgians—and I should not leave out the Syrian. Go into an African town of any size and you will find the retail business pretty much controlled by Syrians just as their blood cousins, the Jews have all the business in American Negro neighborhoods.[17]

To Barnett, the lack of a business ethos among blacks was a byproduct of earlier colonial relations, and this state of affairs was reproduced in minority markets in the United States. In fact, Wirth made a similar observation concerning internal colonial conditions on the South Side of Chicago, "The Negro, like the immigrant, is segregated in the city into a racial colony. Economic considerations, racial prejudice, and cultural differences combine to set him apart."[18] Barnett adds an additional dimension to this perspective, pointing out that life in a racial colony entails disincentives for black entrepreneurs, since economic and social institutions are controlled by outsiders. However, Barnett recognized that middleman groups, such as Jews, were in a unique position in minority markets. Their middleman role allowed them to hold a certain degree of economic power in minority markets, although they faced animosity from whites in mainstream society.

Racial and Ethnic Cleavages in Minority Markets

Barnett addressed this issue in a discussion of how blacks and Jews shared a common experience with discrimination in society:

Some weeks ago I made a brief talk and showed a movie to a branch of the American Jewish Congress up on the Northwest Side in Logan Square. I suggested that Jewish merchants ought to be interested in the problems of colored people because they handled perhaps 65 percent of the money which is spent in our districts. I told them that Jews and Negroes had a lot in common, in the discrimination which we both suffered and that in many ways we seem to have a kinship..... I told these people of the American Jewish Congress that they ought to join hands closer with us. They should use our greater numbers and combine to make a solid front. They should teach us the secret of how to do business and how to make money so as to get ahead too. When I told them to teach us how to do business, they let out a big laugh. It really tickled them. It was the only time they laughed while I was talking but no one suggested they had any idea of teaching us anything.[19]

The common experience that blacks and Jews had with discrimination did not bridge the structural barriers dividing them on the South Side of Chicago. Inequality inherent in the structure of the economy limited the degree to which groups confined to minority markets could unite around social issues. Black and Jewish entrepreneurs occupied distinct economic niches in minority markets. Because of this, they focused on addressing specific issues and economic constraints. In addition, black and Jewish entrepreneurs faced a different social context in minority markets. For example, Jews filled a middleman minority role on the South Side of Chicago, while blacks did not. These issues limited the ability of black and Jewish entrepreneurs to build coalitions.

Interactions between blacks and Jews were structured by minority markets and the social environment that produced them. Jewish merchants concentrated on attracting black consumers to their stores, and paid little attention to other matters. They saw black consumers as desirable customers, since Jewish merchants felt that blacks spent their money "freely, and usually had some to spend."[20] Because of this attitude, Jewish merchants actively pursued black business. Jewish merchants used a variety of mechanisms to attract black customers to their stores. They were price competitive with their neighbors, oriented their stores to the buying habits of black consumers, and they offered credit to customers. However, some Jewish merchants were brazen toward black customers. For instance, in the 1920's a Jewish clothing merchant commented that, "A dollar is just as good whether a black hand or a white hand hands it over," adding, "Anyway, their hands are white on the inside."[21] This blend of dispassionate economic behavior mixed with racial stereotyping fostered animosity between black customers and Jewish merchants.

One repercussion of the emerging impasse between blacks and Jews, was that Jewish merchants became the focus of discussions concerning the plight of black business. In some instances, this debate became entwined with calls for black consumers to patronize black-owned businesses.[22] The scapegoating of Jewish merchants because of capital constraints that black consumers and entrepreneurs faced became exaggerated during periods of economic scarcity. For example, during the Great Depression black boycotts of Jewish merchants and large chain stores on the South Side of Chicago grew in numbers.[23] During the civil rights movement, similar conflicts grew out of non-economic events. For instance, after the assassination of Martin Luther King Jr. in 1968, Jewish stores were looted in the Maxwell Street market.[24] Although these conflicts unfolded at the parochial level, they occurred in direct response to events taking place in mainstream society. The collateral effect of such conflicts was the acceleration of the flight of Jewish merchants from South Side neighborhoods.[25]

Despite the departure of Jewish merchants from South Side neighborhoods in the late 1960's and early 1970's, the underlying forces that shaped minority markets remained intact. During this period, the entrenchment of internal colonial conditions on the South Side of Chicago blocked ethnic succession for blacks. Capital constraints stemming from racial barriers that blacks faced in mainstream society kept black entrepreneurs from filling the void created by the exodus of Jewish merchants from the South

Side of Chicago. However, there was a need for the departing
Jewish merchants to be replaced, since Jewish merchants filled a
critical middleman role in minority markets on the South Side of
Chicago. In addition to operating small businesses, they functioned as a buffer between black consumers and mainstream institutions.

FROM THE CIVIL RIGHTS MOVEMENT TO THE GLOBAL ECONOMY, THE KOREAN SUCCESSION OF JEWISH MERCHANTS ON THE SOUTH SIDE OF CHICAGO

International Trade and the Korean Wig Industry

While the Jewish merchants were departing from the South Side of
Chicago, other middleman groups were gaining a foothold in the
area. In fact, potential black entrepreneurs faced competition from
better capitalized middleman minorities in the early-1970's. Many
of these middleman minorities were recent immigrants from
Korea.[26] Korean immigration began to grow rapidly in Chicago
and other cities in the United States following the passage of the
Immigration Act of 1965. However, many Korean immigrants
experienced setbacks in the mainstream economy and began to
pursue entrepreneurship in minority markets. Racial discrimination produced a number of social and economic constraints for
Korean immigrants just as it had for black Americans. The presence of racial barriers led to a number of social and economic
adaptations among Korean immigrants. One was the assumption
of a middleman role in minority markets on the South Side of
Chicago.

Koreans assumed the role of middleman minority on the South
Side of Chicago as Jewish merchants left the area. Korean entrepreneurs crowded black entrepreneurs out of the market, since
they were able to pay higher prices for the businesses that Jewish
merchants were selling. At the same time, Korean entrepreneurs
developed business networks in Korea that black entrepreneurs
had no access to. Using these business networks, Korean entrepreneurs established a niche in the minority markets on the South Side
of Chicago during the early-1970's. This niche was in the wig
industry.[27] By the early 1970's the demand for wigs in the black

community was at an all time high.[28] Black women were interested in purchasing inexpensive wigs, and synthetic hair manufacturers in Korea actively pursued black customers. During this period, Korean manufacturers and retailers expanded their economic activity in minority markets:

> Korean manufacturers sent their sales representatives to black areas to open retail stores. Korean wig-importers actively recruited Korean immigrants as retailers and peddlers in black areas to expand their businesses. They even supplied wigs to Korean retailers on credit, so that Korean immigrants could start their own wig businesses with very little initial capital.[29]

In the early-1970's, Korean wig stores began to appear in the shopping districts on the South Side of Chicago. During this period, the following observation was made in the Maxwell Street market, "A Korean man, quiet and with a cowlick, owns the wig store, that odd little dreamworld of glass cases with shelf upon shelf of bodiless heads containing unblinking eyes and flowering hair."[30] There are similar examples of early Korean merchants found throughout the minority markets on the South Side of Chicago. For instance, the story of a Korean man, Mr. Ku, who operated a wig store in the Englewood mall is representative of how Korean entrepreneurship began on the South Side of Chicago:

> It was 1971, he was 28 years old, and as a kind of sales rep for a Korean wig manufacturers back home, he had roots in a potentially lucrative business and all of the stock he needed. At the time, Afro wigs were a hot item in the black community, and the cheapest were those made in Korea. It did not matter that Ku's English then was spotty. His wigs cost less. His business boomed.[31]

The sale of wigs in the black community was profitable during the early 1970's, and many Korean merchants gained a foothold in the minority markets on the South Side of Chicago by opening wig stores. However, by the late-1970's, competition became intense among Korean merchants who operated wig businesses. Price slashing reduced profits in the wig industry, and sales dropped off further when the demand for wigs decreased at the end of the decade. When the wig industry became less profitable Korean entrepreneurs began to sell other merchandise in the black community, such as handbags, jewelry, clothing, beauty supplies, and general merchandise. At this critical point in time, some Korean merchants elected to stay on the South Side of Chicago and expand their middleman role, rather than risk entering the mainstream economy.

Incentives to Remain in the Black Community

Despite the declining demand for wigs in the black community, Korean merchants expanded their economic activity on the South Side of Chicago in the late 1970's. In part, this was because the opportunity to take over Jewish-owned stores was present. But at a more fundamental level, Korean entrepreneurs were responding to racial antagonism that they found in mainstream society. Korean immigrants elected to pursue entrepreneurship in the black community since they perceived less racial animosity there. In his study of Korean businesses in Chicago, Yoon describes this issue in detail:

> In fact, one of the important reasons for Koreans to site their businesses in black areas was the lower level of discrimination and hostility against Koreans in those areas compared with white areas. Blacks were perceived by Koreans to be simple and easy to please, whereas whites were seen to look down on Koreans. Some of the respondents in this study attributed the mild attitudes of blacks toward Koreans to the sharing of the common minority status in a white-dominated society.[32]

Korean immigrants found it difficult to gain access to jobs in the mainstream economy, although many came to the United States with professional training and experience. This caused many Koreans to withdraw from mainstream society. In part, their problems in the mainstream job market stemmed from language barriers and unsuitable professional credentials. However, as indicated above, they also sensed latent discrimination from whites, which discouraged them from pursuing jobs in the mainstream economy.

Like other middleman minorities, Korean entrepreneurs developed a preference for doing business in minority markets. This grew out of alienation that they experienced in mainstream society. Korean merchants found the absence of mainstream companies in minority markets to be comforting, and beneficial to their own economic interests. In fact, black neighborhoods and other minority areas are more important sources of income for Korean merchants than their own Korean community.[33] By creating a niche in minority markets, Korean entrepreneurs were able to earn greater incomes and improve their childrens' chances of obtaining upward mobility. Furthermore, Korean entrepreneurs fill the "business vacuum" created by the absence of mainstream companies in minority markets, and they actively developed minority markets by introducing a variety of cheap products manufactured in Korea or other developing countries.[34] By assuming this middleman role, Korean merchants buffer mainstream institutions and insulate them from pressure from the black community for systematic change.

Like the Jewish merchants who preceded them, the impact of Korean entrepreneurs on the South Side of Chicago is immense. In 1986, it was estimated that Korean-owned stores accounted for 85 percent of the businesses in the Madison-Pulaski shopping district, 41 percent of the stores in the Englewood mall , and 80 percent of the stores in the Maxwell Street market.[35] Several other Korean-owned stores are dispersed throughout other shopping areas on the South Side of Chicago. In 1991, it was estimated that there were between 850 and 1,000 Korean owned stores on the South Side of Chicago.[36] This is in sharp contrast to the number of black-owned stores on the South Side. For instance, in 1992, it was reported that in the Englewood mall, "blacks own only 10 percent of the stores, and most of these are cafes and barber shops."[37] The economic relationship that existed before the 1970's between blacks and Jews has been reproduced between blacks and Koreans. Today, there is a visible presence of Korean merchants on the South Side of Chicago. This presence, and the daily interactions that it entails, is the key to understanding how middleman groups buffer dominant institutions when conditions of internal colonialism exist.

THE POLITICAL OVERTONES OF MINORITY MARKETS

Korean businesses are found adjacent to some of the most impoverished neighborhoods in Chicago. This poverty is chronic and institutionalized. Historically, mainstream institutions have made few efforts to eradicate the conditions that produce poverty on the South Side of Chicago. When societal resources have been injected into the South Side, they have been limited. In effect, this type of public policy has contained poverty in South Side neighborhoods, and produced few opportunities for blacks. The institutional relationships that have developed between South Side residents and mainstream institutions have a strong influence on the structure of minority markets. Because of these relationships, Korean businesses serve a specific clientele on the South Side of Chicago:

> The marginal position of Korean immigrant businesses is indicated by the ethnic composition of their customers. Korean businesses in black areas cater to heavily lower-class blacks. A majority of these blacks are said to be dependent upon welfare. Therefore, the fate of Korean businesses in these areas depends heavily on the economic condition of the local black residents. After the Reagan Administration began cutting welfare expenditures for minorities in the middle of the 1980s, Korean businesses in black areas experienced a recession because of the deteriorating economic conditions of lower-class blacks. In a simple illustration, Korean businesses are said to experience a brief "sales boost" shortly after blacks receive their welfare checks.[38]

There are a number of ramifications that grow out of this situation. First, minority markets exist in a state of economic dependence. In part, this is because minority markets are driven by the welfare economy. In this respect, minority markets are captive markets that respond to shifts in public policy emanating from mainstream institutions. Second, minority markets, and the middleman merchants in them, buffer mainstream institutions from the grievances of residents in poverty stricken communities. As a result, when impasses emerge between poor members of the black community and mainstream institutions, middleman merchants become the targets of subsequent social unrest.

A variety of conflicts between black and white America can result in the scapegoating of middleman minorities. One example involves disputes over the welfare system, and its impending reform. In other instances, the frustrations of blacks, and other oppressed groups, with the criminal justice system can affect middleman entrepreneurs. For instance, Min drew the following conclusions about the causes of rioting on the South Side of Chicago during the summer of 1992:

The repercussions of the Los Angeles riots came to Chicago even later. When the Chicago Bulls clinched the NBA championship on the evening of June 14, African American fans rioted in South Chicago. Approximately forty Korean stores were subjected to destruction, looting, and arson in the so-called Bulls Riot.[39]

As mainstream institutions have exhibited indifference and authoritarianism toward disenfranchised communities, middleman minorities have become the focus of public frustration. However, the mechanics of this relationship are not as well understood as their outcomes.

This chapter has argued that minority markets developed on the South Side of Chicago in response to social isolation, which was the product of racism and racial discrimination experienced by minority entrepreneurs and consumers. A discussion of some of the factors that have contributed to the development of underdevelopment on the South Side of Chicago was presented in support of this argument. In addition, factors contributing to the historical development of black, Jewish and Korean businesses on the South Side of Chicago were identified in order to frame this argument. The remainder of this study focuses on contemporary black, Jewish and Korean businesses in Chicago's ethnic beauty aids industry, with reference to the theoretical and historical framework outlined in chapters 1 through 3. In the next chapter, this discussion will begin by highlighting the linkage between mainstream institutions and minority markets. This relationship is illustrated through an examination of contemporary middleman minorities and the welfare economy on the South Side of Chicago.

NOTES

[1]William Julius Wilson, *The Truly Disadvantaged, The Inner City, The Underclass, and Public Policy*, (Chicago: University of Chicago Press, 1990).

[2]"Business in Bronzeville," *Time*, April 18 (1938): 70. St. Clair Drake and Horace R. Cayton, *Black Metropolis, A Study of Negro Life in a Northern City*, (Chicago: University of Chicago Press, 1993): 63.

[3] St. Clair Drake and Horace R. Cayton, *Black Metropolis, A Study of Negro Life in a Northern City*, (Chicago: University of Chicago Press, 1993); Allan H. Spear, *Black Chicago, The Making of a Negro Ghetto 1890-1920*, (Chicago: University of Chicago Press, 1967).

⁴Claude A. Barnett's Speech to the Chicago Negro Chamber of Commerce, 21 May 1950, Claude A. Barnett Collection, Chicago Historical Society, Chicago, IL, Box 405, Folder 1.

⁵ Marcus Alexis, "The Black Consumer," in Harold G. Vatter and Thomas Palm ed, *The Economics of Black America.*, (New York: Harcourt Brace Jovanovich, Inc., 1972): 151-154; E. Franklin Frazier, *Black Bourgeoisie, The Rise of a New Middle Class in the United States*, (New York: Collier Books, 1962).

⁶ Marcus Alexis, "The Black Consumer," in Harold G. Vatter and Thomas Palm ed. *The Economics of Black America*, (New York: Harcourt Brace Jovanovich, Inc., 1972): 151-154.

⁷ Ibid, 151-154.

⁸ Ibid, 152.

⁹ Allan H. Spear,*Black Chicago, The Making of a Negro Ghetto*, (Chicago: University of Chicago Press, 1967): 112.

¹⁰ Lizabeth Cohen, *Making a New Deal, Industrial Workers in Chicago, 1919-1939*, (New York: Cambridge University Press, 1990): 149-152; St. Clair Drake and Horace R. Cayton, *Black Metropolis, A Study of Negro Life in a Northern City*, (Chicago: University of Chicago Press, 1993): 438; Eugine P. Foley, "The Negro Businessman, In Search of A Tradition," *Daedalus*, 95 (1962): 107-144.

¹¹ Allan H. Spear, *Black Chicago, The Making of a Negro Ghetto*, (Chicago: University of Chicago Press, 1967): 184.

¹² St. Clair Drake and Horace R. Cayton, *Black Metropolis, A Study of Negro Life in a Northern City*, (Chicago: University of Chicago Press, 1993): 432.

¹³ Louis Wirth, *The Ghetto*, (Chicago: University of Chicago Press, 1956); Ira Berkow, *Maxwell Street, Survival in a Bazaar*, (New York: Doubleday and Company, Inc., 1977).

¹⁴ St. Clair Drake and Horace R. Cayton, *Black Metropolis, A Study of Negro Life in a Northern City*, (Chicago: University of Chicago Press, 1993): 443-445.

¹⁵ Claude A. Barnett's Speech to the Chicago Negro Chamber of Commerce, 21 May 1950, Claude A. Barnett Collection, Chicago Historical Society, Chicago, IL, Box 405, Folder 1.

¹⁶ Ibid.

¹⁷ Ibid.

¹⁸ Louis Wirth, *The Ghetto*, (Chicago: University of Chicago Press, 1956): 230.

[19] Claude A. Barnett's Speech to the Chicago Negro Chamber of Commerce, 21 May 1950, Claude A. Barnett Collection, Chicago Historical Society, Chicago, IL, Box 405, Folder 1.

[20] Louis Wirth, *The Ghetto*, (Chicago: University of Chicago Press, 1956): 230.

[21] Ibid, 230.

[22] Lizabeth Cohen, *Making a New Deal, Industrial Workers in Chicago, 1919-1939*, (New York: Cambridge University Press, 1990): 151-154; St. Clair Drake and Horace R. Cayton, *Black Metropolis, A Study of Negro Life in a Northern City*, (Chicago: University of Chicago Press, 1993): 439-453.

[23] Ibid.

[24] Ira Berkow, *Maxwell Street, Survival in a Bazaar*, (New York: Doubleday and Company, Inc., 1977): 523-532.

[25] Howard Aldrich and Albert J. Reiss, Jr., "The Effect of Civil Disorders on Small Business in the Inner City," *Journal of Social Issues*, 26.1 (1970): 187-206.

[26] For a general discussion of Korean immigration to the United States and Chicago see Brian Lehrer, *The Korean Americans*, (New York: Chelsea House Publishers, 1988); Joseph Ahne, "Koreans of Chicago, The New Entrepreneurial Immigrants," in Melvin G. Holli and Peter d'A. Jones ed, *Ethnic Chicago, A Multicultural Portrait*, (Grand Rapids: William B. Eerdmans Publishing Company, 1995): 463-500.

[27] Ku-Sup Chin, In-Jin Yoon and David Smith, "Immigrant Small Business and International Economic Linkage, A Case of the Korean Wig Business in Los Angeles, 1968-1977," *IMR*, 30.2 (1996): 485-510.

[28] In-Jin Yoon, "The Growth of Korean Immigrant Entrepreneurship in Chicago," *Ethnic and Racial Studies*, 18.2 (1995): 315- 335.

[29] Ibid, 322.

[30] Ira Berkow, *Maxwell Street, Survival in a Bazaar*, (New York: Doubleday and Company, Inc., 1977): 31-32.

[31] Ben Joravsky, "Koreans Sell, Blacks Buy, A Clash of Cultures at the 63rd Street Mall," *Reader*, February 13 (1987): 3.

[32] In-Jin Yoon, "The Growth of Korean Immigrant Entrepreneurship in Chicago," *Ethnic and Racial Studies*, 18.2 (1995): 327.

[33] Ibid, 316; In-Jin Yoon, "The Changing Significance of Ethnic and Class Resources in Immigrant Businesses, The Case of Korean Immigrant Business in Chicago," *IMR*, 25.2 (1991): 303.

[34] Kwang Chung Kim and Won Moo Hurh, "Ethnic Resource Utilization of Korean Immigrant Entrepreneurs in the Chicago Minority Area," *IMR*, 19.1 (1985): 86-87.

[35] In-Jin Yoon, "The Growth of Korean Immigrant Entrepreneurship in Chicago." *Ethnic and Racial Studies,* 18.2 (1995): 325- 326.

[36] In-Jin Yoon, "Self-Employment in Business, Chinese-, Japanese-, Korean-Americans, Blacks, and Whites," Dissertation, (Chicago: University of Chicago, 1991): 169; Joseph Ahne, "Koreans of Chicago: The New Entrepreneurial Immigrants," in Melvin G. Holli and Peter d'A. Jones ed. *Ethnic Chicago, A Multicultural Portrait,* (Grand Rapids: William B. Eerdmans Publishing Company, 1995): 488.

[37] R. C. Longworth, "One Street, Two Different Paths of Success," *Chicago Tribune,* (17 September 1992): Section 1.

[38] In-Jin Yoon, "Self-Employment in Business, Chinese-, Japanese-, Korean-Americans, Blacks, and Whites," Dissertation, (Chicago: University of Chicago, 1991): 184.

[39] Pyong Gap Min, *Caught in the Middle, Korean Communities in New York and Los Angeles,* (Berkeley: University of California Press, 1996): 94.

CHAPTER 4:

Sojourning And The Welfare Economy

MERCHANTS ON CHICAGO'S SOUTH SIDE

This chapter examines two issues that are critical to understanding the social and institutional forces that reproduce internal colonialism on the South Side of Chicago, sojourning on the part of middleman minorities and the role of the welfare economy in producing economic dependence in the black community. The central argument of this chapter is that the relationship between middleman merchants, black consumers, and the social welfare system reenforces internal colonial conditions in the black community. This argument focuses on the nexus between middleman minorities and the welfare economy. This relationship entails a unique set of perceptions and attitudes about minority markets, which middleman minorities hold.

Middleman minorities identify many of the same characteristics of the black community as Tabb does in his discussion of internal colonialism.[1] In particular, middleman minorities perceive the black community as a place where incomes are low, businesses are underdeveloped, and where a high demand exists for consumer goods. Middleman minorities also see the black community as separate and remote from mainstream society. The isolation of the black community from mainstream society opens economic opportunities for middleman minorities. These opportunities are furthered since economic competition is limited in the black community. In part, this is because middleman minorities have fewer large white-owned companies to compete with in minority markets, and also because they do not view black entrepreneurs in minority markets as serious competitors. In addition, middleman minorities perceive the black community as being economically dependent on mainstream institutions. In particular, they view the black community as a place where there is a high rate of welfare dependence, and they focus on supplying goods and services to the poor. These attitudes and perceptions draw middleman minorities to minority markets, but they also contribute to the development of a sojourning orientation in the black community. In part, this orientation develops in response to the risks middleman minorities associate with doing business in minority markets.

Middleman minorities are aware of cleavages that exist between blacks and whites in society, and perceive the black community as subordinate to mainstream society. Middleman minorities also have their own experiences with discrimination in mainstream society, and feel disenfranchised from it. Because of this, they understand that the minority markets they do business in are volatile markets, where they may become scapegoats during periods of conflict between blacks and whites, so they set out to make economic activity in them temporary. This is the essence of sojourning behavior as it is discussed by scholars.[2] It should be stresses that sojourning behavior grows out of the institutional structure of internal colonialism, and this is the product of racial stratification in society.

The link between sojourning on the part of middleman minorities and institutional forces is important to recognize, since it highlights how conflicts that occur at the parochial level stem from broader institutional structures. This relationship is brought to light through a comparison of black and Korean merchants on the South Side of Chicago. An examination of some of the similarities and differences between black and Korean merchants on the South Side of Chicago highlights the importance of an initial sojourning orientation among middleman entrepreneurs. Such an examination also distinguishes between general characteristics of entrepreneurship and the middleman minority role that Korean entrepreneurs assume in minority markets.

SIMILARITIES AND DIFFERENCES BETWEEN MIDDLEMAN AND BLACK ENTREPRENEUR

Common Characteristics

There are a number of similarities between the black and Korean merchants who were interviewed on the South Side of Chicago. They were all well educated. In fact, most had earned a bachelors degree. The black and Korean merchants came from similar age cohorts, and entered business at a similar stage in their lives. All of the informants reported working long hours, often in excess of seventy hours a week. Both the black and Korean merchants employed family members in their stores, although this was usually limited to a spouse or another immediate family member. In addition, both the black and Korean merchants reported that they raised the initial capital for their businesses using personal savings and with the assistance of family members.

The similarities between black and Korean merchants are striking when compared to one and other. For instance, a Korean merchant on the South Side of Chicago made these comments when discussing how he raised the capital to start his business:

> Actually, I've been in business since I was like nine, my parents had a store. Basically, on weekends and summer vacation I would go and help my parents out. So, I was, you know, I was in business for a long time. And then, during the college years I was in economics, and I was thinking about opening up my own business. And, that's what happened. After college I opened up my shoe store, opened up a shoe store. My father financed it for me.

In many respects, the factors this individual discussed concerning his introduction to entrepreneurship are similar to those raised in the literature on ethnic entrepreneurship.[3] Interestingly, many of the themes in the previous statement made by a Korean merchant are also found in the following statement made by a black merchant, while describing how he raised the capital to start a business with his brother:

> My brother came from the University of California, he got a job with a long time beauty supply company, and he needed help. I had a little money I saved, my wife and I had saved, and we loaned him the money to go buy merchandise to start

the business. He bought the merchandise and he asked me to
help him, and I did. I liked it. So I went into business, my
brother and myself.

On a litany of issues concerning their businesses and entrepreneurship in general, black and Korean merchants held similar
opinions. For instance, all of the merchants felt that a strong work
ethic helped their businesses. When asked why his business had
been successful, a Korean merchant commented, "I've been in this
business 14 years, I never off a day, never late." This sentiment was
shared by a black merchant who attributed the success of his business to "My stubborn attitude, and my ability to perform, and
work, and to have the intellect of a hard working black genius."

Clear Distinctions

Despite their similarities in attitudes and experiences, there were
important distinctions to be made about the black and Korean
merchants who were interviewed. The stores operated by Koreans
in the ethnic beauty aids industry were larger than those operated
by black merchants. In addition, half of the Korean merchants
who were interviewed reported that they owned more than one
beauty supply store on the South Side of Chicago, while the black
merchants did business on a smaller scale, from a single store. The
stores operated by black and Korean entrepreneurs differed in
other respects as well. Korean-owned stores were located in the
center of established business districts on the South Side of
Chicago, while black-owned businesses were more dispersed.
Korean-owned stores carried a wider variety of products than were
found in black-owned stores. In addition, Korean merchants
claimed to offer lower prices than black merchants. These characteristics indicate that although there were some similarities
between black and Korean merchants, there were also important
distinctions to be made about the context of their businesses.

   One of the more important contrasts between the black and
Korean merchants concerned the attitudes that each group of
entrepreneurs held about doing business on the South Side of
Chicago. These attitudes helped to define the role of each group of
entrepreneurs in the black community. The difference in the attitudes of black and Korean entrepreneurs with respect to minority
markets is the key to understanding why Korean entrepreneurs fill
a middleman minority role in the black community, as well as to

understand why black entrepreneurs do not. One of the most important distinctions to be made concerning attitudinal differences between black and Korean merchants on the South Side of Chicago involves the transient outlook of Korean entrepreneurs. Several of the Korean merchants who were interviewed discussed how a great deal of uncertainty surrounded the future of Korean entrepreneurship in the black community. This stemmed from concerns about economic conditions worsening in the black community, and from concerns about the possibility of becoming scapegoats if tensions were to heighten between blacks and whites in society.

SOJOURNING AND ENTREPRENEURSHIP

Mainstream Society and Attitudes Toward Business in the Black Community

The perception that economic instability might lead to scapegoating contributed to the adoption of a sojourning orientation among Korean merchants. This was in sharp contrast to black merchants, who had concerns about economic conditions in the black community, but little anxiety about the consequences that racial conflict would have for their businesses. However, a sojourning orientation is not simply adopted in response to conditions that Korean merchants find once they have opened businesses in minority markets, it grows out of the experiences they have in mainstream society prior to pursuing entrepreneurship in an internal colonial setting. These experiences have an important effect on the attitudes and perceptions of Korean entrepreneurs. The Korean merchants who were interviewed were socialized as middleman minorities through interactions in mainstream society. This is how they acquired the attitudes and perceptions necessary to assume a middleman role in the black community. This orientation distinguishes Korean entrepreneurs from black entrepreneurs in minority markets.

The Korean merchants' attitudes and perceptions were affected in two important ways by mainstream institutions. First, when they originally immigrated to the United States, they found it difficult to access jobs in the mainstream economy. This experience generated feelings of animosity toward mainstream society, since, in part, many of the Korean merchants attributed their difficulties in the economy to discrimination in mainstream society. Second, the Korean merchants learned about the black community through mainstream institutions. Through this process they internalized many of white America's stereotypes and prejudices about black America. Because of the stigma attached to the black community, many of the businesses opened by Korean entrepreneurs on the South Side of Chicago were intended to be transitional businesses. Some intended to operate a business in the black community until they saved enough money to open a business in the Korean community, and serve co-ethnic customers. Others opened businesses in the black community to raise capital so they could later enter the import-export business. Still, others opened businesses in the black community to earn an income while pursuing jobs and establishing businesses in mainstream society. For instance, one Korean merchant discussed plans to open a dry cleaning establishment in a white neighborhood, another had recently purchased a motel near downtown Chicago, and another Korean merchant was scaling down his store since he had recently been hired by an engineering firm in a suburb of Chicago.

Although the Korean merchants who were interviewed had different goals for their businesses, they all held similar views of their economic role in the black community. They initially viewed the South Side of Chicago as a temporary place to do business. Even though some of the Korean merchants operated businesses in the black community for years, they retained the desire to pursue economic activity elsewhere. The sojourning orientation among the Korean merchants became more apparent when the attitudes of Korean merchants were compared to black merchants. The black merchants hoped to expand their existing stores, and expand the scope of their businesses in the black community.

Another important distinctions between the black and Korean merchants, involved the relationship between their businesses and their children. Many of the Korean merchant had children who were enrolled in American universities, and they helped out at the family business sporadically, on weekends and during holidays. However, in the long run, most of the Korean merchants hoped that their children would have careers outside of the black community. Many of the Korean merchants pursued entrepreneurship to finance their childrens' education. They saw entrepreneurship in the black community as a way of sacrificing for the next generation.

In contrast, the children of the black merchants played a more active role in the family business. For example, one of the daughters of a black merchant worked daily in the family store, and both the daughter and grandson of another black merchant effectively ran the family store. Like their parents, the children of black merchants pursued an education, but the family businesses played a more central role in their lives. Most of the black entrepreneurs were future oriented with respect to their businesses, and they desired to maintain the family business and pass it on to their children and grandchildren. For the black merchants, entrepreneurship in the black community was not considered a personal sacrifice for the betterment of the next generation. On the contrary, black-owned businesses were seen as a safety net for the family. The black merchants hoped their children would be successful, and they saw the family business as one path to economic stability in the future.

Black and Korean merchants held divergent attitudes. Korean merchants viewed their businesses as stepping stones. They were transitional businesses used to finance future economic activities outside of the black community, and they facilitated their childrens upward mobility and entry into mainstream society. On the other hand, black merchants saw their businesses as the bedrock of economic stability. Their businesses allowed them to gain a level of economic autonomy in spite of racial barriers in society, and they offered a similar form of security for their children to fall back on, if racial barriers continued to impede the progress of blacks. This is an important distinction, since it highlights how the attitudes of middleman minorities differ from black entrepreneurs on the South Side of Chicago. To more fully understand how the attitudes of Korean entrepreneurs are shaped by mainstream society, and how this results in sojourning behavior, it is useful to examine the factors that cause Korean immigrants to pursue entrepreneurship in more detail.

Barriers on the Surface

The Korean merchants who were interviewed cited a number of barriers they faced to entering the mainstream economy. Many of these barriers have been identified in the past by other scholars.[4] However, others have not, and require further elaboration. For instance, many of the Korean merchants identified language as an obstacle to entering the mainstream economy. They discussed how language barriers hampered their ability to find jobs in white America, and how a limited proficiency in English made it difficult for them to communicate with potential employers, and inform them about their work history. This issues was compounded, since many of the Korean merchants held advanced degrees from foreign universities; however, these credentials were not recognized in the United States. The ability to transfer records and credentials to the United States was a common problem for the Korean merchants, and extended beyond issues related to employment and education.

Some of the Korean merchants pointed out that when they immigrated they had no records to verify their financial status. They had no credit history and no record of paying taxes in the United States. In fact, one Korean store owner reported that several years transpired between the time he immigrated to the United States and when he obtained a Social Security card. Because of these problems, many of the Korean merchants reported that they initially found it difficult to obtain credit in America. One merchant pointed out that he could not get a credit card in the United States for years, so he had to use one from a bank in Korea. Although he paid his bills regularly, this did not help him build a credit history in the United States. The lack of a credit history made it difficult for new immigrants to borrow money from large financial institutions in American.

The inability to borrow money from banks in the mainstream economy affected Korean immigrants in several ways. Many of the Koreans who were interviewed reported that they were forced to pay cash for all of their purchases after arriving in America. They paid cash for daily purchases such as food and clothing. In addition, they paid cash for larger purchase such as automobiles and homes. One Korean merchant on the South Side of Chicago commented in detail about his financial situation when he first came to America:

> I bought my house in Madison, Wisconsin for cash because I don't have any credit in the United States. And, the bank they never gave me a loan, and only from bringing all the money from Korea, I bought the house in Madison, Wisconsin. First I rent the apartment, but some apartment, they don't approve my credit, because I don't have any credit. So, I'm looking for the house, because I have a lot of money only. I bought the

owned house in Madison, Wisconsin. Only cash. Five or six years I only spend money I bring from Korea, I need almost $5 thousand cash a month. I don't have any mortgage for my house or payment for my car, I bought by cash.

This highlights an important characteristic of the Korean merchants who were interviewed. Most of the Korean merchants who were interviewed on the South Side of Chicago had achieved a middle-class lifestyle before coming to America. However, once arriving in America, they found it difficult to maintain that lifestyle. They spent their savings, but could not find jobs similar to those they left behind in Korea. This situation caused them to consider entrepreneurship in the black community, since the costs of opening a business there was lower than in the white community. In the black community, Korean entrepreneurs could invest their personal savings, and money borrowed from family members in a small business. While operating that business, they could establish a credit history and save money for the future. To many of the Koreans who were interviewed, businesses in the black community were initially seen as stepping stones.

Submerged Barriers

In addition to language barriers, issues surrounding credentials, and barriers to obtaining credit, many of the Korean merchants also perceived racial barriers to entering the mainstream economy. In fact, the Korean merchants' perception of anti-Korean sentiment in white American is a reflection of what scholars have identified as "host hostility."[5] The belief among some Korean merchant that racism existed in white American, and that this created additional barriers to entry in the mainstream economy, limited the scope of economic alternatives available to them. When the issue of host hostility was taken into consideration, the social benefits of doing business in the black community were congruent with the financial benefits.

The Korean merchants who were interviewed focused on business activities in the black community, with most of them claiming that 99 percent of their customers were black. Some Korean merchants indicated that they felt more comfortable doing business with blacks than with whites. For example, a Korean merchant on the South Side of Chicago made the following comment:

I'm afraid to speak English to the white people, always I'm afraid they look at me low. Only if I go trip, or if I go to restaurant, or I go to McDonald's or something, and I buy something it's easy. But I meet for business, and I meet white people to buy business or something, difficult. But I will try to learn English. It's too difficult, because I have no job and no business in the United States.

Two important issues are raised in this statement. First, the informant identifies the anxiety that he feels when conducting business with whites, as opposed to blacks. Second, this merchant draws a clear distinction between the status of a business in the white community, when compared to a business in the black community. Although this informant operated a business in the black community, he states that he has "no job and no business in the United States." For all effective purposes, this Korean merchant did not think of the black community as a part of mainstream society.

The Korean merchants were aware of the marginal status of their businesses in mainstream society, and this affects the manner in which they interact with white-owned business. Because of this issue, some Korean merchants considered doing business with whites more strained than doing business with other minorities. A comment made by a Korean merchant, who was asked if white-owned businesses discriminate against minority-owned businesses, illustrates how this issue manifests itself:

I think they do. I think, I think more, actually I firmly believe that we get more respect from the Afro-American distributors than a caucasian company. I think the Caucasian manufacturers, I don't know, they sort of look down on you. I know they don't want to, but that's the feeling we get. Where, the ethnic distributor, they know they need us to distribute the item. Where with the Caucasian, they know the industry, they know the Koreans are the South Side, and they have Afro-American products they need to sell. So, they know that we are imperative in their company. Ethnic, they would treat us better, with more respect, saying please take this. But I think when you deal with more like a (name of large white-owned company), or a company in the caucasian market, they look at you as if they're doing you a favor. Like, I have my general market, and your market's only ahh, but I'll still sell it to

> you kinda thing. I can tell when I try to open up accounts, I
> get totally different treatment from them.

This informant went on to explain that the differential treatment
that he received from white-owned, as opposed to black-owned,
companies in the ethnic beauty aids industry, grew out of the stigma that whites attached to the industry and the black community.
Because his business was located on the South Side of Chicago, this
Korean merchant believed that white-owned companies were
reluctant to do business with him.

Other Korean merchants also indicated that white-owned companies attached little status to businesses in minority markets.
These businesses were considered to be small, unstable, and
remote from the mainstream economy. However, some of the
Korean merchants were concerned that as their businesses grew in
size, whites would become more interested in entering the ethnic
beauty aids market. One Korean merchant thought that "white
people" would become "afraid" if his business grew too quickly,
and they would use "some other government power to reduce
competition" from minority businesses. He explained how whites
might mobilize institutional resources to reduce competition from
minority-owned businesses:

> White people doing the other competition own big company,
> and they afraid minority company growing up. They do cut,
> don't give more, extend the lease, something. For example,
> somebody leases a building and they open the store, they
> growing up their business, and their business is very good.
> Some other company push the building owner, they don't
> extend the lease.

Concerns about whites taking actions to limit the economic activities of minorities grow out of prior experiences that Korean merchants had with host hostility. These attitudes affected later
interactions between Korean merchants and mainstream institutions. For instance, some of the Korean merchants were not enthu-
siastic about local government, finding it to be unresponsive. Such
feelings of alienation from mainstream society pushed Korean
merchants to insulate themselves from white America, and locate
their businesses in the black community. However, the Korean
merchants who were interviewed did not consider the black community to be their permanent home.

Learning Stereotypes from Whites

Although host hostility drives Koreans entrepreneurs out of the mainstream economy, the exposure that Korean immigrants have to mainstream institutions infused stereotypes about blacks in their minds. Stereotypes and mainstream characterizations of black Americans are learned by Korean immigrants, and this encourages them to adopt a sojourning orientation. There are a number of ways that the Korean merchants who were interviewed learned about the black community before coming to America. Some of the Korean merchants reported that they had seen black soldiers during the Korean War. However, the wartime experiences that Koreans had with black soldiers was not always positive. One Korean merchant commented that, "Some of the Korean lady marry with the black soldier, and they immigrate to the United States, almost all divorced." In fact, he attributed this to a lack of commitment on the part of blacks, stating that, "Most of the black people, they don't like the married life." Jo's research indicates that the stereotypes that Koreans internalized about black Americans during the Korean War were reenforced through later contact that Koreans had with mainstream institutions.[6]

In fact, a number of mainstream institutions were identified as sources of information about black Americans. Many of the Korean merchants reported that they learned a great deal about the black community through the media before they decided to open their businesses. In some cases, Korean immigrants learned about black Americans by watching popular movies, American televisions shows, and thorough stories on the evening news and in the mainstream press. In others cases, Korean immigrants found information about the black community in the Korean American media. More recent immigrants also learned about the black community while still in Korea, since the American media is increasingly accessible overseas. One Korean merchant pointed out that the growing presence of news stories about the black community was discouraging some Koreans from immigrating to the United States. He went on to say that more recent Korean immigrants were less willing to open businesses in the black community, because of negative press coverage in the mainstream media. He described how some people in Korea perceived the black community as an extremely dangerous place to do business. They thought of the black community as a place where Korean merchants wear "flack jackets and carrying guns every day."

Mainstream institutions had a powerful influence on how Korean immigrants perceived the black community. Some Korean retailers discussed how they came to the black community with negative perceptions of blacks, and later moderated these attitudes as they learned more about the neighborhoods where their businesses were located. One Korean merchant commented on how his views of black America had changed:

> Right now my wife and I, I think very good coming to the South Side of Chicago, because at first my wife and I hate all black people, but right now I like the black people. Before I open (store's name) in South Side area, I never like black people. I never know about the black people. But, right now I know the black society, the black people. And, a couple times I went to black people church, and prayed. We prayed and sing song together. Usually, the black people don't like the other skin color. The white people they are afraid, the oriental and some other skin color they don't like.

After spending a period of time in the black community, the Korean merchants became sensitized to the subtleties of racial discrimination in America society. This was true in the case of black-white cleavages in society, as well as in the case of Korean-white cleavages. On occasion, such cross-cutting issues generated a limited degree of social cohesion between Korean merchants and black consumers. However, the development of solidarity between Korean merchants and the black community was limited by the middleman role that Korean merchants filled. The importance of this role becomes visible when social and economic tension grows between blacks and whites.

From the Assassination of Martin Luther King Jr. to OJ Simpson

The sojourning orientation of Korean entrepreneurs in minority markets is reenforced by the presence of racial cleavages in society. When asked about their future business plans, a number of the Korean retailers expressed an interest in doing something different, outside of the black community. Many Korean merchants expressed concern about the unpredictable nature of black-white relations in society, and the possible effect that social cleavages would have on their businesses. One Korean merchant commented that he was hesitant to purchase property in the black community and make other long term investments. In the following statement, it is clear that he was mainly concerned about racial tension in mainstream society:

> But buildings, I cannot invest in it down here. I don't know when we are gonna move out. That's bad business. You know in California, sometimes trouble and we have to move out if something go wrong.

Other Korean merchants made reference to the 1992 Los Angeles Riot, when they discussed the risks of doing business in the black community. However, they also had more general concerns related to their perception of a deteriorating racial climate in the 1990's.

In fact, the perceived threat of riots occurring in Chicago was, in part, based on prior history. For example, rioting resulted on the South Side of Chicago in 1968 after Martin Luther King Jr. was assassinated, and it also occurred after the Chicago Bulls won the NBA championship in 1992.[7] One Korean merchant described how the perceived threat of rioting affects the business climate on the South Side of Chicago:

> Everyone is somewhat scared about that type of problem. Trying to take as much caution as possible. Typically those kind of things happen at night, hopefully those things happen at night. So nobody will be there. Once the initial shock is done and over with, nobody's gonna come back out again and do the same thing again. For example, when OJ Simpson verdict came out, everybody was ready to fly. I shit you not. Everybody was literally one step out before cars were out there. And, they said if the verdict came out they were gonna just shut the door and get the hell out of here.

Conflicts between blacks and whites are inherently linked to tensions that emerge between blacks and Koreans at the parochial level. Even issues that seem to be independent of mainstream institutions, such as differences in cultural traits and communication styles between blacks and Koreans, are tainted by stereotypes of blacks and Koreans which emanate from white America.[8]

WELFARE AS ECONOMIC DEVELOPMENT?

Structural Change and the Welfare Economy

Tension between the black community and mainstream society comes from a number of institutional sources. One of the more important involves the role of the social welfare system in the maintenance of internal colonialism. In the black community, economic dependence on mainstream institutions is, in part, facilitated through the social welfare system. For instance, Drake and Cayton pointed out that joblessness and dependence on welfare expanded on the South Side of Chicago for blacks during the Great Depression.[9] According to Wilson, these condition have intensified during the contemporary period, and they surpass those of the depression in some South Side neighborhoods.[10]

The visibility of economic dependence in the black community increased during the 1970's and 1980's. In part, the heightened visibility of economic dependence in the black community resulted from broad economic and political shifts in society. One of these shifts involved the restructuring of the economy in the United States.[11] Economic restructuring had a disproportionate impact on the black community. On the South Side of Chicago, this was reflected in larger increases in unemployment and greater losses in manufacturing jobs for blacks, than for whites during the 1970's and 1980's.[12] These economic shifts were accompanied by political shifts in society. The most important involved extensive cuts in government expenditures for education and social welfare programs during the 1970's and 1980's.[13]

By the end of the 1980's, welfare became a divisive issue in mainstream society. One of the results of the welfare debate was that poor urban blacks were demonized by conservative scholars.[14] In fact, "urban poverty" became a buzz word for black poverty during this period. At this time, some scholars claimed that, "increasingly concentrated urban poverty poses a special threat to the well-being of the country," and they proposed that social welfare programs be drastically cut, "in the interest of the poor."[15] The growing turmoil over welfare reform had two implications in the black community. One was that the rhetoric surrounding the welfare debate magnified cleavages between blacks and whites in society. The other was that in actual practice, cuts in social welfare spending ensured that minority markets would remain underdeveloped. Cutting welfare undermined economic development in the black community, since funds that were dispersed in the black community through the welfare system created an economic stimulus. When these funds were taken away, the stimulus disappeared.

Korean Merchants and the Welfare Economy

Welfare augmented the disposable income of poor blacks. Welfare cuts caused minority markets to stagnate, since poor blacks dependent on transfer payments made up a sizable segment of the consumers in those markets. The Korean merchants on the South Side of Chicago had a clear understanding of the relationship between welfare and minority markets. In fact, one of the main incentives for them to do business on the South Side of Chicago was the presence of a large consumer base, composed of poor blacks, many of whom were on some form of public assistance. The vitality of the minority market attracted Korean entrepreneurs interested in selling nondurable goods to blacks, such as toiletries, clothing, and basic household items. In fact, many of the Korean merchants who were interviewed identified social welfare expenditures as an important gauge of the health of their businesses. One Korean merchant made this comment:

> Actually my customers, they spend money, they spend. First of all, they are happy to spend a lot of money for hair. I know they spend money for shoes and cloths, but I think they spend money for hair. Economy's good, lot of people are working, lot of people got government check, I'm doing good. Otherwise, economy's bad.

All of the Korean merchant brought the issue of welfare to the forefront. The dependent relationship between the black community and the social welfare system was raised spontaneously by all of the Korean merchants interviewed on the South Side of Chicago.

All of the Korean merchants who were interviewed considered government transfers to be important sources of disposable income for their customers. In fact, the Korean merchants who were interviewed recognized that surges in sales corresponded to the times when their customers received government cheeks. One Korean merchant described the scenario this way:

> Every month, the fifteenth and the end of month, very busy.
> Welfare day. Just a couple of days. A lot of welfare customers.
> They get money from government, they exchange it at cur-
> rency exchange, they get cash. Then they spend everything.
> Eating, enjoying, drug, drink, strip shows, they buy clothing,
> shoes, they broke that day.

The first of the month and the fifteenth of the month was the most frequently mentioned time period by the Korean merchants on the South Side of Chicago. During the course of a conversation, one Korean merchant said her customers were, "poor, most of them on welfare, lots of them, so we get busy every first few days every month, and then it slows down." When another Korean merchant was asked about when his store was busy he replied, "beginning of the month, I'm sure you've heard that a lot, that's got a lot to do with the social security checks and welfare checks."

All of the Korean merchants who were interviewed on the South Side of Chicago thought a large percentage of their cus-tomers received welfare. One commented, "I think 70 percent are welfare people." Another Korean merchant believed that since his store was adjacent to a large public housing project that over 80 percent of his customers were on welfare. Other Korean merchant estimated the number of customers on welfare to be approximate-ly 50 percent. The lowest estimate of customers on welfare came from a Korean merchant in a middle-class neighborhood on the South Side of Chicago, and he believed that 30 percent of his cus-tomers were on welfare. Although some of the estimates may be inflated, the locations of the Korean merchants' stores corre-sponded with the community areas on the South Side of Chicago that Wilson identified as having 45 percent or more of their resi-dents living in poverty in 1990.[16]

The close relationship between welfare and sales was articulat-ed in other ways by the Korean merchants on the South Side of Chicago. For example, all of the respondents attributed recent declining profits to cuts in government spending and social welfare programs. More striking, they were all in agreement about when this situation worsened. Economic conditions became acute on the South Side of Chicago between 1990 and 1992. According to reports from the Korean merchants who were interviewed in mid-1996, the black community, and their business, still had not recov-ered from the economic downturn of the early 1990's. One Korean merchant commented, "I think five years ago, or six, it was OK, but right now too slow, slow. And you know why? Black guys always received government money, welfare money. That down, down, down, down. That's why." Another Korean merchant pointed out that in the 1980's business was good, but by the mid-1990's he had seen the volume of his sales decline sharply. He identified the cause of this decline clearly:

> The reason is, this beauty supply is especially for black people. Most of the beauty supply located in the South part. Most of the main reason is the cutting in welfare support by the government. The other one is the losing job, cutting down, layoffs of the employee. I think that's the reason.

The decline in his business was accompanied by a general decline in economic conditions on the South Side of Chicago. For instance, the merchant cited above, commented that a number of fast food chains had closed near his store recently, and business in the area was "dead."

The perceived effect of welfare cuts on sales in Korean-owned businesses was drastic. One Korean merchant estimated the effect of welfare cut on his business between 1986 and 1996. He believed that he had seen at least a 30 percent drop in sales, and estimated that depending on the size of a given store, the effect of welfare cuts for other Korean merchants during that period ranged between a 20 percent and a 50 percent decline in sales. This drop in sales drove many Korean merchants out of business, and it forced others to pursue new customers more aggressively. One Korean merchant whose business is located in a middle-class neighborhood on the South Side of Chicago, discussed how expanding his advertising changed the composition of his clientele:

> I knew my market was limited. So once I advertised through newspaper, through in stores, and through radio, and having some lost-leader items I was promoting, I was getting a lot of customers from out of my area. So once I did that, the lower income bracket people would come into my store. So, our first of the week, first of the month, and third of the month, our sales would rise because that's when they would get their welfare checks. But, in also doing that, my level of losses went up.

He went on to explain how the arrival of these new customers was accompanied by a rise in shoplifting in his store. He also identified a number of other issues that were unique to businesses that served the poor:

> The first week and the third week customers, they're more price conscious, and you really have to keep an eye on them because we do have. We're not too far from the Englewood area which is a rougher area, very welfare oriented. So they try to do it. They want a product, but they don't want to pay, so they would have to steal. So, that's when I have the sensoring system, that's when I installed all of that, when my business went up. And, it's been very effective.

There were trade-offs involved in focusing on serving the poor. Increased profits often meant that Korean merchants had to invest more time and money in security systems and crime prevention. However, the Korean merchants considered these issues to be part of doing business in minority markets.

THE WELFARE ECONOMY AND SOJOURNING

The Korean merchants were extremely perceptive about the institutional context that their businesses were embedded in. This understanding of the nature of economic dependence was clearly expressed in their discussions of the welfare system. Although Korean merchants' profits were tied to welfare expenditures, they voiced criticisms concerning the role of the social welfare system in black America. One Korean merchant pointed out that, "the welfare system is good for my business, but it is not good." Some of the Korean merchants directed their criticism of the welfare system at white America, viewing the welfare system as "the white people's responsibility." To some it was seen as a poorly conceived system that government had little interest in improving. However, most of the Korean merchants interviewed on the South Side of Chicago had a more pragmatic view of the welfare system. They saw it as a source of economic relief for the poor. Unfortunately, they also bore witness to its erosion.

The decline of the social welfare system is one source of growing instability in minority markets. Another source relates to declining incomes and rising unemployment in the black community. Both indicate that economic conditions in minority markets are worsening. These conditions are magnified by black-white cleavages in society, that results in the demonization of the black community by mainstream institutions. Combined, these issues raise the stakes for middleman minorities, and reenforce their predisposition to sojourn in minority markets. However, another effect of the growing economic and political subordination of minority markets was also identified in this chapter. The stigmatization of the black community by mainstream institutions, and the repercussions of social welfare cuts in the black community, have resulted in declining sales and profits for entrepreneurs in minority markets. In the next chapter, the effects of these changes for black and Korean merchants will be discussed. In particular, the effect of growing competition on the level of ethnic solidarity among black and Korean entrepreneurs will be examined.

NOTES

[1]William K. Tabb, *The Political Economy of the Black Ghetto*, (New York: W.W. Norton and Company, 1970): 21-34.

[2]Paul C. P.Siu, "The Sojourner." *The American Journal of Sociology,* LVIII, 1952: 33-44; Rose Hume Lee, *The Chinese in the United States of America,* (Oxford: Oxford University Press, 1960), 69-85; Hubert Blalock, *Toward a Theory of Minority-Group Relations*, (New York: Capricorn Books, 1967); Edna Bonacich, Edna, "A Theory of Middleman Minorities," *American Sociological Review*, 38, 1973: 583-594.; Light, Ivan. and Edna Bonacich, *Immigrant Entrepreneurs, Koreans in Los Angeles, 1965-1982*, (Berkeley: University of California Press, 1988), 294-297; Marlene Sway, *Familiar Strangers, Gypsy Life in America,* (Champaign: University of Illinois Press, 1988): 21-23 and 125-126; and Walter P. Zenner, *Minorities in the Middle, A Cross-Cultural Text,* (Albany: State University of New York Press, 1991): 15-17.

[3] Ivan Light, *Ethnic Enterprise in America, Business and Welfare Among Chinese, Japanese, and Blacks,* (Berkeley: University of California Press, 1972); Ivan Light, "Asian Enterprise in America, Chinese, Japanese, and Koreans in Small Business," in Scott Cummings, ed. *Self-Help in Urban America, Patterns of Minority Business Enterprise,* (Port Washington: National University Publications, 1980), 33-57; Light, Ivan. and Edna Bonacich,*Immigrant Entrepreneurs, Koreans in Los Angeles, 1965-1982*,

(Berkeley: University of California Press, 1988); John Sibley Butler, *Entrepreneurship and Self-Help Among Black Americans, A Reconsideration of Race and Economics,* (Albany: State University of New York Press, 1991): 22-26.

⁴ Kwang Chung Kim and Won Moo Hurh, "Ethnic Resources Utilization of Korean Immigrant Entrepreneurs in the Chicago Minority Area,"*IMR,* 19.1, 1985: 82-109; P.G. Min and C. Jaret, "Ethnic Business Success: The Case of Korean Small Business in Atlanta," *Sociology and Social Research,* 69 (1985): 412-435; Ivan Light and Edna Bonacich, *Immigrant Entrepreneurs, Koreans in Los Angeles, 1965-1982.*, (Berkeley: University of California Press, 1988), 344-347; Pyong Gap Min, *Ethnic Business Enterprise, Korean Small Business in Atlanta,* (New York: Center for Migration Studies, 1988); In-Jin Yoon, "The Changing Significance of Ethnic and Class Resources in Immigrant Businesses: The Case of Korean Immigrant Businesses in Chicago," *IMR,* 25.2 (1991): 303-331; In-Jin Yoon, "The Growth of Korean Immigrant Entrepreneurship in Chicago," *Ethnic and Racial Studies,* 18.2 (1995): 315-335.

⁵ Hubert Blalock,*Toward a Theory of Minority-Group Relations,* (New York: Capricorn Books, 1967); Edna Bonacich, Edna, "A Theory of Middleman Minorities," *American Sociological Review,* 38 (1973): 583-594.; Edna Bonacich, *The Economic Basis of Ethnic Solidarity, Small Business in the Japanese American Community,* (Berkeley: University of California Press, 1980); Marlene Sway,*Familiar Strangers, Gypsy Life in America,* (Champaign: University of Illinois Press, 1988); and Walter P. Zenner, *Minorities in the Middle, A Cross-Cultural Text,* (Albany: State University of New York Press, 1991).

⁶ Moon H. Jo, "Korean Merchants in the Black Community, Prejudice Among the Victims of Prejudice," *Ethnic and Racial Studies,* 15.3 (1992): 395-411.

⁷ Howard Aldrich and Albert J. Reiss, Jr., "The Effect of Civil Disorders on Small Business in the Inner City," *Journal of Social Issues,* 26.1 (1970): 187-206; Ira Berkow, *Maxwell Street, Survival in a Bazaar,* (New York: Doubleday and Company, Inc., 1977): 523-532; Pyong Gap Min, *Caught in the Middle, Korean Communities in New York and Los Angeles,* (Berkeley: University of California Press (1996): 94.

⁸ Ella Stewart, *Ethnic Cultural Diversity, An Interpretive Study of Cultural Differences and Communication Styles Between Korean Merchants/Employees and Black Patrons in South Los Angeles,* Masters Thesis, (Los Angeles: California State University, Los Angeles, 1989).

[9] St. Clair Drake and Horace R. Cayton, *Black Metropolis, A Study of Negro Life in a Northern City*, (Chicago: University of Chicago Press, 1993): 88-89.

[10] William Julius Wilson, *When Work Disappears, The World of the New Urban Poor*, (New York: Alfred A. Knopf Publishing, 1996): 18-20.

[11] Barry Bluestone and Bennett Harrison, *The Deindustrialization of America, Plant Closing, Community Abandonment, and the Dismantling of Basic Industry*, (New York: Basic Books, 1982); Thomas M. Stanbeck and Thierry J. Noyelle, *Cities in Transition: Changing Job Structures in Atlanta, Denver, Buffalo, Phoenix, Columbus (Ohio), Nashville, and Charlotte*, (Totowa: Allanheld, Osmun And Co. Publishers, 1982); Barry Bluestone and Bennett Harrison, *The Great U-Turn, Corporate Restructuring and the Polarizing of America*, (New York: Basic Books, 1988).

[12] William Julius Wilson, *The Truly Disadvantaged, The Inner City, The Underclass, and Public Policy*, (Chicago: University of Chicago Press, 1987); Gregory D. Squires, Larry Bennett, Kathleen McCourt and Philip Nyden, *Chicago, Race, Class, and the Response to Urban Decline*, (Philadelphia: Temple University Press, 1987); William Julius Wilson, *When Work Disappears, The World of the New Urban Poor*, (New York: Alfred A. Knopf Publishing, 1996).

[13] Michael B. Katz, *The Undeserving Poor, From the War on Poverty to the War on Welfare*, (New York, Pantheon Books, 1989).

[14] Charles Murray, *Losing Ground, American Social Policy 1950-1980*, (New York: Basic Books, 1984); Richard J. Herrnstein and Charles Murray, *The Bell Curve: Intelligence and Class in American Life*, (New York: Free Press, 1994).

[15] Paul E. Peterson and Mark C. Rom, *Welfare Magnets, A New Case for a National Standard*, (Washington D.C.: The Brookings Institute, 1990).

[16] William Julius Wilson, *When Work Disappears, The World of the New Urban Poor*, (New York: Alfred A. Knopf Publishing, 1996): 12-13.

CHAPTER 5:

The Effects Of Competition On Ethnic Solidarity

WHEN MINORITY MARKETS STAGNATE

This chapter examines how perceptions of economic stagnation during the early 1990's affected ethnic solidarity among black and Korean merchants on the South Side of Chicago. The central argument of this chapter is that perceptions of economic stagnation led to growing competition and declining ethnic solidarity among Korean merchants, while they had no effect on competition and increased ethnic solidarity among black merchants. This distinction is explained by differences in the availability and utilization of ethnic and class resources between black and Korean entrepreneurs in minority markets.[1] It will be argued that the middleman minority role that Korean merchants fill in the black community reduces the role of ethnic resources in their businesses. This is the case, since Korean merchants in the black community do not have a co-ethnic clientele.

In contrast, black merchants in the black community serve co-ethnic customers, which to some extent buffers them from shifts in the economy. The ability to mobilize ethnic solidarity during periods of economic stagnation, and appeal to co-ethnic consumers, is an important resource for minority businesses. In the context of minority markets, persistent racial hostility in mainstream society elevates the role of ethnic solidarity between black merchants and black customers. However, Korean merchants do not benefit from ethnic solidarity in this way, since they are middleman minorities in the black community. In fact, they often became scapegoats for black-white conflict in society. Because of these factors, the absence of co-ethnic customers is the principle distinction to be made between black and Korean merchants in minority markets when discussing ethnic resources.

Although Korean merchants do not have co-ethnic customers in the black community, there is still a great deal of similarity in the way black and Korean merchants mobilize other types of ethnic resources. For example, many of the similarities between black and Korean merchants on the South Side of Chicago were identified in chapter 4. It was pointed out that both groups of merchants employ family members in their businesses. Also, black and Korean merchants raise the initial start-up capital for their business in similar ways, using personal savings and loans from family members. In addition, both groups of merchants possess a strong work ethic. In fact, the mobilization of ethnic resources by black and Korean entrepreneur has been discussed by several scholars.[2] Historically, each group has mobilized ethnic resources for economic ends.

Despite the use of ethnic resources, economic outcomes for black and Korean entrepreneurs have been different. Bates attributes this to differences in the levels of capital that black and Korean entrepreneurs are able to raise for business start-ups.[3] This highlights an important distinctions between black and Korean businesses in minority markets. Black merchants benefit from the ability to mobilize ethnic resources in minority markets that Korean merchants do not have access to. In particular, black merchant benefit from ethnic solidarity with black customers in minority markets. However, Korean merchants benefit from class resources that black merchants do not have access to. This was particularly apparent when the black and Korean merchants who were interviewed on the South Side of Chicago discussed issues related to capital.

There was a noticeable disparity in the amount of capital that the black and Korean merchants could leverage for their businesses. For instance, some of the informants discussed how they came to the United States with large blocks of capital from the sales of homes and property in Korea. This capital was used to start their businesses in the black community. In addition, some of the Korean merchants discussed paying over $50 thousand in cash for their businesses. In contrast, the black merchants discussed investing smaller amounts of venture capital in their businesses. For instance, two of the black merchants said that they started their businesses with less than $5 thousand, and another had less than $20 thousand to start his business. The disparity in capital between black and Korean merchants was also clear when they discussed how much they invested in the monthly inventory for their stores. Again, several of the Korean merchants bought over $10 thousand worth of inventory per month, while the black merchants discussed how they spent considerably less on monthly inventory.

The size and location of the stores owned by black and Korean merchants also reflected differences in access to capital. Most of the Korean merchants ran larger stores than the black merchants. For instance, all black merchants had less than 1,500 square feet of retail space in their stores, while over half of the Korean merchants ran stores with more retail space. In addition, all of the stores run by Korean merchants were located in the center of business districts on the South Side of Chicago, while the stores of black merchants were located on the edges of these business districts and on side streets. The advantages that the Korean merchants accrued due to such class resources helped them compensate for the lack of a co-ethnic clientele. On the other hand, the black merchants clearly benefitted from the presence of co-ethnic customers. The presence of co-ethnic customers seemed particularly important when their capital constraints were taken into consideration.

The differences in class and ethnic resources among black and Korean merchants shaped their response to the economic stagnation which resulted from declining social welfare spending in the early 1990's. During this period, the black and Korean merchants adopted different strategies to sustain their businesses. The Korean merchants focused on developing class resources. In particular, they invested capital in their businesses, in order to expand them and take advantage of economies of scale. In contrast, the black merchants focused on developing ethnic resources in the black community. In part, this entailed reducing the scope of their businesses and focusing on sales to black beauticians and barbers.

However, this ethnic strategy also meant that black merchants promoted their businesses as "black-owned," in order to attract co-ethnic customers. In the following sections, the strategies of black and Korean merchants will be discussed in greater detail.

GROWING TO SURVIVE

Korean Merchants Respond to Welfare Cuts

All of the Korean merchants who were interviewed reported that consumer spending on the South Side of Chicago was down during the early 1990's. They attributed this to cuts in social welfare programs and job losses in the black community. These changes resulted in declining incomes for poor blacks, who were their core customers. Some Korean-owned businesses were more susceptible to these changes than others. For instance, one Korean merchant pointed out that before the early 1990's, there were many Korean-owned shoe stores and clothing stores on the South Side of Chicago. But as black consumers began spending less, the sales in these types of businesses declined. This Korean merchant went on to explain that the ethnic beauty aids industry was considered more resilient during economic downturns. Beauty supplies were less expensive than other consumer items, and consumers needed to purchase them on a regular basis. In fact, the Korean merchant pointed out that, "As time went by and business started to get slower and slower, the people who were in the beauty supply industry were still doing strong." The perception that the ethnic beauty aids industry was resistent to economic downturns attracted many Korean merchants to it during the early 1990's.

Korean merchants drew on two distinct strategies to expanded their role in the ethnic beauty aids industry during the early 1990's. In one strategy, Korean merchants attempted to diversify their stores. In doing this, they shifted from selling one or two types of products, such as wigs and beauty supplies, to selling an entire line of general merchandise. Some sold clothing, shoes, consumer electronics, household appliances, toys, dollar items, and a full line of beauty supplies. The goal of this business strategy was to sell some products, usually beauty supplies, at the merchant's cost, and others at a regular mark-up. The items sold at the merchant's cost, known as "loss leaders," were used to attract black customers to the store. Once in the store, the customers would buy the loss leaders as well as other products at regular prices. The other type of business strategy adopted by Korean merchants involved specializing in the sale of one type of product, ethnic beauty aids. The goal of this strategy was to purchase large quantities of beauty supplies direct from manufacturers at a discount, and then pass those discounts on to the consumer in the form of lower prices. Using this strategy, a merchant could sell a large volume of ethnic beauty aids. Even though this approach lowered a merchant's profits on each item that was sold, the store's overall sales were higher and profits increased.

Although each of these strategies is distinct, they both had a similar effect on retail prices in the ethnic beauty aids industry. As Korean merchants expanded their stores, they created downward pressure on the price of beauty supplies. Korean-owned general merchandise stores drove the price of beauty supplies down, since they were using them as loss leaders, and selling beauty supplies at cost. Similarly, large Korean-owned beauty supply stores caused prices to fall, since they purchased large volumes of merchandise directly from manufacturers, selling them at discount prices. The result was that small beauty supply stores were being priced out of the market. One Korean merchant reflected on the effect of these changes:

> I think we've seen a process where a lot of businesses closing down, or markets getting tougher in a way. So only few I think, not that many of them is gonna survive through the next five or ten years. Even though you gonna have plenty of them out here, the percentile I think it's gonna be, either big ones are gonna survive or niche markets gonna survive.

The process this Korean merchant described began in the early 1990's. At that time, retailing in the ethnic beauty aids industry became increasingly polarized. Large Korean-owned stores began to emerge which specialized in volume sales at discount prices, and a smaller niche market matured which specialized in the sale of professional beauty supplies to black beauticians and barbers.

Competition and the Need for Capital

These two sides of the ethnic beauty aids industry became increasingly distinct in the early 1990's. Each side of the industry was unique in both function and in terms of the ethnic composition of its merchants. Korean merchants became concentrated in the larger retail segment of the industry, and black merchants specialized in the smaller professional side of the ethnic beauty aids industry. This segmentation was driven by differences in ethnic and class resources. The development of a separate niche in the ethnic beauty aids industry for black merchants, based on ethnic resources, is discussed later in this chapter. Before this discussion, several points about the niche that Korean merchants occupy in the ethnic beauty aids industry should be made.

First, the role of class resources in the development of a retail niche for Korean merchants requires further discussion. As retailing in the ethnic beauty aids industry became more price competitive, the success of a merchant's business became dependent on his or her ability to mobilize capital. This was the case both for Korean merchants who sold a full line of general merchandise, and for those who specialized in volume sales of ethnic beauty aids. Because they sold a number of different products, Korean general merchants had to invest heavily in their inventory. They also needed additional capital to purchase ethnic beauty aids from local distributors, which would later be sold at cost. The capital requirements for Korean merchants who specialized in volume sales of ethnic beauty supplies were also high. In order to offer the lowest possible prices to consumers, the Korean merchants had to buy products in large volumes, directly from the manufacturers. In both cases, the ability to mobilize capital was critical to the maintenance of their businesses.

The issue of capitalization became more important as the spending power of black consumers declined in the early 1990's. As downward pressure on prices increased, the need to leverage capital became magnified. These market conditions made black consumers and Korean merchants highly price conscious. The primacy of price was clearly identified by one Korean merchant, "I'm looking for all the time, same kind, how can I buy the merchandise cheaper." The ability to buy merchandise at the lowest possible price was directly related to the level of capital a merchant had on hand at a given time. This was the case, since merchants received volume discounts from suppliers when they bought large amounts of merchandise at once. One Korean discussed this issue in detail:

> It's all based on volume. The more you buy it, then you can
> start to deal directly with the factory. So you are basically cut-

ting out the middleman by that time. Every time a good
changes hands it's gonna take a markup some, so they can
justify their existence. So, good or bad, that will take time.
But if we get bigger, and we can do enough volume, factory is
gonna want to deal directly with you. That way you can save
some money, and you can undercut the competition, in a way.

In the early 1990's, price competition increased in the ethnic beauty aids industry, and there were pressures on Korean merchants to
expand their businesses. However, business expansion had to
occur without reducing the pool of operating capital that was used
to buy monthly inventory. The Korean merchants who were interviewed discussed a number of strategies they adopted for business
growth that kept their operating capital stable.

Some of the Korean merchants who were interviewed avoided
many strategies for business expansion, since they tended to reduce
the level of operating capital available to a business. For instance,
many were cautious about borrowing money and acquiring debt
from banks. In part, their suspicion of major financial institutions
grew out of negative experiences in the past. But even after some
of the Korean merchants established a business and a credit history in the United States, they remained pessimistic about borrowing
from mainstream banks. One Korean merchant who had been in
the United States for over a decade discussed how business loans
were eventually offered to him by banks, but he turned them down
since the interest payments took money away from the operating
capital necessary to run his business. He made the following comment:

American company, American bank, they want me for a loan.
But I never tread into the loan business. No, that's no good.
First time it looks good. After, your business cannot follow up
with that money. Maybe, not easy.

The need to maintain a high cash flow to meet the operating costs
of a business made borrowing money and servicing a debt unattractive to the Korean merchants who were interviewed. This was
seen as a drain on operating capital and cash reserves.

The Relative Importance of Class Resources to Korean Merchants

Because retailing in the ethnic beauty aids industry was cash intensive, the ability to mobilize class resources was important to the
Korean merchants on the South Side of Chicago. Initially, they
establish their businesses using money from personal savings and
money borrowed from friends and relatives. For instance, Min
points out that, "most Korean merchants depend primarily on
their own savings for their start-up capital," and to a lesser extent
on personal loans from friend and family members.[4] He goes on to
explain that loans from mainstream lending institutions and ethnic
associations, such as rotating credit associations, do not play a
major role in the initial capitalization of their businesses.[5] The
investment of personal savings was sometimes large enough to
allow Korean merchants to purchase businesses with monthly
operating costs in excess of $10 thousand. In fact, some of the
Korean merchants reported a monthly cash flow in excess of $50
thousand. Much of this capital was used to purchase inventory,
and this was done in two general ways. Inventory was either purchased for cash, or on occasion with a 30 day line of credit from a
supplier. But, purchasing inventory for cash was preferred, since
paying cash sometimes meant that a merchant would get a lower
price. The ability to pay cash for inventory opened several additional avenues to Korean merchants.

One Korean merchant discussed how having cash on hand
allowed him to purchase products from other Korean merchants
when their stores went out of business. This created several advantages. The most important was that when he purchased beauty
supplies from stores that went out of business, he got a lower price
than a regular supplier would offer, "sometimes four times, five
times" less. Once these products were purchased, they could be
sold at regular retail prices. This allowed the merchant to increase
his overall profits. However, this was not the only flexible buying
strategy mentioned. Other Korean merchants coordinated their
purchases from manufacturers in groups, so they could acquire a
wide range of inventory for their stores at the lowest price.

This strategy, although appearing to be based on ethnic
resources, was actually dependent on class resources. One Korean
merchant described how this purchasing strategy worked. He said

that about six of his friends owned large beauty supply stores, and each month they would buy merchandise from manufacturers in the ethnic beauty aids industry. Each Korean merchant would buy several thousand dollars worth of merchandise from a different manufacturer, and receive a volume discount. After each of the Korean merchants made their individual purchases, the group would divide the products up. This strategy allowed all of the Korean merchants who participated in the buying group to benefit from the discounted prices that individual manufacturers offered for volume sales, without having to make several large purchases on an individual basis. However, this buying strategy was based primarily on the class resources that these merchants could mobilize, rather than on broad based ethnic resources available to all Korean merchants.

Only a small segment of the Korean merchants on the South Side of Chicago could participate in these buying groups, since they were first required to mobilize the prerequisite class resources to gain access to them. In particular, these merchants had to have enough cash on hand to buy close to $20 thousand worth of merchandise from a manufacturer at a time. This meant that at minimum, a merchant had to own one of the larger beauty supply stores on the South Side of Chicago, or own several stores, to be able to participate in a buying group. Korean merchants who owned smaller stores were not able to raise the required capital to join a buying group. Less than half of the Korean merchants who were interviewed owned businesses that sold enough merchandise to participate in a buying group. Although other merchants were aware of buying groups, they did not have the capital to participate in them. In this sense, it was class resources, and not ethnic resources, that allowed merchants to join buying groups. Only Korean merchants able to leverage large blocks of capital could participate.

This type of a relationship is in sharp contrast to business strategies based on ethnic resources, since these types of strategies are opened to all members of an ethnic group regardless of class position. Business strategies opened to only a segment of a population of ethnic entrepreneurs are predominantly based on class resources.[6] For instance, one Korean merchant discussed how class resources determined the type of supplier a merchant would buy products from:

> When I first came into the business I used the distributor, but
> then I started to open up my own accounts with the manu-
> facturer because we were doing that kind of volume then. I
> could buy 30, 40, thousand items per company. In this busi-
> ness it's basically money talks, the more you buy the more dis-
> counts you get. So a lot of the smaller guys usually cannot
> utilize the manufacturer because they have a certain, if they
> buy at a $1 thousand dollar level you might as well buy from
> a distributor, because you getting cheaper from a distributor.
> Unless you are gonna buy at the $50 thousand and then $200
> thousand bracket, then your saving 15, 20, percent.

The type of supplier an individual Korean merchant used was
based on how much capital he or she had, and not on the merchant's ethnicity. In fact, disparities in the ability to mobilize class
resources generated a number of cleavages among the Korean merchants on the South Side of Chicago.

INTRA-ETHNIC COMPETITION

The Schism between Class Resources and Ethnic Solidarity

In some instances, differences in the ability to mobilize class
resources among the Korean merchants had a detrimental impact
on ethnic solidarity. For example, one Korean merchant describe
how owning a large beauty supply store allowed him to push merchants who owned smaller stores out of the market:

> Well, I think that's the advantage of having a bigger store, is
> you can carry more a variety of beauty supplies. I mean, they
> might carry 20 items, where I carry 4000 items. To me it
> doesn't really matter, because, if they carry 20 items, I can put
> 20 items at cost, and I know they can't put it at cost. But, I
> can still make money on the other 3800 products.

This strategy was based on the merchant's capital position. By
mobilizing capital and slashing prices, he was able to push smaller
merchants out of the market. However, this behavior had a detrimental effect on the level of ethnic solidarity among Korean merchants. Most of the smaller Korean merchants expressed concern
over this type of market behavior. They perceived it as an expres-
sion of "greed" on the part of "rich" Koreans, and felt animosity
toward them. As the economy on the South Side of Chicago stagnated in the early 1990's, the Korean merchants said that this type

of market behavior became more intense. As a result, ethnic solidarity among the Korean merchants weakened.

The schism between class and ethnic resources is illustrated by the experience of a Korean merchant whose business suffered when a Korean distributor of ethnic beauty aids opened a large retail store next door to her. When the better capitalized Korean distributer began to compete directly with her smaller beauty supply store, her sales and profits dropped. In response, she went to the Korean distributor and implored him to adjust his prices so her store could compete, but he ignored her appeal and continued to slash the prices in his store. The owner of the smaller store was upset about the Korean distributor's actions. She stated that, "It was not right, it was just out of greed, that's what I thought at that time, and I was very angry at him." This experience caused her to sever business ties with other Koreans. She discussed this in the following comment:

> I had some problems with the Korean distributors, because one of the biggest Korean distributors opened up his business right next door to me a couple years ago. I had to deal with him anyway. So, I don't deal with the Korean distributors.

This was not an isolated incident. Other Korean merchants discussed trepidations they had when doing business with Korean distributors, since they feared that some day those larger businesses would become their competition.

For instance, one Korean merchant gave a detailed description of how he and other small retailers reacted to Korean distributors who opened retail stores near them. He said that merchants would avoid doing business with such distributors. While discussing the issue he stated, "I don't want to make my competitors rich by buying from them, when I know they are gonna get the price break better than what I can." In fact, Korean distributors who enter the retail market face the possibility of being boycotted by other Korean merchants. The Korean merchant cited above discussed how other Korean merchants were suspicious of such Korean distributors:

> I know a couple of stores, they totally don't do business with a certain wholesaler because one of their brother, brother-in-law, opened up a store down here. So they say, the hell with you guys, I'm not doing any business with you whatsoever.

> And, since everybody basically sells the same thing at just about the same pricing level, unless you are getting desperate about certain worn out items, you are not going to have that much effects by stopping business with a certain wholesaler.

Ethnic solidarity broke down when better capitalized co-ethnics entered the market place. In fact, the Korean merchants competed almost exclusively with among themselves. Other types of retail stores, such as large chain stores, had a limited role in the retail side of the ethnic beauty aid industry. According to the Korean merchants who were interviewed, chain stores carried fewer products than the Korean merchants and sold them as slightly higher prices.

Intra-Ethnic Competition and the Limited Scope of Business Organizations

However, the absence of chain stores as serious competitors did not mean that competition was lacking in minority markets. In fact, as the economy stagnated during the early 1990's on the South Side of Chicago, competition between Korean merchants intensified. Growing competition created an environment where Korean merchants became wary of one and other. For instance, one Korean merchant discussed how he avoided advertising his prices, because when his competitors saw what items he had on sale they would undercut his prices. Several other Korean merchants were cautious about joining Korean business organizations because of concerns they had about competition. One Korean merchant expressed his belief that such organizations focused on the needs of larger businesses. He commented, "I don't want to participate in that kind of a group, because my business is so small."

The nature of price competition among Korean merchants limited the economic role of Korean business organizations. One Korean merchant pointed out, "This is free competition, we're not going to sit around and set the price. You know, let's mark it up 50 percent on this item." Because of the business climate on the South Side of Chicago, the role of Korean business organizations was narrow. They existed primarily for community relations purposes and for conflict resolution vis-a-vis the black community. One Korean merchant made this comment about the role of Korean business associations on the South Side of Chicago:

> As long as you don't have riots or whatever, or mass demon-
> strations about certain things, you'll never ever really have
> dealings with those business associations. When you have
> typically community based problems, that's when you need
> them as representatives. I sat on one of those things for a cou-
> ple of times. What good they do. I really cannot tell you.

Ironically, Korean business organizations may have become more
active on the South Side of Chicago during the early 1990's, since
black-Korean conflict expanded as a result of economic stagnation.[7] However, the same economic conditions that increased the
need for Korean business organizations to address black-Korean
conflict, also caused competition among Korean merchants to
intensify. The growth of competition among Korean merchants
undermined the ethnic solidarity necessary for many types of
cooperative business activities.

THE ETHNIC BEAUTY AIDS INDUSTRY IS A BLACK INDUSTRY

Black Perceptions of the "Korean Invasion"

Intensified competition between Korean merchants highlighted
disparities in class resources. The role of class resources became
more central to Korean merchants as the economy on the South
Side of Chicago stagnated. Increasingly, the level of capital that an
individual Korean merchant held determined how the merchant's
business would perform. In contrast, there was little change in the
role of class resources for black merchants on the South Side of
Chicago during this early 1990's. In part, this is because black
merchants have been undercapitalized for decades. However, economic change during the early 1990's did affect the manner in
which black merchants approached business. As stagnation in the
economy persisted, the black merchants on the South Side of
Chicago focused on a specific niche in the ethnic beauty aids industry, the sale of professional products to black beauticians and barbers. This segment of the ethnic beauty aids industry was smaller
and less price competitive than the general retail market that
Koreans merchants occupied. By focusing on the professional market, black merchants needed less capital to sustain their businesses. In addition, the ability of black merchants to mobilize ethnic

resources protected their niche in the ethnic beauty aids industry from an influx of better financed Korean entrepreneurs.

The Korean merchants who were interviewed knew about the professional market for ethnic beauty aids, but they showed little interest in entering it. Instead, they specialized in selling beauty supplies to black consumers in the general retail market. In fact, the Korean merchants who were interviewed did not consider black merchants to be their competitors. When asked about black merchants, one Korean merchant replied, "I haven't seen one, I hardly ever seen one." However, the black merchants who were interviewed were quite aware of the presence of Korean merchants on the South Side of Chicago. The black merchants felt that Korean merchants controlled the general retail market in the ethnic beauty aids industry, since they had more capital to invest in their businesses. This disparity in capital motivated the black merchants to concentrate on developing their niche on the professional side of the ethnic beauty aids industry.

The black merchants were overwhelmed by the amount of capital that Korean merchants had to invest in their businesses. In fact, a number of myths circulated in the black community concerning the source of this capital. One of the more prevalent was that Korean businesses were subsidized by the United States government. Although there is no evidence to support this story, it helped to affiliate Korean merchants with mainstream institutions in the eyes of some members of the black community. This myth was clearly articulated in the following comment by one black merchant:

> They had great deals of money. From some source. I have ascertained it came from our government. They had tax free operations. Terrific investment capital. I can't see how a guardian nation like Korea, who lost a war, could have that kind of money. But they came here with great deals of money. That money I think came from our government. Like a lend lease type of thing. I think, but I can't prove any of this. But there's no way in the world a guardian people could have that kind of money. $30, $40, $50 thousand to buy a business. Or to do like they do across the street, a million dollar inventory in 6 or 7 years. You don't grow that fast. So the source of money came from somewhere. They came, they had great deals of money, they moved in, bought most of the black distributors out, those who would sell. Those who didn't sell, they competed with them. Unlimited supplies of money.

This myth functioned to heighten the black community's awareness of capital disparities between black and Korean merchants. In doing so, it created a clear contrast between the two groups. Korean merchants were characterized as outsiders in the black community, and their presence was seen as destabilizing to black business. In contrast, black merchants were portrayed as co-ethnics who were under siege by what was described as a Korean "invasion" of the black community. This myth served to strengthen ethnic solidarity in the black community.

The Symbolic Value of Black-Owned Business

In addition to the role of myths about Korean merchants, there were other mechanisms that helped black merchants mobilize ethnic resources in the black community. For instance, many of the black merchants on the South Side of Chicago advertise their businesses as black-owned. One of the most common ways black merchants did this was by hanging signs in the windows of their stores that read, "BLACK-OWNED." However, this theme was incorporated into other forms of advertising for black- owned stores. For instance, one black merchant circulated a flyer to her customers discussing the plight of black-owned businesses on the South Side of Chicago, and the role Korean merchants played in their demise. The following excerpt illustrates the tone of the letter:

> In the past, the Beauty Business was predominantly African American owned. Largely due to the fact that we, people of color, set the fashion and beauty trends. However, in the mid-1980's, the invasion of Korean merchants took place in our neighborhoods, replacing many Black owned businesses.

The flyer touched on a number of themes, highlighting the need for ethnic solidarity in the black community. In one part of the flyer, the black merchant explained how her business faced direct competition from Korean merchants, and how ethnic solidarity in the black community would curb this competition. The black merchant identified several benefits that ethnic solidarity would produce. The flyer pointed out that Korean merchants did not "have command of the English language," and that Korean merchants were rude to black customers. The flyer argued that blacks who patronized black-owned stores did not confront these issues. The letter ended with an appeal to black consumers to shop in black-owned stores. It asked black consumers, "Think about it — Could we operate and flourish in their community as they have done in ours? NO! NO! NO!!!" In effect, this was a clear attempt to mobilize ethnic resources in the black community.

All of the black merchants who were interviewed on the South Side of Chicago discussed the importance of mobilizing ethnic resources. The role of ethnic resources became more important in the early 1980's, after Korean merchants "began their invasion" on the South Side of Chicago, and again in the early 1990's when the economy stagnated. The black merchant described a number of business strategies they adopted which focused on mobilizing ethnic resources in the black community. They pointed out that black merchants had a better understanding of trends and products in the ethnic beauty aids industry, since they had access to informal networks in the black community. Many of these benefits stemmed from the fact that they lived in the black community. However, the black merchants also had a better understanding of the products in the ethnic beauty aids industry, since they used the products that they sold. In addition, the black merchants focused on segments of the ethnic beauty aids industry where sales were influenced more by a merchant's ability to build rapport with consumers, than by price. This led them to focus on selling professional products to black beauticians and barbers. One black merchant discussed the decision to focus on this niche:

> We've cut back, and concentrated most on the professional items. The Koreans who are a force in this industry, they habitually low ball prices, and because of that there's no profitability in retail products, or products that are readily available to most. So, we saw the need, if we don't want to give the impression that we are thieves, and ripping off people, we had to redirect our focus, so we focus on salons and professional items.

Rather than attempting to mobilize capital and compete directly with Korean merchants, black merchants chose to confine their business activities to a smaller economic niche where the ability to mobilize ethnic resources had a greater effect on business success.

In part, Korean merchants limited their access to this niche by cutting prices in the general retail market. Because of their aggressive price cutting, black consumers began to associate Korean merchants with low quality products and a lack of commitment to the long term stability of the ethnic beauty aids industry. This reduced the credibility of Korean merchant on the professional side of the ethnic beauty aids industry. The business style of Korean merchants was not compatible with the image of black beauticians and barbers. In the black community, black beauticians and barbers were seen as providers of professional services and quality products. In order to maintain this image, they sought to use products that black consumers trusted. This trust was developed in two ways. First, black beauticians and barbers made sure that the products they used worked. Second, black beauticians and barbers mobilized ethnic resources to build consumer confidence in those products. Black merchants were an important component of building consumer trust and confidence.

The business style of black merchants complemented the salon market in two important ways. First, black merchants focused on selling professional products, and distanced themselves from the retail merchandise that Korean merchants sold. In fact, an important selling point of the professional products that black merchants sold was that they were not available in the retail stores owned by Korean merchants. Second, the black merchants emphasized the ethnic dimension of the products they sold, highlighting that the ethnic beauty aids industry was a homespun industry. In fact, an important service that black merchants provided to black salons was that they delivered merchandise to the stores. This was important for practical and symbolic reasons. In terms of convenience, delivery services made it easier for black salon owners to get products. More importantly, when black merchants delivered products to black salons, black customers saw them. This added value to the products they sold, and it reenforced the image of the ethnic beauty aids industry as a black industry. One black merchant discussed the importance of this image, and the role of ethnic resources in the black community:

> Right now I've seen the Koreans, which I don't think they had a lot of good intentions initially coming in the industry. They just wanted to make money, and they didn't want to enhance and maintain. Where as I am black, I am compelled to do so, and I think it's the only area in which we don't necessarily control, but we should control. You know, we are the ones

using the products, we are the ones, our loved ones are the ones utilizing it, so we should always be a part of the puzzle I think. So, because of that affiliation, I love to see, I don't know if you have traveled too much around here but if you want to see a woman, a black woman in the morning, one of the first things that you could observe is that her hair is well done. Almost to the T. Unless she's a little bit crazy or something. You can go to Robert Taylor Homes, or anywhere, when they come out their hair's at least done. So, they do take pride in that. And I think over the years, not having straight hair, and it's so difficult to comb and all that, they're taking pride in fixing their hair. And, I think we should be a part of that, I really think we should be a part of that.

Black merchants filled an important symbolic role in the ethnic beauty aids industry. They were the black representatives of a black industry. Being black helped create an economic niche for the products they sold. In contrast, Korean merchants did not have access to ethnic resources in the black community. In order to compete, they mobilized class resources to carve out an economic niche in the black community.

DIVERGENT PATHS

The development of separate niches in the ethnic beauty aids industry for black and Korean merchants began to crystalize in the early 1990's. During this period, economic stagnation forced black and Korean merchants to refocus their businesses. In doing this, they mobilized the ethnic and class resources available to them. In some respects, black and Korean merchants drew from similar types of resources. For example, both groups of merchants invested their personal savings in their businesses, hired family members to work in their stores, and worked long hours. However, black and Korean merchants had different levels of access to some types of class and ethnic resources. For instance, the Korean merchants on the South Side of Chicago had more capital to invest in their businesses. Initially, this capital came from personal saving and money borrowed from family members. Later, it came from profits in their existing businesses. On the other hand, the black merchants on the South Side of Chicago were able to mobilize ethnic resources in the black community more easily. This was because the minority markets on the South Side of Chicago were composed of black consumers. This large pool of co-ethnic customers created opportunities for black merchants to mobilize ethnic resources that Korean merchants could not.

The result of these differences in class and ethnic resources was that black and Korean businesses developed on separate paths. Korean merchants focused on selling discount merchandise in the black community, and black merchants focused on selling professional products to black beauticians and barbers. The development of these separate economic niches for black and Korean merchants in minority markets highlights how structural changes are linked to individual agency. Black and Korean merchants mobilized ethnic and class resources in response to shifts in mainstream society. These shifts were identified in chapter 4. During the 1970's and 1980's economic restructuring occurred.[8] This was accompanied by cuts in social welfare spending in the 1980's, and the demonization of poor blacks by some scholars in the early 1990's.[9] The impact of these changes caused the economy on the South Side of Chicago to stagnate in the early 1990's. As a result, black and Korean merchants followed divergent paths, based on their differential access to class and ethnic resources.

Issues concerning access to class and ethnic resources continue to constrain the businesses of black and Korean merchants on the South Side of Chicago. For instance, black merchants still face capital constraints, despite the fact that they have secured an economic niche in the ethnic beauty aids industry. Similarly, cleavages exist between Korean merchants and black customers on the South Side of Chicago. In some ways, many Korean merchants have attempted to address these cleavages by hiring blacks to work in their stores. The next chapter will discuss how Korean merchants combine their class resources with the ethnic resources of black employees to reduce tension with black customers.

NOTES

[1]Ivan Light, "Asian Enterprise in America, Chinese, Japanese, and Koreans in Small Business," in Scott Cummings, ed. *Self- Help in Urban America, Patterns of Minority Business Enterprise*, (Port Washington: National University Publications, 1980), 33-57; In-Jin Yoon, "The

Changing Significance of Ethnic and Class Resources in Immigrant Businesses: The Case of Korean Immigrant Businesses in Chicago," *IMR*, 25.2, 1991: 303-331; In-Jin Yoon, "The Growth of Korean Immigrant Entrepreneurship in Chicago," *Ethnic and Racial Studies*, 18.2, 1995: 315-335.

[2] Ivan Light, *Ethnic Enterprise in America, Business and Welfare Among Chinese, Japanese, and Blacks*, (Berkeley: University of California Press, 1972); Ivan Light, "Asian Enterprise in America, Chinese, Japanese, and Koreans in Small Business," in Scott Cummings, ed. *Self-Help in Urban America, Patterns of Minority Business Enterprise*, (Port Washington: National University Publications, 1980), 33-57; Light, Ivan. and Edna Bonacich, *Immigrant Entrepreneurs, Koreans in Los Angeles, 1965-1982*, (Berkeley: University of California Press, 1988); Pyong Gap Min, *Ethnic Business Enterprise, Korean Small Business in Atlanta*, (New York: Center for Migration Studies, 1988); John Sibley Butler, *Entrepreneurship and Self-Help Among Black Americans, A Reconsideration of Race and Economics*, (Albany: State University of New York Press, 1991).

[3] Timothy Bates, "An Analysis of Korean-Immigrant-owned Small-Business Start-ups with Comparisons to African-American- and Nonminority-Owned Firms," *Urban Affairs Quarterly*, 30.2, 1994: 227-248.

[4] Pyong Gap Min, *Caught in the Middle, Korean Communities in New York and Los Angeles*, (Berkeley: University of California Press, 1996): 102.

[5] Ibid.

[6] In-Jin Yoon, "The Changing Significance of Ethnic and Class Resources in Immigrant Businesses: The Case of Korean Immigrant Businesses in Chicago," *IMR*, 25.2, 1991: 318.

[7] Joseph Ahne, "Koreans of Chicago, The New Entrepreneurial Immigrants," in Melvin G. Holli and Peter d'A. Jones eds., *Ethnic Chicago, A Multicultural Portrait*, (Grand Rapids: William B. Eerdmans Publishing Company, 1995): 492-499.

[8] Barry Bluestone and Bennett Harrison, *The Deindustrialization of America, Plant Closing, Community Abandonment, and the Dismantling of Basic Industry*, (New York: Basic Books, 1982); Thomas M. Stanbeck and Thierry J. Noyelle, *Cities in Transition: Changing Job Structures in Atlanta, Denver, Buffalo, Phoenix, Columbus (Ohio), Nashville, and Charlotte*, (Totowa: Allanheld, Osmun And Co. Publishers, 1982); Barry Bluestone and Bennett Harrison, *The Great U-Turn, Corporate*

Restructuring and the Polarizing of America, (New York: Basic Books, 1988).

[9] Charles Murray, *Losing Ground, American Social Policy 1950-1980*, (New York: Basic Books, 1984); Michael B. Katz, *The Undeserving Poor, From the War on Poverty to the War on Welfare*, (New York, Pantheon Books, 1989); Paul E. Peterson and Mark C. Rom, *Welfare Magnets, A New Case for a National Standard*, (Washington D.C.: The Brookings Institute, 1990); Richard J. Herrnstein and Charles Murray, *The Bell Curve: Intelligence and Class in American Life*, (New York: Free Press, 1994).

CHAPTER 6:

The Interdependence Of Korean Merchants And Black Employees In Minority Markets

KOREANS AND BLACKS AT THE CROSSROADS

This chapter examines the relationship between the class resources that Korean merchants bring to minority markets and the ethnic resources that black employees bring to minority markets. The central argument is that a symbiotic relationship has developed between Korean merchants and black employees. In this relationship, Korean merchants bring capital to the black community which is used to finance small businesses and create jobs, while black employees bring ethnic resources which are mobilized to reduce tension with black customers. This relationship grows out of the middleman role that Korean merchants fill in the black community, and it illustrates how Korean merchants and black employees exercise agency in order to cope with the internal colonial conditions they are embedded in. In this context, black employees provide an important mediating function for Korean merchants in the black community. They are instrumental in defusing conflicts arising between Korean merchants and black customers. This mediating role is pronounced in minority markets, since black customers make up the clientele of Korean-owned businesses. In fact, several studies have discussed how Korean merchants hire black employees to reduce tension with black customers.[1]

Despite their importance as mediators in Korean-owned stores, black employees remain in a subordinate position to their employers. The equilibrium between Korean merchants and black

145

employees is maintained by a number of social controls. For example, Korean merchants control information and capital in their stores, which gives them authority over black employees. In addition, before opening their businesses, many Korean merchants learned stereotypes about blacks through contact with mainstream society. These stereotypes influence how Korean merchants assess the abilities of black employees and evaluate their work. Although the mediating function of black employees creates incentives for Korean merchants to hire them, stereotyping and the mobilization of class resources by Korean merchants closes other opportunities to black employees in Korean-owned stores. Yoon addresses this situation in his study of ethnic entrepreneurship in Chicago.[2] In this study, he makes the following comments about the relationship between Korean merchants and black employees:

> Korean business owners in black areas almost invariably have one or more black employees. In fact, black employees account for 70 percent of the total paid employees (N=240) of Korean stores in black areas. Korean Business owners quickly recognize the advantages of having black employees: they protect the stores and the owners from criminal attacks from blacks, they sometimes mediate between Korean owners and black customers in disputes, and they demonstrate that Korean stores contribute to the local economy. In the midst of growing black hostility toward Korean businesses, now being blamed for draining resources out of black neighborhoods, hiring blacks is a tactic Koreans use to improve public relations. Nonetheless, Korean business owners complain about black employees. They are often regarded as lazy and unreliable in their work habits. Absenteeism and high turn-over are frequently referred to as problems with black employees. Shoplifting by black employees and by their friends is another common problem. Despite some costs of having black employees, benefits or social pressure to hire black employees usually overwhelm such costs.[3]

A number of incentives exist in minority markets which encourage Korean merchants to hire black employees, and these inducement outweigh factors which would otherwise deter Korean merchants from hiring black employees. However, despite the identification of such conditions, it is difficult to explain this situation using current theories about immigrant entrepreneurship and hiring queues.

These theories do not address the conditions that encourage Korean merchants to hire black employees in minority markets. In fact, they argue against such behavior. For example, Cheng and Espiritu offer the "immigrant hypothesis" as an explanation for why Korean merchants in Los Angeles preferred to hire Latino workers over black workers, arguing that Korean merchants preferred to hire Latinos over blacks since they share a common immigrant experience.[4] However, the immigrant hypothesis does not explain the hiring preferences of Korean merchants on the South Side of Chicago. In fact, many of the Korean merchants who were interviewed in this study preferred to hire black employees over Latino employees in their stores. This preference existed despite the presence a large pool of Latino workers. In fact, in 1990, Latinos made up 19.2 percent of the population of Chicago, and over 143,000 Latinos lived in neighborhoods adjacent to Korean-owned stores on the South Side of Chicago.[5]

The hiring preferences of Korean merchants on the South Side of Chicago were influenced by their perceptions of the black community. To a large extent, these perceptions were based on stereotypes of black Americans which are prevalent in mainstream society. A close examination of the effects of these stereotypes on the hiring practices of Korean merchants illustrates how the dominant-subordinate relationship between mainstream society and the black community influences minority markets. In this chapter, Korean merchants' ties to black employees are examined in relation to attitudes and stereotypes held in mainstream society. This is done to better understand how mainstream institutions influence black-Korean relations.

STEREOTYPING

Before discussing the mediating function of black employees in Korean-owned stores, it is important to examine how stereotypes shape the perceptions that Korean merchants have of their black employees. In chapter 4, it was pointed out that Korean immigrants learned stereotypes about black Americans through mainstream institutions. In fact, Jo discussed how this learning process began in Korea, where Koreans were exposed to stereotypes about black Americans in the popular media.[6] Once Korean immigrants arrived in the United States, these stereotypes were reenforced through contacts that they had with white Americans. By the time

Korean immigrants opened businesses in the black community, they had developed a schema for interpreting their interactions with black Americans which was heavily influenced by stereotypes.

These stereotypes became cognitive tools for interpreting the actions of black Americans. The strength of these stereotypes became apparent when Korean merchants generalized to me about their black employees and the black community. Although some of the stereotypes had been modified to fit the context of black-Korean relations, they were clearly derivatives of more popularized stereotypes of blacks found in mainstream society. For example, a common stereotype of black Americans is that they are uneducated and illiterate. Several of the Korean merchants on the South Side of Chicago subscribed to this view. For example, one Korean merchant expressed his view that, " A lot of people don't want to read, a lot of black people they don't read a letter, a book." This Korean merchant went on to explain how his black employees shared this general trait, "I have eight employees, one employee reads very poor, three employees can't read." This stereotype was reenforced by a more general view that blacks lacked a work ethic and were unreliable. For instance, one Korean merchant stated that blacks "are very lazy." Another Korean merchant commented on how black employees were unreliable, "they don't care if they come, sometimes they take off and they never call me."

Other stereotypes were also articulated about black employees, and blacks in general. For example, one Korean merchant described how his black employees were unable to manage their finances. He attributed their inability to save money to character flaws, and not to low incomes. The Korean merchant discussed this issue in detail:

> There's no bank account, only they use cash. They don't want to open their bank account, because a lot of people living all together. A lot of the black peoples' families live in one house, and they keep some cash, and they wondering if it steal by the other family member. They make money, they want to use, they want to spend immediately. This is a life, very simple, very simple life. First they make money, and they want to spend. All of them. But next day, they don't have any money. Even the food money, they don't have food money. They want to beg for food money, one dollar, two dollar. The first time

of the day they have a couple hundred of money. A couple hundred cash, they buy clothing, beauty supply, everything. Next day, they don't have any money, even the lunch money.

It is important to highlight how this Korean merchant's discussion of his black employees quickly drifted into a general discussion of the black community. In addition, the Korean merchant's comments focused on his perceptions of the individual traits of black Americans, and on the institutional causes of poverty in the black community. For example, the unstable financial situation of his employees, and the black community in general, was attributed to individual shortcomings rather than depressed incomes. No connection between low wages and poverty was made. The ability to apply stereotypes, and attribute poverty in the black community to the impulsive spending habits of blacks, made it easier for some Korean merchants to justify the low wages they paid their employees.

The use of stereotypes reenforced the wage structure in Korean-owned stores, and stereotyping also limited the scope of employment for blacks. For example, one stereotype that was prevalent among the Korean merchants on the South Side of Chicago was that blacks were dishonest and would steal. For example, one Korean merchant expressed his belief that among blacks, "70 percent or 80 percent, they have the experience of being locked up, in a jail. Lot of black people, they have the experience in jail life." Because of this type of perception, some Korean merchants perceived employee theft as a severe problem, and they were reluctant to let black employees handle money in their stores. One Korean merchant commented on this issue:

> Some people don't put certain people in the register, they don't trust them. I had problems, a lot of times they steal, dishonest. Their relatives come, or their family comes, they just don't ring up the merchandise and they give it in a bag.

However, other Korean merchants allowed black employees to handle money, but they watched them closely. Some Korean merchants installed elaborate surveillance systems for this purpose. For instance, one Korean merchant had a television monitor next to his desk in the back of his store. The monitor was hooked up to a number of surveillance cameras in the store, including a camera mounted behind the cash register. He used this surveillance system to monitor black customers and black employees. Other Korean merchants used similar surveillance systems.

Although employee theft is a concern found in all businesses, the stereotypes that Korean merchants held about the black community exaggerated this concern. In fact, many of the Korean merchants on the South Side of Chicago used stereotypes to interpret a number of situations they encountered while doing business in minority markets, and this affected their interactions with black Americans. Black Americans were characterized as uneducated, unreliable, impulsive and dishonest. These perception of the black community generated a paternalistic style among some of the Korean merchants. This was reflected in the tenor of the interactions between Korean merchants and black employees. In one way, the paternalistic style of Korean merchants is illustrated by the missionary role that some Korean merchants assumed in the black community.

Stereotyping caused some of the Korean merchants on the South Side of Chicago to downplay the effects that structural unemployment and racial discrimination had on poverty in the black community. Instead, they focused on how cultural traits and character flaws caused black Americans to remain poor. Because of this, some of the Korean merchants assumed a missionary role in the black community. This was most prevalent among the Korean merchants who identified themselves as born again Christians. These Korean merchants took it upon themselves to "save" their black employees, and set a Christian example for them. This blend of evangelism and paternalism grew out of attitudes that Korean merchants held about the black community. For example, one Korean merchant who identified herself as a born again Christian discussed how she applied Christian values to the operation of her store, and to the management of her black employees. She describes responding to black employees who stole from her store with "love." In doing this, she would "train them, train them, and train them, and they change eventually."

Because many Korean merchants stereotyped black Americans as lacking in moral character, some Korean merchants felt that black employees required close supervision and moral training. Some of the Korean merchants who were born again Christians used this rationale to justify their missionary work in the black community. For example, one Korean merchant discussed how he read the Bible with his employees:

> I always pray to Jesus with all the employees every morning, before we start working. Every morning for about fifteen or twenty minutes we pray, all together. Sometimes, some customer join us. Every morning before we start the work. All employee, all customer, are very good neighbor.

Religious training became a mechanism to monitor and control the behavior of black employees. In this respect, it had a similar social control function as the surveillance systems in the stores of Korean merchants. However, the use of religion was a more effective and flexible form of social control. It helped to ameliorate problems such as employee theft, but it also fostered trust between Korean merchants and black employees which became a valuable resource when conflicts with black customers occurred. However, religion did more than function as a form of social control in some of the Korean-owned stores, it also functions as a screening device for employees when hiring decisions were made.

SCREENING AND RETENTION

An employer often evaluates potential employees based on a variety of subjective standards, and religion is sometimes one of these. However, the Korean merchants on the South Side of Chicago used several additional criteria to evaluate employees, and most were based on informal mechanisms. In fact, none of the Korean merchants reported using formal mechanisms to recruit black employees, such as newspaper advertisements or local employment agencies. Korean merchants were wary of attracting "bad" workers through such sources. In many respects, a "bad" worker was one who fit the stereotypes associated with black Americans. In order to reduce the chances of hiring such a worker, the Korean merchants relied on informal hiring mechanisms. In most instances, they identified potential black employees through personal references from regular customers or existing employees. Because of this, a black employee needed to establish a relationship with a Korean merchant before being hired. This could be either a direct relationship, or one established through family members and friends.

The Korean merchants who were interviewed on the South Side of Chicago indicated that when black employee were hired in this manner, they remained employed for long periods of time. Despite Yoon's observation, that black employees had high rates of turnover in Korean-owned stores, the Korean merchants interviewed in this study reported that several of their black workers were long-term employees.[7] In fact, one Korean merchant described how his black employees had worked for him for three to five years each. Another Korean merchant discussed the long-term relationship he had with his black employees:

> This business start in 1984 and at that time his name was Michael, and he went to high school. He helped me. Now he finished school, and he's been working for me more than 10 years. And the lady, she started working for me about 8 years ago, and she still working for me. Her name's Michelle.

Another Korean merchant stated that four of his black employees had worked for him for "more than five years," and he rarely fired people. He indicated that sometimes a black employee would quit, and in other instances one would be fired for absenteeism or theft. However, the informal screening mechanisms that the Korean merchants used reduced many of the risks associated with hiring black employees. In addition, Korean merchants had an interest in retaining black employees for long periods of time.

Despite the effectiveness of informal screening devices and the desire of Korean merchants to retain black employees, the existence of long-term employment in Korean-owned stores was principally the result of economic underdevelopment in the black community. In fact, the jobs in Korean-owned stores had many shortcomings. They paid low wages, they were unstable due to shifts in the economy and they entailed few fringe benefits. These jobs had many of the characteristics associated with those in the secondary sector of the economy.[8] However, they were some of the only jobs available on the South Side of Chicago, and this meant that many blacks who lived there were interested in working for Korean merchants. In fact, several of the Korean merchants who were interviewed pointed out that blacks regularly came to their stores asking for jobs.

The surplus of black workers on the South Side of Chicago allowed Korean merchants to maintain a flexible labor force in their stores. In part, this meant that wages were kept low, with most jobs starting at minimum wage. For instance, one Korean merchant pointed out that he preferred to hire blacks from the neighborhood near his store because they would accept lower wages. He contrasted the wages that he could pay black employees with the wages Korean employees demanded, pointing out that Korean workers, "are looking for big money, so I can't hire them." However, the low wage structure of Korean- owned stores on the South Side of Chicago was an artifact of the structure of the economy in minority markets. In fact, when the economy on the South Side of Chicago stagnated in the early 1990's, some Korean merchants reported that they had to cut back on the number of employees in their stores. Others reported that they had to reduce the number of full-time employees in their stores, and rely more heavily on part-time workers.

Despite the changes in the economy in the early 1990's, the Korean merchants indicated that it was important to retain as many employees as possible. In part, this was because a certain number of employees were required to operate a merchant's store. One Korean merchant discussed this issue:

> It is true, it's very difficult to find people you can trust well enough to do the work for you. Wage is not much better than minimum wage. We really cannot pay them a whole lot more than that to be competitive. For this size of a store, I hire a lot more people than a lot of stores. This is necessary overhead. I think sometimes you need the salesperson to do the right job. To make the actual sales.

It was especially important to retain black employees, since Korean merchants benefitted from the ethnic resources they brought to their stores. In the ethnic beauty aids industry, the role of black employees was of particular importance. In fact, many of the Korean merchants indicated that they preferred to hire black employees, since black customers felt more comfortable being served by them.

LABOR MARKET SEGMENTATION

The nature of the ethnic beauty aids industry, and minority markets in general, created a demand for black employees in Korean-owned stores on the South Side of Chicago. In part, the

demand for black employees is related to their knowledge of ethnic beauty aids, and because they filled a mediating role in their
stores. This will be discussed further in the next section, but first
the nature of labor market segmentation in the ethnic beauty aids
industry should be explained in more detail. Hiring queues in the
ethnic beauty aids industry are distinct from those found in other
industries, since the ethnic beauty aids industry focuses on developing products for black consumers. In fact, black women are the
primary consumers of ethnic beauty aids. As a result, they have a
great deal of knowledge about such products. In part, this knowledge explains why black women make up the majority of the
workers in Korean-owned beauty supply stores on the South Side
of Chicago.

Although there were black men employed in these stores, and a
small numbers of Latino and Korean workers, black women were
the largest group of employees in the Korean-owned beauty supply
stores on the South Side of Chicago. This observation is in line
with Yoon's finding that, 70 percent of the paid employees in
Korean-owned businesses on the South Side of Chicago were
black.[9] In fact, on the South Side of Chicago, growing immigrant
populations had little effect on the hiring preferences of Korean
merchants. They continued to prefer to hire blacks to do jobs
where workers interacted directly with black customers. As a
result, immigrants found it difficult to gain access to these positions.

The position of blacks in the hiring queue remained stable,
despite the fact that Korean merchants had access to immigrant
workers. In fact, one Korean merchant clearly indicated that she
had access to a variety of employees:

> I have some Koreans, I have some Mexicans, and I have some
> blacks. Blacks, most of my employees, they work here for a
> long time, as they come in they don't want to go. Most of my
> employees work here about four or five years. Blacks I found,
> a lot of people coming in, walk-ins they ask for jobs. I hire
> sometimes through that, or sometimes when they go out for
> some reason, they quit, then bring in one of their friends.
> Koreans, you get to know them through Korean community.
> Mexicans, I know them through Koreans, because a Korean
> knows them. They hire Mexicans, a lot of Koreans own dry-
> cleaning shops, and they hire a lot of Mexicans. I get to know
> some Mexican connection and they give me the names of

some Mexican people. So, I have Mexicans, Koreans, and blacks.

Despite the access that this Korean merchant had to immigrant and black workers, she continued to hire predominantly black women in her store. This was because of the nature of labor market segmentation in the ethnic beauty aids industry. Blacks and immigrants filled different roles in the ethnic beauty aids industry. For example, many of the Korean merchants hired black women to work directly with black customers, either as clerks, cashiers or floor managers. Black men also interacted with black customers, but this was generally on a more limited level. For the most part, black men were hired as uniformed security guards and to stock shelves. A smaller number of Korean workers found jobs in Korean-owned stores on the South Side of Chicago. They usually worked as cashiers or store managers. Similarly, Latinos had limited access to jobs in Korean-owned stores on the South Side of Chicago. On occasion Korean merchants hired Latino men to do general construction and odd jobs. Despite the presence of immigrant workers, the majority of the paid employees in Korean-owned store on the South Side of Chicago were black.

These finding contradict predictions made by more conventional theories concerning hiring queues and immigrant succession.[10] For instance, Waldinger describes hiring queues as somewhat deterministic, where immigrants enter the bottom of the economy, pushing native groups up the job ladder.[11] However, blacks continued to obtain entry level positions in the beauty supply stores run by Korean merchants on the South Side of Chicago. This situation brings Waldinger's conceptualization of immigrant succession into question. In a similar manner, the immigrant hypothesis identified by Cheng and Espiritu is also brought into question, since it does not explain why the Korean merchants on the South Side of Chicago continued to show a preference for hiring black workers over immigrant workers. In order to understand the presence of a hiring queue on the South Side of Chicago that favors black workers over immigrant workers, the context of minority markets must be taken into consideration.

Minority markets are important to the maintenance of such a hiring queue, since they insulate black workers from competition with immigrant workers. In part, this particular hiring queue emerged because of the exclusively black clientele in minority markets, and since Korean merchants were often unable to resolve conflicts with black customers. The social impasse between Korean merchants and black customers resulted from the internal colonial context that minority markets are embedded in, and the middleman role that Korean merchants filled in that setting. However, these same conditions create a hiring queue favorable to blacks, since they could mobilize ethnic resources in minority markets that helped to reduce tension between Korean merchants and black consumers. Because black workers were able to build rapport with black customers, they filled an important mediating role in Korean-owned stores.

BLACK OMBUDSMAN

Black employees act as mediators in Korean-owned stores. Their ombudsman function in minority markets secures their position in the hiring queue. Korean merchants understand that black employees are needed to prevent disputes with black customers, and this moves blacks up the hiring queue in their stores. In fact, the effectiveness of black employees as ombudsman allowed Korean merchants to minimize their contact with black customers and focus on other aspects of their businesses. Many of the Korean merchants who were interviewed on the South Side of Chicago described how hiring black employees to handle customer relations issues in their stores allowed them to focus their attention on paperwork and the financial management of their stores.

Several of the Korean merchants on the South Side of Chicago benefitted from such a division of labor in their stores. One Korean merchant commented that, "I'm rarely out on the floor, because I have managers out on the floor do my stuff. I can't, it's very hard to run the store and do paperwork, then do the ordering, it's very hard." Other Korean merchants also made this point, stressing that paperwork, placing orders and dealing with salesmen took up a large amount of their time. However, some of the Korean merchants also pointed out that they preferred to maintain a low profile in their store, in order to avoid conflicts with black customers. The presence of black employees allowed Korean merchants to delegate work in their stores more efficiently, but the primary benefit of hiring black employees was that they limited the level of contact that Korean merchants had with black customers.

This became apparent during an interview with a black employee in a Korean-owned beauty supply store. This interview was arranged by a Korean merchant and it took place in her store. When the interview began, the store had no customers. The interview was being conducted in the back of the store, while the Korean merchant and a Korean employee were standing at the cash register in the front of the store. The ombudsman role of the black employee was clearly demonstrated when a black customer entered the store. As the black customer walked through the front door, the Korean merchant left the cash register to find the black employee. She quickly directed the black employee to the black customer. While the black employee was helping the black customer, another black customer came into the store. Again, the Korean merchant brought this customer to the black employee's attention. The Korean merchant and the Korean employee stood at a distance, limiting their contact with the black customers. In fact, the only contact between this Korean merchant and the black customers was when cash was exchanged. In this arrangement, the black employee was primarily responsible for providing direct assistance to black customers, while the Korean merchant and the Korean employee focused on the monetary aspects of the business.

Similar observations were made in other Korean-owned stores. In fact, some Korean merchants described how they deliberately stayed in the back of their stores, away from black customers. For example, one Korean merchant who adopted this practice explain, "most of the time I am here hiding, doing something else." Another Korean merchant made this comment:

> If you look around my store, you don't have Koreans, you don't have five, six Koreans walking around watching customers. So basically I have my manager's black, and all my workers are black. So I try to, lot of people come to the store, they get impression that it's a black-owned store.So I try to stay out as much as I can. They'd rather it be a black-owned store than Korean-owned.

A demand for black employees was created by the perception that black customers resented Korean merchants. In order to avoid conflicts with black customers, many Korean merchants limited their contact with them, and some Korean merchants retreated to the backs of their stores. This situation expanded the role of black employees in Korean-owned stores. Black employees assumed an ombudsman function, since they could mobilize ethnic resources in the black community. However, the mediating role that black employees filled in Korean-owned stores was balanced by the ability of Korean merchants to mobilize class resources.

One way Korean merchants maintained this equilibrium was by controlling information and decision-making in their stores. In particular, some of the Korean merchants on the South Side of Chicago felt it was important to be seen as knowledgeable by their black employees. One Korean merchant commented on how he had to learn as much as possible about the products he sold, so that his black employees would rely on him for information. For example, he explained how black customers would asks questions about products and his black employees would relay them to him:

> They ask me, well (merchant's name), this customer needs this and this, what do I need? They're coming to me, they're basically looking up to me and giving me respect, and saying well you know more than me so I'm going to listen to you. I think that's very important. I think that's one of the keys to having good employees, is that you have to know more than your employees.

Knowledge of products and store policies was an important resource to this Korean merchant. Other Korean merchant made similar points, and they also focused on other resources that allowed them to make up for the inability to mobilize ethnic resources in the black community.

The ability to mobilize capital was the most important resource that Korean merchants brought to the black community. The capital that they brought to the black community, and their business management skills, allowed the Korean merchants to maintain a certain level of authority in their stores. In fact, the delegation of customer service functions to black employees elevated the need for Korean merchants to mobilize class resources on the South Side of Chicago. It was important for Korean merchants to be better informed and better financed than black employees and customers, so that they could be seen as legitimate authority figures in their stores. This issue became more important since the inability to mobilize ethnic resources in the black community reduced the authority of Korean merchant.

THE LIMITS OF CLASS RESOURCES

The inability of Korean merchants to mobilize ethnic resources in the black community exaggerated conflicts with black customers. For instance, several of the Korean merchants in this study reported that in addition to complaining about general issues such as return policies and the quality of merchandise, black customers also complained about a discrete set of issues linked to ethnicity. Black customers complained about "Koreans" following them in stores and watched them as if they were criminals. Black customers complained about "Koreans" being rude. In addition, black customers complained about "Koreans" not speaking English well. All of these complaints emphasized to cultural differences between blacks and Koreans, which increased the likelihood that tension would emerge in the course of business transactions in Korean-owned stores.[12]

The dynamics of the interactions between Korean merchants and black customers were observed during the course of the field work for this study. Although some of the Korean merchants on the South Side of Chicago made efforts to address the complaints of black customers, many others did not. For instance, some Korean merchants were observed following customers in their stores, and watching them. In other instances, black customers became visibly frustrated with Korean merchants, because they did not speak English well. In addition, some Korean merchants were involved in arguments with customers over returned items. In all of these situations, the Korean merchants' inability to mobilize ethnic resources in the black community added tension to otherwise minor instances. For example, one Korean merchant entered into a long discussion of how a dispute over a returned item escalated, in part, because he could not mobilize ethnic resources in the black community:

> A customer buy some merchandise, and ten days later they want to exchange. But, what I sold they use, it's messed up. I tell them I can't refund or I can't exchange other thing. So they call the police, and the police come to here, and only the police hear about the customer. The customer wanted the cash back. I explained to them, we can't cash back because it's messed up. But, the police office doesn't care. Sometimes he used a bad, very bad word. the "F" something. "Why don't you give cash back, ** cash back now." OK police office, I'm

> going to call your commander, and they said, "shut up, cash
> back right now." Immediately I say this terrible situation,
> they don't want to listen. The two police officers are black
> people, and the customer are black people. And, I called my
> manager, and my manager explained the same situation, and
> they never tried to listen to the situation. One hour they are
> here, and they go back and I never pay for it because it's not
> fair. Two hours later they come again with two more police
> cars, and five or six police officer come together. Very tough
> guys come to me. "Why don't you cash back." And, there's a
> lot of customers there, very bad situation there. I cash back
> then.

In this situation, the Korean merchant felt paralyzed by his inability to mobilize ethnic resources with the black customers and the
black police officers. In fact, as the situation escalated, even the
Korean merchant's black manager was unable to bridge the
impasse. The only recourse the Korean merchant had was to
refund the black customer's money.

Many of the Korean merchants described disputes that they had
with black customers, and some of them said they felt blacks were
more confrontational with Korean merchants than with white
merchants. One Korean merchant remarked, "I might be wrong,
but if I'm a Caucasian, they try just one, two times, but because
I'm a foreigner they might try more." The belief that black customers were more confrontational with Korean merchants grew
out of other complaints they voiced about Korean merchants. For
instance, some black customers accused Korean merchants of prof-
iteering in the black community. One Korean merchant made this
comment:

> They try to watch Koreans, because they think we're getting
> into their neighborhood and we're getting into their market.
> They think that we take all their money. They think them-
> selves like victims. That's this market, beauty supplies,
> because all the Koreans own beauty supply stores, clothing
> stores in all black areas.

On the surface, these accusations reflected the lack of rapport that
existed between Korean merchants and black customers. On a
more fundamental level, these types of complaints also indicated
that black customers drew a clear distinction between minority
markets and the mainstream economy. In fact, both black con-

sumers and Korean merchants had a clear understanding of the middleman minority role that Korean merchants filled in the black community. This increased the level of tension between black consumers and Korean merchants on the South Side of Chicago.

Many of the Korean merchants felt that they were treated unfairly by some blacks because of the middleman role they filled in the black community, and they identified a number of complaints that they had about black customers. For example, several of the Korean respondents reported that they were insulted by blacks who referred to them as "Chinese," or told them to go back to Korea. Other Korean merchants complained that black customers were rude to them, and yelled at them. One Korean merchant discussed how ethnic differences made it more difficult for her to run her businesses:

> When I first opened up, they complained a lot because I was Korean. They didn't treat me right, because I didn't speak English. I was little, I looked like a little girl to them. And, I have no male working in my store. I was myself with one black girl. They ignored me, tried to humiliate me.

The inability to mobilize ethnic resources in the black community hampered the businesses of Korean merchants in minority markets. It took years for some Korean merchants to build informal ties with their black employees and customers. Once established, these ties allowed them to partially overcome the ethnic barriers between blacks and Koreans. For instance, the Korean merchant cited above commented that the she experience less ethnic hostility as she interacted with her black employees, "After ten years, I know their grandmas, and a lot of families. I know their daughters and families, grandmas, who got married, who got divorced. I know that. I get familiar with the people." However, this was a long process.

In the short-term, Korean merchants found it advantageous to hire black employees to reduce tension with black customers. There were few other options available to Korean merchants that allowed them to take advantage of ethnic resources in the black community. In fact, most of the other strategies that Korean merchants used to reduce tension with black customers relied on their ability to mobilize capital, or to develop some other type of system based on material rewards. For instance, many of the Korean mer-

chants gave small gifts and sample items to black customers. Some
of the Korean merchants on the South Side of Chicago also reported giving items such as old clothing to their customers and contributing to local charities.

One Korean merchant described how he would recruit blacks
from the neighborhood near his store to do informal work. This
merchant would sell clearance items to blacks who participated in
the informal economy, in order to reduce the chances that they
would steal from his store. He described this in detail:

> Some professional thief comes to my store, they try to steal
> something. I don't like them. But I give job to some of them.
> Sometimes I want them to sweep the outside. Sometimes I
> supply some very cheap merchandise, clearance items, and
> regular price is $20, sale price is $10. I gave to them $1 or $2,
> and they sell it $10 to somebody outside. I give them some
> job, and I told them, hey come here. There are several kids
> there, and I knew them, I knew their face. I recommend to
> them the sale price for the merchandise $10, I gave to them
> $1. They come in teams and they sell it very good. I give them
> for $3 some item, and they sell it $15, $20 outside on street.
> They sell it to passenger.

The Korean merchant's ability to initiate such activities was based
on his access to capital, and not ethnic resources. The relationship
between Korean merchants and black consumers was based on
economic trade-offs, and not ethnic solidarity. In order to access
ethnic resources in the black community, Korean merchants had to
hire black employees. The benefits of ethnic solidarity with black
customers came to them vicariously through their black employees.

THE EFFECT OF INTERNAL COLONIALISM ON
CLASS AND ETHNIC RESOURCES

The role of ethnic and class resources in the ethnic beauty aids
industry is shaped by the internal colonial context of minority
markets. Internal colonialism limits the ability of blacks to mobilize class resources in minority markets. This is highlighted by the
disparity between the class resources blacks have access to and the
class resources Koreans have access to in minority markets.
Internal colonialism also limits the ability of Korean merchants to
mobilize ethnic resources in minority markets, since their customer

base is almost entirely composed of black customers. The importance of ethnic resources is elevated for Korean merchants, since they are middleman minorities in the black community. Because Korean merchants are middleman minorities in an internal colonial setting, the potential for tension between them and black customers is elevated. However, the ability to control this tension is limited, since much of it emanates from mainstream society.

Because of the volatile relationship that exists between middleman minorities and colonized groups, Korean merchants act to reduce tension with black customers. In undertaking this action, they demonstrate that although mainstream institutions create internal colonial conditions in the black community, these conditions are not entirely deterministic. In fact, there is room for agency within the parameters of an internal colonial setting. Korean merchants illustrate this in two ways. In one, they mobilize class resources, using capital to reduce tension with black customers. In the other, they take advantage of the ethnic resources present in the black community, and hire black employees to fill an ombudsman role in their stores. These ways of mobilizing class and ethnic resources are unique to minority markets, and they illustrate the impact that internal colonialism has on economic behavior. This adds dimension to the discussion of the relationship between internal colonialism and class and ethnic resources. So far, this discussion has focused on the experiences of merchants in the ethnic beauty aids industry. In the next chapter, these issues will be examined from the perspective of distributors in the ethnic beauty aids industry, to illustrate how internal colonialism effects economic behavior in larger scale organizations.

NOTES

[1] In-Jin Yoon, *Self Employment in Business, Chinese, Japanese, Korean-American, Blacks, and Whites*, Dissertation, (Chicago: University of Chicago, 1991); Pyong Gap Min and Andrew Kolodny, "The Middleman Minority Characteristics of Korean Immigrants in the United States," *Korea Journal of Population and Development*, 20.2 (1994): 179-202; Ivan Light, Hadas-Har Chvi, and Kenneth Kan, "Black/Korean Conflict in Los Angeles," in Seamus Dunn, ed.,*Managing Divided Cities*, (Newbury Park: Sage Publications, 1994); Joseph Ahne, "Koreans of Chicago, The New Entrepreneurial Immigrants," in Melvin G. Holli and Peter d'A. Jones, eds, *Ethnic Chicago, A Multicultural Portrait, Fourth Edition*,

(Grand Rapids: William B. Eerdmans Publishing Company, 1995); Kyeyong Park, "The Re-Invention of Affirmative Action, Korean Immigrants' Changing Conceptions of African Americans and Latin Americans,"*Urban Anthropology*, 24.1 (1995): 59-92.

[2]In-Jin Yoon, *Self Employment in Business, Chinese, Japanese, Korean-American, Blacks, and Whites*, Dissertation, (Chicago: University of Chicago, 1991).

[3] Ibid, 200-201.

[4] Lucie Cheng and Yen Espiritu, "Korean Businesses in Black and Hispanic Neighborhoods, A Study of Intergroup Relations," *Sociological Perspectives*, 32.4 (1989): 521-534; Park highlights some of the limitations of the immigrant hypothesis. In particular, he discusses how political mobilization in the black community and increasing animosity between Latinos and Koreans after the L.A. Riots, resulted in a shift in the hiring preferences of Korean employers. See Kyeyong Park, "The Reinvention of Affirmative Action, Korean Immigrants' Changing Conceptions of African Americans and Latin Americans." *Urban Anthropology*, 24.1 (1995): 59-92.

[5] Jorge Casuso and Eduardo Camacho, "Latino Chicago," in Melvin G. Hilli and Peter d'A. Jones, eds., *Ethnic Chicago, A Multicultural Portrait*, (Grand Rapids: William B. Eerdmans Publishing Company, 1995): 346-377.

[6] Moon H. Jo, "Korean Merchants in the Black Community, Prejudice Among the Victims of Prejudice," in *Ethnic and Racial Studies*, 15.3 (1992): 395-411.

[7] In-Jin Yoon, *Self Employment in Business, Chinese, Japanese, Korean-American, Blacks, and Whites*, Dissertation, (Chicago: University of Chicago, 1991): 200-201.

[8] Robert T. Averitt, *The Dual Economy, The Dynamics of American Industry Structure*, (New York: Norton, 1968); Bennett Harrison, *Education, Training and the Urban Ghetto*, (Baltimore: Johns Hopkins University Press, 1972); R.C. Edwards, M. Reich and D.M. Gordon, eds., *Labor Market Segmentation*, (Lexington: Health, 1975).

[9] In-Jin Yoon, *Self Employment in Business, Chinese, Japanese, Korean-American, Blacks, and Whites*, Dissertation, (Chicago: University of Chicago, 1991): 200-201.

[10] Lucie Cheng and Yen Espiritu, "Korean Businesses in Black and Hispanic Neighborhoods, A Study of Intergroup Relations." *Sociological Perspectives*, 32.4 (1989): 521-534; Roger Waldinger, *Still The Promised City*, (Cambridge: Harvard University Press, 1996).

[11] Roger Waldinger, *Still The Promised City*, (Cambridge: Harvard University Press, 1996).

[12] Ella Stewart, *Ethnic Cultural Diversity, An Interpretive Study of Cultural and Communication Styles Between Korean Merchants/Employees and Black Patrons in South Los Angeles*, Thesis, (Los Angeles: California State University, Los Angeles, 1989).

CHAPTER 7:

Middleman And Black Distributors

TWO SEPARATE NICHES

As discussed in chapter 5, the ethnic beauty aids industry is divided into two distinct economic niches, a niche focusing on retail sales and a niche focusing on the sales of professional products to black beauticians and barbers. Traditional middleman groups, such as Koreans and Jews, are concentrated in the retail niche, and blacks entrepreneurs are clustered in the professional niche. The tendency for middleman and black entrepreneurs to cluster in these economic niches became more pronounced during the early 1990's, when the economy on the South Side of Chicago stagnated. However, this effect was not limited to merchants in the ethnic beauty aids industry. The development of separate niches for middleman and black entrepreneurs was also found at other levels of the ethnic beauty aids industry. In this chapter, the development of separate economic niches for middleman and black distributors in the ethnic beauty aids industry is examined. The central argument of this chapter is that these economic niches developed for distributors of ethnic beauty aids in response to each group's ability to mobilize class and ethnic resources, just as they did for merchants. As a result there is a close relationship between the economic role of middleman and black distributors and that of middleman and black merchants. Korean and Jewish distributors sell ethnic beauty aids primarily to Korean merchants who own retail stores in the black community, and black distributors sell ethnic beauty aids to black merchants and black salon owners in the black community.

In order to grasp the relationship between distributors and merchants in minority markets, it is helpful to examine the role of class and ethnic resources in the ethnic beauty aids industry. In past research, the link between the merchant-distributor relationship and the role of class and ethnic resources in minority markets was somewhat underdeveloped. In fact, the conventional view of this relationship was forwarded by Hurh and Kim in their discussion of Korean merchants in Chicago.[1] They pointed out that Korean merchants bought some kinds of merchandise from Korean distributors and other kinds from white distributors. Hurh and Kim argued that this merchant-distributor relationship existed since Korean distributors specialized in low-priced merchandise suitable to low-income communities, while white distributors did not.[2] They also pointed out that Korean merchants preferred to do business with Korean distributors since they experienced fewer language barriers, and Korean distributors offered credit.[3] These observations were made in later studies and remained relatively unchanged.[4] However, the merchant- distributor relationship discovered in this study did not reflect these findings.

The Korean and Jewish distributors of ethnic beauty aids who were interviewed in Chicago sold the same products to Korean merchants, and offered them similar credit terms and services. Most importantly, the Korean merchants indicated that their decision to purchase ethnic beauty aids from a distributor was driven primarily by price, and the ethnicity of the distributor was not a major factor. Because of this, the success of Korean and Jewish distributors was based on their ability to mobilize capital and remain price competitive. The ability of a distributor to mobilize ethnic resources with Korean merchants was secondary. The presence of Jewish distributors in the ethnic beauty aids industry illustrated the secondary role of ethnic resources in the purchasing decisions of Korean merchants in the retail niche of the ethnic beauty aids industry. In fact, the presence of Korean and Jewish distributors highlighted the middleman minority role that each group filled in the ethnic beauty aids industry.

Pressures on middleman entrepreneurs to mobilize capital in minority markets was magnified by the internal colonial setting that such markets were embedded in. In minority markets, the ability to mobilize ethnic resources was reduced for middleman entrepreneurs, since poor blacks made up the customer base for their businesses. On the other hand, the role of capital was enhanced, since poverty in minority markets intensified price competition which distributors and merchants had to cope with in the retail niche of the ethnic beauty aids industry.

The ability to mobilize capital determined the long-term success of middleman businesses in minority markets, since price competition in minority markets created pressure on middleman entrepreneurs to expand their businesses. This relates to the substitutive relationship identified by Yoon in his discussion of ethnic and class resources.⁵ He pointed out that as businesses become larger, ethnic resources become less important to their success, and class resources become more important. In contrast, black merchants and distributors in the ethnic beauty aids industry were more insulated from price competition, and less dependent on class resources than middleman businesses. This was because they were primarily active in the professional niche of the industry, rather than the retail niche. Although black merchants and distributors found it more difficult to access capital than middleman businesses, they focused on economic niches where there was less price competition. As a result, their survival was more closely tied to the mobilization of ethnic resources in the black community.

The ability of black merchants and distributors to remain competitive in the professional niche of the ethnic beauty aids industry is directly related to this issue. The professional niche in the ethnic beauty aids industry is not as price competitive as the retail niche. However, black beauticians and barbers place a higher value on goods manufactured and sold by blacks than those that are not. This distinction concerning the importance of class and ethnic resources for middleman and black entrepreneurs is crucial to the analysis of minority markets. It highlights how economic behavior is shaped by the internal colonial conditions that minority markets are embedded in. The following discussion focuses on this connection by examining how middleman and black distributors mobilized class and ethnic resources during the early 1990's, in order to adapt to economic stagnation in the black community.

THE RETAILERS' SILENT SPRING

Welfare Cuts and Business Viability

Chapters 4 and 5 discuss how the economy on the South Side of Chicago stagnated during the early 1990's. The implications of economic stagnation for black distributors is discussed later in this chapter. But first, the implications of this stagnation for middleman distributors is discussed. Yoon described how interdependence among Korean merchants and distributors was "similar to the food chain in ecology."⁶ In this discussion, he pointed out that, "Korean retailers in minority areas are heavily dependent on the economic condition of blacks."⁷ This created a situation where:

> Korean wholesalers are affected by the business sales of
> Korean retailers in minority areas. During economic reces-
> sions, Korean wholesalers have difficulty in collecting delayed
> payments for their supplies from Korean retailers.[8]

As a result, deteriorating economic conditions for blacks have a
negative effect on Korean merchants in minority markets, and subsequently impact middleman distributors.

This analogy captures the relationship between businesses and
consumers in minority markets, as well as their mutual dependence
on public spending in the economy, since economic stagnation was
due in part to cuts in welfare and public employment. The relationship between social welfare spending and business viability
was also found among middleman distributors in the ethnic beauty aids industry, in addition to the merchants discussed in chapters
4 and 5. For instance, all of the middleman distributors who were
interviewed discussed how the market for ethnic beauty aids tight-
ened during the early 1990's, and some connected this trend with
declining economic conditions in the black community. One
Jewish distributor made this comment about how his business had
changed:

> It definitely has changed, it has slowed down. There's a lot
> more products, and people don't have as much money. I've
> gotta be honest with you. People that buy ethnic beauty sup-
> plies, a lot of them are on welfare. There's been a lot of
> changes. There's all these little things. It has been diluted. But
> a lot has to do with. Obviously, the main reason is, obvious-
> ly, the welfare structure.

A Korean distributor made a similar comment, linking economic
conditions in the black community to declining consumer spending, "I'm doing business for only ethnic groups. I think their
money depends on the federal money, or drug money, or some kind
of certain employment, or something like that." All of the middleman distributors indicated that as economic conditions worsened
in the black community, and Korean merchants experienced
declining sales, their businesses were forced to adjust.

The Effects of Economic Stagnation on the Merchant-Distributor Relationship

In particular, all of the middleman distributors indicated that economic stagnation in the black community forced them to adjust
their credit policies and pricing structures. The soft economy in the
black community created a great deal of downward pressure on

prices in the ethnic beauty aids industry, and declining sales cause many Korean merchants to experience trouble paying their bills. For example, one Korean distributor pointed out that as the economy in the black community slowed down in the 1990's, he had to offer more flexible credit terms to merchants. This was not an issue of ethnicity, but of scarcity. Often, merchants would not be able to pay their bills on time, so middleman distributor would have to extend their payment periods.

The issue of credit came up with other middleman distributors. One pointed out that sales to merchants, "used to be all cash," but they increasingly asked for credit beginning in the early 1990's. The need to purchase products using credit was caused by economic stagnation in the black community, since declining sales reduced the levels of working capital available to merchants. The middleman distributors in Chicago relaxed their credit policies in response to the slow economy in the black community. As long as a merchant paid his or her bills, credit was extended to him or her by the middleman distributors. Credit was only denied in extreme cases. For instance, a Jewish distributor commented that, "if they bounce a check here, they bounce a check, sometimes we let them bounce it twice, but after that it's all cash." All of the middleman distributors had relatively lenient credit systems in place. However, some middleman distributors reported that they could not offer credit to a large proportion of the merchants in the ethnic beauty aids industry, despite the lenient credit policies. One Korean distributor pointed out that, "roughly about 20% to 25% I cannot extend any credit at all." The lack of credit worthiness among some of the merchants in the ethnic beauty aids industry was a stark reminder of the ramifications of economic deprivation on the South Side of Chicago for middleman entrepreneurs. In addition to increasing the demand for credit, economic scarcity also contributed to price competition in minority markets.

Price competition among Korean merchants was discussed in detail in chapter 5. It was pointed out that as the market for ethnic beauty aids began to contract in the early 1990's, intra-ethnic competition expanded. This resulted in downward pressure on prices in the retail niche of the ethnic beauty aids industry. Pressure to reduce prices was felt among middleman merchants and distributors. For instance, one Korean distributor discussed how merchants began comparing the prices of different middleman distributors in the early 1990's, in order to find the middleman distributor offering the lowest possible prices on ethnic beauty aids. This distributor described how the emphasis on finding the lowest possible prices was relatively new:

> About 10 years ago they have different situation, but now really tough. That's why they at the retail shop, the owner has to compete with somebody else. That's why they are very sensitive to pricing. About ten years ago somebody selling at some higher prices they don't care, because they are doing their job, I am doing my job. At this time, we cannot insist in that way. We have to be very sensitive.

Increased competition among merchants in the ethnic beauty aids industry, which grew out of economic stagnation in the black community, created downward pressure on the prices middleman distributors could offer to merchants. Price competition among merchants affected middleman distributors in other ways as well.

Some middleman distributors indicated that some merchants would put pressure on them to lower prices on merchandise. This became such a problem for the middleman distributors that they eventually adopted formal pricing structures to curb such requests. For example, all of the middleman distributors who were interviewed published catalogs that listed their prices and discounts. This was done as a defensive measure to protect them from merchants who wanted to negotiate for lower prices on an individual basis. One Jewish distributor discussed this issue in detail:

> One of the trends in the beauty supply business, it's changed, and we were the ones to actually change this. At the beginning people come in and say, there use to be a lot of low balling, footballing, where somebody would come into my place, wherever, and say (another distributor is) selling this for $2 what will you sell it to me for. So if you sold it to him for $1.95 or $1.90 he'd buy it from you. And, this was a common practice for a long time. We decided, we're not going to do this anymore. Because what happens is, they tell everyone else. So we get everyone who we're selling it for $2 to, and now they want it for $1.90. $1.90 becomes the price. So we decided, we're gonna publish prices and this is gonna be it. If people don't like it, then they won't buy it. This way we got the price, and everybody's got the same price, and we put stuff on sale. So basically, that's what we started doing. So nobody can come in here now and say to me, this guy's got it for $3 what are you going to do, I'll pay cash.

The adoption of formal pricing structures was an indication of the primacy of class resources for middleman distributors. Formal pricing structures were adopted to deter merchants from attempting to negotiate informally with middleman distributors for lower prices. By emphasizing that prices were not flexible, middleman distributors signified that the mobilization of capital was a prerequisite to entering the retail niche in the ethnic beauty aids industry. The ability to mobilize capital was important to middleman distributors in other areas as well.

During the early 1990's, there was a great deal of pressure on middleman distributors to expand the size of their businesses. This was the result of a tighter market for ethnic beauty aids and heightened competition among merchants. Because of the pressure to expand, a number of middleman distributors experienced financial difficulties and eventually closed their businesses. While this process was unfolding, many of the distributors who experienced financial difficulties began to liquidate their inventories. One middleman distributor described how a sudden drop in a distributor's prices was often an indication that he was in debt, and about to go out of business. In fact, during the early 1990's, a number of distributors went out of business after a failed attempt at expansion. One Korean distributor estimated the rate of business failure among middleman distributors of ethnic beauty aids at one business per year between 1990 and 1996. Another Korean distributor confirmed this, pointing out that in Chicago, the number of middleman distributors in the industry had been cut in half during that time period. The middleman distributors who survived that period operated businesses that were larger and better capitalized.

In the early 1990's, the capital requirements increased for middleman distributors in the ethnic beauty aids industry. In order to survive in the industry, middleman distributors had to expand their businesses and develop economies of scale. One Korean distributor discussed how increased price competition created a business climate that made medium sized distributorships obsolete:

> We have to take two choice, getting less or getting larger. This time I'm gonna take getting smaller. You know, to save my body. As a wholesaler, this time is really tough to stay middle point, too tough. We should go to the giant size of the business, or really tiny business. Wholesaler means middleman. This is a really tough situation to survive in this kind of competition.

Pressures to develop economies of scale discouraged some middleman distributors, while others expanded their businesses rapidly. However, the decision to expand was ultimately tied to a middleman distributor's ability to mobilize class resources.

CLASS RESOURCES

As the ethnic beauty aids industry consolidated in the early 1990's, the growth and survival of middleman distributorships was increasingly determined by class resources. This is distinct from findings of past research which correlate business success among middleman minorities with ethnic resources such as, family labor, ethnic patronage and rotating credit association. These ethnic resources have declined in importance as business survival has become dependent on expanding the size of businesses and developing economies of scale. The middleman distributors who were interviewed provided a great deal of insight into these issues when they discussed the importance of mobilizing class resources as opposed to ethnic resources in the ethnic beauty aids industry. For instance, one Korean owner of a small ethnic beauty aids distributorship pointed out that in order for his business to grow he would, "have to make better communication with a banker, or something like that." This was because business expansion depended on gaining access to mainstream sources of capital. In fact, none of the middleman distributors who were interviewed indicated that they mobilized ethnic resources to raise investment capital for their businesses. In fact, all of the middleman distributors used either personal savings or loans from mainstream lending institutions as sources of investment capital.

In contrast to the Korean merchants discussed in chapter 5, bank loans were an important class resource that middleman distributors used to establish and expand their businesses. One Korean distributor commented that when he opened his business, "the bank help me a lot, more than 90 percent, I borrow the money from them." He went on to explain that he was able to borrow money from a mainstream bank because he had a great deal of collateral to attract the loan with. These comments were punctuated by a Jewish distributor, who added that the retail niche of the ethnic beauty aids industry was, "dominated by Koreans because they just have more money." He discussed the source of their capital this in some detail:

> They come here with a lot more money to start with. When they come over, the homes are very expensive in Korea. So they sell their homes, they've got a lot of cash. They bring so much into the country. Yeh, they start with more money.

It was necessary to mobilize class resources to remain competitive in the retail niche of the ethnic beauty aids industry. In fact, none of the middleman distributors attributed their ability to leverage capital to informal associations, such as the rotating credit associations that Velez-Ibanez discussed.[9] Typically, such borrowing networks do not have the capacity to leverage the amount of capital necessary to open a large retail store or distributorship. Among the middleman distributors who were interviewed, venture capital was raised by mobilizing class resources, not ethnic resources.

In addition to capital, the demand for employees with specialized skills also increased as middleman businesses expanded in size. For instance, Human capital was increasingly important to business success. As middleman businesses expanded, the need for employees with specialized business and management skills became more important. These skills fall into the category of class resources. One Korean distributor highlighted this issue in the following comment:

> In my school background I didn't take my major in economics. Actually, I was a metallurgical engineer in my country. I had a real different background. So, that would be a problem if I were gonna have more people, more sales. In that case, I'd have to hire more professional backgrounded person.

Another Korean distributor described how formalized business systems needed to be adopted before he could expand his company, " Number one is the management, I'm now set up with the management." He was a strong advocate of professionalizing his staff in order to grow, since he believed that "all business is run by the people, so I have to have a strong management team." Pressures to expand and develop economies of scale made ethnic resources less important than class resources. This became clear as Korean and Jewish distributors of ethnic beauty aids discussed their experiences with business expansion.

The increasing importance of class resources for middleman distributors resulted from heightened competition in the retail niche of the ethnic beauty aids industry. In contrast, the economic circumstances that black distributors faced in the professional niche of the ethnic beauty aids industry elevated the importance of ethnic resources for business success. The business strategies of blacks in the ethnic beauty aids industry helps clarify the role of ethnic resources in business development. This is ironic, since popular images and scholarly works have often downplayed the role of such resources in the black community.

THE DOCTRINE OF THE DOUBLE-DUTY DOLLAR

Ethnic Solidarity in Black America

Light distinguished between Chinese, Japanese and black entrepreneurs along the lines of ethnic resources.[10] He concluded that a lack of ethnic cooperation curtailed business development among blacks. In many ways, this theme was a rearticulation of earlier scholarly work on black entrepreneurship. For instance, DuBois made references to the marginality of black-owned businesses in several passages of *The Negro in Business*, and Frazier portrayed the black businesses that emerged in cities like Chicago and New York during the early 1900's in a similar light.[11] These characterizations perpetuated negative stereotypes of black entrepreneurs, particularly those focusing on critiques of ethnic cooperation in the black community. However, there is little evidence to support conclusions that the black community lacks a business tradition based on mutual aid and ethnic solidarity. In fact, several scholars have documented the existence of such a tradition.[12] In particular, Butler identified a tradition of mutual aid and self-help in his study of entrepreneurship in the black community.[13]

In the past, some scholars failed to identify the importance of ethnic solidarity in the black community. This is unfortunate, since an entire ideology has developed in black America based on ethnic solidarity. In many respects, the development of this ideology was a byproduct of the deprivation and exploitation that black Americans face in society. This ideology is articulated in many ways. When used in reference to black entrepreneurship, it is expressed through the concept of the doctrine of the double-duty dollar.[14] Drake and Cayton described how the doctrine of the double-duty dollar stressed, "the virtues of buying from Negroes - of making the dollar do 'double-duty': by both purchasing a commodity and, 'advancing The Race.'"[15] Historically, this doctrine was articulated by prominent black leader such as Booker T. Washington, as well as local black ministers.[16] Through the years, it has become a component of popular sentiment in the black community.

The doctrine of the double-duty dollar reflects the desire of blacks to maintain a strong ethnic economy in the black community. Because of this, it is an important element in the maintenance of a black niche in the ethnic beauty aids industry. The importance of supporting an ethnic economy in the black community was identified by many of the black entrepreneurs on the South Side of Chicago. For instance, many the black entrepreneurs on the South

Side of Chicago advertised their businesses as black-owned businesses, and they highlighted the fact that they sold products made by black companies. The marketing strategies of black entrepreneurs focused on tapping into ethnic networks, and black consumers were responsive to them. In fact, the support black consumers displayed for a strong ethnic economy in the black community was also identified by some of the middleman distributors in the ethnic beauty aids industry. For instance, one middleman distributor described how the doctrine of the double-duty dollar was articulated in the market place. He described how it precluded his entry into the professional niche in the ethnic beauty aids industry since, "many black retailers and customers prefer to buy from black-owned companies." The black distributors who were interviewed stressed this same point. The doctrine of the double-duty dollar was internalized by their customers and professional clientele, and it affected decisions concerning who to they did business with.

The doctrine of the double-duty dollar is crucial to understanding why some black businesses succeed, despite the fact that many are undercapitalized and surrounded by larger better financed middleman businesses. Black distributors in the ethnic beauty aids industry are at a disadvantage when compared with Korean and Jewish distributors. In fact, they find few customers in the retail niche of the ethnic beauty aids industry, since they cannot mobilize enough capital to compete with middleman distributors in the industry. However, black distributors dominate the professional niche in the ethnic beauty aids industry, which focuses on selling professional products to black beauticians and barbers. For example, one black distributor pointed out that, "95 percent of our business is professional." Another black distributor pointed out that her business serviced over five-hundred black salons. Despite the fact that some black distributors combine the servicing of salons with the operation of small retail shops, the primary focus of their businesses is on distributing professional products to black beauticians and barbers.

The Benefits of Being Black

This is a relatively small niche in the ethnic beauty aids industry. However, it is dominated by black businesses. The black distributors who were interviewed pointed out that there were only five or six black distributors in the Chicago area. Despite the small number of black distributors, they serviced almost all of the black salons in the metropolitan area. Although it was small in size, the professional niche was important to the long-term survival of the ethnic beauty aids industry. This was because manufacturers of ethnic beauty aids used black salons to test market and launch new products. Black distributors filled a vital role in the marketing of products to black salons, since they were responsible for organizing classes for black beauticians and demonstrating how to use new products. Being black made it easier for distributors to fill this role in the ethnic beauty aids industry. Black beauticians and barbers preferred to learn about new products through black distributors, and they had more confidence in the abilities of black distributors to demonstrate new products and answer questions about their nuances, since they were designed exclusively for people of African descent. Because ethnic resources facilitated the development of rapport between black distributors and black beauticians, the professional niche of the ethnic beauty aids industry remained insulated from competition with middleman merchants and distributors.

In order to limit their exposure to competition from middleman distributors, black distributors focused on selling professional products. Although the professional niche of the ethnic beauty aids industry was based on a small market with limited opportunities for business growth, it was also a more stable market. In part, this was because black beauticians and barbers preferred to do business with black distributors. However, these characteristics made the professional niche of the ethnic beauty aids industry unattractive to middleman entrepreneurs. Their inability to mobilize ethnic resources limited the access of middleman entrepreneurs to the professional niche, and other characteristics of the professional niche of the ethnic beauty aids industry discouraged middleman entrepreneurs from entering. For instance, the small size of the professional niche and its limited potential for sales made it unattractive to middleman entrepreneurs.

One black distributor made a number of comments about how the nature of the professional niche in the ethnic beauty aids industry discouraged middleman entrepreneurs from entering. For example, he pointed out that "Koreans" stay out of the professional market since they specialize in volume sales. He believed that "Koreans" did not try to sell to black beauticians and barbers because, "it's not enough money for them." This black distributor also believed black beauticians preferred to buy from other blacks when given the opportunity, and this discourage middleman merchants from attempting to do business with them. Because of these traits, black distributors believed it was advantageous to do business in the professional niche of the ethnic beauty aids industry. One black distributer made this comment:

> Most of the history of the industry states that if you are dear to the salons and the stylists, you tend to have a longer reign. More so than if you focus on retail. Because as I said, retail is awfully expensive, and if you limit yourself, and not get the salons in your corner, it's a short lived endeavor. That's what I'm finding out.

This distributor went on to discuss how the professional niche of the ethnic beauty aids industry was more stable than the retail niche, since there was less price competition. In fact, many manufacturers gave individual black distributors exclusive rights to sell their professional products to black beauticians and barbers. This enabled the distributor to have a monopoly on the sales of a particular product. Because of this, the use of exclusive rights limited price competition in the professional niche of the ethnic beauty aids industry. However, when a professional product developed name recognition in the black community, its manufacturer would begin to market it as a retail product. When this occurred the professional sales of a product would rapidly diminish. In this manner, black salons were effectively serving as test markets for products that would ultimately end up on retailer's shelves. Of course, moving an established professional product to the general market increased the demand for new professional products, which created a cycle of new business for black distributors.

Although black distributors were concentrated in a smaller segment of the market, it was a more stable business environment. This was the case, since there was a steady demand for professional products and exclusive rights to sell then insulated black distributors from price competition. The professional niche of the ethnic beauty aids industry also buffered black distributors in other ways. For instance, the presence of the doctrine of the double-duty dollar allowed black distributors to survive in an otherwise hostile marketplace. One black distributor made this point, "Because we are a force, especially manufacturers who are professionals, if they were to come to Chicago, they know they'd have to see a few of us (black distributors), if they want the professional business." In fact, being black was an important asset to distributors in the professional niche of the ethnic beauty aids industry. One black distributor pointed out that although all manufacturers understood the value of black distributors in the professional market, white manufacturers were extremely interested in developing a name for their professional products by selling them through black distributors. This black distributor emphasized that when a white manufacturer identifies a black distributor, "they'll break your door down to get into your shop."

In addition to the benefits black distributors gained from their ability to mobilize ethnic resources in the professional niche of the ethnic beauty aids industry, the professional niche also had lower capital requirements than the retail niche. This was because black salons carried fewer products and had less turnover than retail outlets. One black distributor discussed the advantages of this smaller market:

> I mean yes we only make X amount, where as we could make a lot more, but it's less headaches because we could rely on those dollars much more than we can rely on the retail dollars. We also don't have to spend quite as much in advertising.

The business strategy that black distributors followed was almost the exact opposite of the strategy adopted by middleman distributors. Black distributors focused on a small market and limited sales, while middleman distributors focused on a mass market and volume sales. Black distributors benefit from exclusive rights to sell professional products and the subsequent stability in demand and prices they produced, while middleman distributors bought products on the open market and they faced high levels of price competition. These business strategies were developed in response to the degree to which each group of entrepreneurs could mobilize class and ethnic resources. The ability of black distributors to mobilize ethnic resources in the black community gave them and advantage in the professional niche of the ethnic beauty aids industry, while the ability of middleman distributors to mobilize class resources gave them an advantage in the retail niche of the industry.

ACCESS TO CAPITAL AND ETHNIC RESOURCES

The ethnic beauty aids industry is an excellent case study of how differences in a group's access to capital and relative levels of ethnic resources affect economic opportunities. For example, class resources were identified as the most influential factors in determining whether middleman distributors would succeed in a business environment characterized by acute price competition and pressures to develop economies of scale. These findings are supported by Bates's study of Korean and black entrepreneurs.[17] In this study, Bates concluded that the long-term survival of both

Korean and black small businesses is most strongly influenced by class resources, since better capitalized Korean businesses were more robust.[18] This chapter refines these conclusions with regard to the relationship between ethnic resources and black entrepreneurship. It has been argued that in specialized niches, such as the professional niche of the ethnic beauty aids industry, ethnic resources were necessary factors in determining whether black distributors would succeed. The doctrine of the double-duty dollar gave them an advantage in this economic niche. In fact, the preference of black beauticians and barbers to do business with black distributors virtually precluded market penetration for middleman distributors. This had the effect of limiting the level of direct competition between black and middleman entrepreneurs, and reducing the importance of class resources for black distributors.

This is an important point, since it highlights the role of ethnic resources for black businesses in minority markets. Despite the ability of middleman distributors to mobilize class resources in the retail niche of the ethnic beauty aids industry, black distributors were able to stabilize their economic position by mobilizing ethnic resources in the professional niche of the industry. The identification of this adaptation emphasizes how capital constraints elevate the role of ethnic resources in black business. This is the essence of the concept of an economic detour.[19] In the next chapter, this discussion and the concept of an economic detour will be expanded upon through an examination of black manufacturers in the ethnic beauty aids industry.

NOTES

[1] Won Moo Hurh and Kwang Chung Kim, "Ethnic Resources Utilization of Korean Immigrant Entrepreneurs in the Chicago Minority Area." *International Migration Review* , 19.1 (1985): 82-109.

[2] Ibid, 99.

[3] Ibid, 99.

[4] Pyong Gap Min, *Ethnic Business Enterprise: Korean Small Business in Atlanta*, (New York: Center for Migration Studies, 1988); In-Jin Yoon, *Self Employment in Business, Chinese, Japanese, Korean-American, Blacks, and Whites, A Dissertation*, (Chicago: University of Chicago, 1991); Pyong Gap Min, *Caught in the Middle, Korean Communities in*

New York and Los Angeles, (Berkeley: University of California Press, 1996).

[5] In-Jin Yoon, "The Changing Significance of Ethnic and Class Resources in Immigrant Businesses: The Case of Korean Immigrant Businesses in Chicago," *Immigration and Migration Review*, 25.2 (1991): 303-331.

[6] In-Jin Yoon, *Self Employment in Business, Chinese, Japanese, Korean-American, Blacks, and Whites*, Dissertation, (Chicago: University of Chicago, 1991): 199.

[7] Ibid, 199.

[8] Ibid, 199.

[9] Carlos G. Velez-Ibanez, *Bonds of Mutual Trust, The Cultural System of Rotating Credit Associations Among Urban Mexicans and Chicanos*, (New Brunswick: Rutgers University Press, 1983).

[10] Ivan H. Light, *Ethnic Enterprise in America, Business and Welfare Among Chinese, Japanese, and Blacks*, (Berkeley: University of California Press, 1972).

[11] E. Franklin Frazier, *The Black Bourgeoisie, The Rise of a New Middle Class in the United States*, (New York: Collier Books, 1962); W.E. Burghardt DuBois, "The Negro In Business," in W.E. Burghardt DuBois, ed., *Atlanta University Publications, Volume 1*, (New York: Octagon Books, Inc, 1968).

[12] M.S. Stuart, *An Economic Detour, A History of Insurance in the Lives of American Negroes,* (College Park: McGrath Publishing Company, 1969); Booker T. Washington, *The Negro in Business*, (New York: AMS Press, 1971); John Sibley Butler, *Entrepreneurship and Self-Help Among Black Americans, A Reconsideration of Race and Economics*, (Albany: State University of New York Press, 1991); St. Clair Drake and Horace R. Cayton, *Black Metropolis: A Study of Negro Life in a Northern City*, (Chicago: University of Chicago Press, 1993).

[13] John Sibley Butler, *Entrepreneurship and Self-Help Among Black Americans, A Reconsideration of Race and Economics*, (Albany: State University of New York Press, 1991).

[14] St. Clair Drake and Horace R. Cayton, *Black Metropolis: A Study of Negro Life in a Northern City*, (Chicago: University of Chicago Press, 1993).

[15] Ibid, 431.

[16] Booker T. Washington, *The Negro in Business*, (New York: AMS Press, 1971); St. Clair Drake and Horace R. Cayton, *Black Metropolis: A Study of Negro Life in a Northern City*, (Chicago: University of Chicago Press, 1993).

[17] Timothy Bates, "An Analysis of Korean-Immigrant-Owned Small-Business Start-Ups with Comparisons to African- American-and-Nonminority-Owned Firms," *Urban Affairs Quarterly*, 30.2 (1994): 227-248.

[18] Ibid.

[19] M.S. Stuart, *An Economic Detour, A History of Insurance in the Lives of American Negroes*, (College Park: McGrath Publishing Company, 1969); John Sibley Butler, *Entrepreneurship and Self-Help Among Black Americans, A Reconsideration of Race and Economics*, (Albany: State University of New York Press, 1991).

CHAPTER 8:

Contemporary Black Manufacturers

AN ECONOMIC DETOUR

Separate economic niches have emerged in the ethnic beauty aids industry for middleman minorities and blacks in response to each group's ability to mobilize ethnic and class resources. Previous chapters focused on this issue. In them, it was pointed out that middleman entrepreneurs dominated the retail niche of the ethnic beauty aids industry because of their ability to mobilize class resources, while black entrepreneurs controlled the professional niche of the industry because of their ability to mobilize ethnic resources in the black community. This chapter expands the discussion of this relationship through an examination of contemporary black manufacturers in the ethnic beauty aids industry. The central argument of this chapter is that contemporary black manufacturers focus on doing business in the professional niche of the ethnic beauty aids industry, since they believed capital constraints and racial discrimination close opportunities in other economic niches to them.

The business orientation of black manufacturers in the ethnic beauty aids industry is explained by the concept of an "economic detour," which was identified in chapter 1. This concept was articulated by Stuart and Butler.[1] Stuart pointed out that during de jure legal segregation, black entrepreneurs were undercapitalized and faced racism.[2] Because of this, they participated in a segregated economy, and they ran businesses where competition from whites was limited. In particular, Stuart identified barber shops, beauty parlors, and other businesses linked to the ethnic beauty aids industry among those where black entrepreneurs historically clustered. The concept of an economic detour was further developed by Butler in his study of black entrepreneurship.[3] Following Stuart's model, Butler pointed out that historically, segregation in American society has affected the development of black entrepreneurship. However, he went further, distinguishing between the characteristics of black entrepreneurship and immigrant entrepreneurship.[4] He stressed that many immigrant entrepreneurs were able to enter into a wider range of businesses than black entrepreneurs. This was because they faced fewer capital constraints, and had a different experience with racial discrimination in American society. Because of this, many immigrant entrepreneurs were able to gain access to consumer markets outside of their individual ethnic communities more readily than black entrepreneurs. These distinctions have broad implications for the study of ethnic entrepreneurship. However, they need to be tested and elaborated upon further.

The ethnic beauty aids industry represents a critical case study for theoretical arguments concerning the concept of an economic detour. If such arguments are valid, one would expect racial attitudes in mainstream society to affect the business strategies of black entrepreneurs at all levels of the ethnic beauty aids industry. In addition, black entrepreneurs would be expected to cluster in segments of the ethnic beauty aids industry where the ability to mobilize ethnic resources in the black community is required for business success. This study has forwarded evidence of such an industry wide effect. In earlier chapters, black distributors and merchants were identified in specialized niches of the ethnic beauty aids industry. These niches were separate from those occupied by middleman merchants and distributors. In this chapter, evidence is presented regarding black manufacturers.

A small but stable base of black manufacturers of ethnic beauty aids has been present in Chicago for over a century. Chapter 2 discussed how black manufacturers of ethnic beauty aids clustered in Chicago historically. This cluster of black manufacturers has remained in place during the contemporary period. For example, in 1991, the American Health and Beauty Aids Institute (AHBAI), identified sixteen black manufacturers of ethnic beauty aids in the United States.[5] Of these, six (37.5%) were based in Chicago. They represented the largest concentration of such firms in the country. Five years later, there was still a heavy concentration of ethnic beauty aids manufacturers in Chicago. In 1996, seven black manufacturers of ethnic beauty aids were identified in the city, and four of them were interviewed for this study.

A common set of themes emerged during these interviews. For instance, the black manufacturers stressed the importance of finding adequate sources of venture capital for their companies. They discussed how undercapitalization hampered their ability to expand their companies and advertise their products. In fact, the black manufacturers who were interviewed clearly contrasted their ability to mobilize capital and the ability of white manufacturers to do so. They described how black-owned companies were often at a disadvantage when compared to better capitalized white-owned companies. This disparity in accessing capital made it difficult for black-owned companies to compete with white-owned companies. As a result, an alternative business strategy was adopted by black entrepreneurs which was based on mobilizing ethnic resources in the black community. This adaptation highlights the nexus between race and capitalization. This is the case, since black entrepreneurs adopted such a strategy due to their limited access to capital and the racial environment that they were embedded in.

RACE AND CAPITAL

The nexus between race and capital explains why black entrepreneurs do business in the context of an economic detour. A better understanding of this nexus is obtained by examining black manufacturers in the ethnic beauty aids industry. All of the black manufacturers who were interviewed in Chicago identified times when limited access to capital from mainstream institutions caused them to change their business strategies. Some of them believed that their inability to attract capital to their companies was partially the result of racial discrimination in society. For instance, one black manufacturer discussed how he was a banker before he started his company in the ethnic beauty aids industry. However, when he started his company he was unable to obtain a loan from a mainstream bank. Instead, he had to rely on personal loans and small contributions from business partners. He made this comment about his experience raising venture capital for his company:

> There were like four of us at the time, we put in $50 a month
> when we were starting out so we could do things like have a
> telephone, get things typed, have business cards, have letter
> heads, things like that. Get incorporated. That we did from
> our own personal cash. But every other thing we did, we bor-
> rowed money, either from friends, or from like, we got the
> company started with an initial $3,000 I borrowed from a
> friend of mine, a business friend of mine. That got us started,
> $3,000.

All of the black manufacturers who were interviewed indicated
that when they started their businesses, they had limited capital. In
itself, such humble beginnings are no different than those of other
entrepreneurs. However, black entrepreneurship is also embedded
in an environment where access to institutions, resources, and networks in mainstream society is limited because of racial discrimination. As a result, racial barriers add an extra burden to black
entrepreneurs, reducing the range of economic opportunities available to them.

In addition to reducing the range of opportunities to black
entrepreneurs, racial barriers also shape their perceptions about
the opportunities that remain open to them. For instance, one
black manufacturer saw a clear connection between capital constraints and issues of race in American society. When asked how he
raised the venture capital for his company, he gave the following
response:

> I didn't have any. You know, when you're black, ethnic, a lot
> of things are not available to you. You have to literally make
> something out of nothing. When I went to get incorporated in
> 1981, I saw my attorney, Mr. A., and I told him what my plan
> was and what I wanted to do. He was at one time a big time
> chemist for the Helene Curtis Company. He looked back at
> me in his big chair and he said, "Well, B. if you want to do
> this thing you need about $20,000." You know, to get a little
> store front, get a piece of equipment, this and that, you know.
> And, he looked at me and he said, "How much do you have?"
> I said, "A. I might be able to scrape up $1,000," and he
> laughed, and he said "Well, I'll incorporate you, you know it's
> nothing about that,"   and I said, "There's nothing wrong
> with testing the market." So that's literally how I started, I
> had $1,000.

The other black manufacturers who were interviewed recanted similar experiences related to the establishment of their companies. Each went into business with limited capital and little access to resources from mainstream institutions.

All of the black manufacturers who were interviewed reported that they had considered borrowing money from mainstream banks to expand their businesses. However, some were unable to borrow, since they need substantial collateral to secure such loans. For instance, one black manufacturer stated, "if you're ethnic and you need money, and you don't have collateral, you have nothing coming." The black manufacturers who could secure loans from mainstream banks often had access to less capital than they desired. Because they initially had limited access to start up capital, the scale of black-owned businesses was small. This made it more difficult to borrow for business expansion later on. In addition to reducing the access that black manufacturers had to commercial loans, the limited growth potential of their businesses also made it difficult for them to qualify for government loans and grants. For instance one black manufacturer pointed out that his business was too small to attract economic development assistance from the City of Chicago. He explained that, "If we're gonna hire three-hundred or four- hundred people, I'm sure the city would step in and help out." But, since his company only employed forty-five people he did not pursue economic development assistance through the city.

The other black manufacturers who were interviewed held a similar opinions about their ability to qualify for public sector loans and grants. Smaller black manufacturers did not participate in government programs, since they perceived such programs as being orientated toward larger companies. In fact, only one of the black manufacturers reported that he secured a loan from the Small Business Administration (SBA), and this was only after his company had grown substantially. He made the following comments about this period of expansion:

> Well, at that time, that we got to this location, we had basically gone through the wars out there. I had started in the basement of my home, and went to a store front from the basement of my home, and kept beating the pavement, and kept trying to expand the business. And then when we got here, when we landed here, we put a package together. We had built (this company) to over 1 million at that point, and

> went to our IRA account and we put an SBA package togeth-
> er. We got the financing to get the facilities and get some
> equipment, and get started.

This black manufacturer was able to attract a loan from the SBA
in the late 1980's, after his company had gone through an extended period of growth. Remarkably, he believed that despite the per-
formance of his company, it would have still been difficult to
access capital if a loan from the SBA had not been available. This
was based on his perception that mainstream banks would be less
willing to loan money to a black-owned company. Unfortunately,
by the time this black manufacturer secured a loan for his business,competition in the ethnic beauty aids industry intensified.
This resulted from a number of changes that occurred in the late
1980's and early 1990's.

In part, growing competition resulted from changes in fashion
trends. For example, in the early 1980's, the Jheri Curl hairstyle
became popular, and many black manufacturers attempted to
expand their businesses by selling such products. However, by the
late 1980's the popularity of the Jheri Curl hairstyle began to
wane, and manufacturers in the ethnic beauty aids industry had to
adapt. One black manufacturer discussed this shift in fashion:

> We were riding on a fad, the curly hair thing. Then, the come-
> dians started jumping on it, and teasing black folks about the
> grease, and the this, and the that. So that thing started to go
> down. At that point, that was all I had. So, here I am, in this
> building, with a $7,000 a month note, and my business start-
> ed to slip. Instead of doing $1.3 million, I ended up doing
> $700,000. So, it put me in a very precarious situation.

Other black manufacturers experienced similar problems. One
commented that his company use to manufacture a number of
Jheri Curl products, but this was no longer the case. He pointed
out that, "During the 80's, early 80's and mid-80's, the Curl was a
very popular item, and when we came into the 90's the Curl died
down." When sales of Jheri Curl products declined, many black-
owned companies experienced financial difficulties. This problem
was compounded since no new product dominated the market for
ethnic beauty aids like the Jheri Curl. As a result, manufacturers
had to offer a wider array of products, and this reduced their ability to develop an economy of scale based on a single product.

However, another factor was also at work in the market. All of the black manufacturers reported that spending among black consumers began to stagnate in the late 1980's and early 1990's. This decline in consumer spending was first felt at the retail level, and later reached distributors and manufacturers in the ethnic beauty aids industry.

A shift in fashion, accompanied by stagnating spending among black consumers in minority markets, created a great deal of stress for black manufacturers. Beginning in the late 1980's, black manufacturers had to develop and establish a market for new products, although they faced softer consumer spending. These problems were compounded, since some black manufacturers had expanded their operations in the 1980's, and acquired debt. Because of these factors, many black manufacturers experienced financial difficulties, and some faced insolvency. At the same time, better capitalized white manufacturers were beginning to discover the market for ethnic beauty aids.[6] By the late 1980's the ethnic beauty aids industry had become increasingly competitive, and disparities between black and white manufacturers in the ability to mobilize capital began to grow. The effect that these disparities had on the competitive position of black-owned businesses is clearly illustrated by examining the nature of competition between black and white manufacturers in the ethnic beauty aids industry during this period.

CHERRY-PICKING AND ADVERTISING

In the late 1980's, competition intensified between black and white manufacturers in the ethnic beauty aids industry. What had traditionally been an industry controlled by small and medium sized black-owned companies, was becoming an industry dominated by larger white-owned conglomerates. During this period, many black manufacturers found it difficult to compete with billion-dollar corporations, and they were acquired, merged or went bankrupt.[7] Others survived, but on a much smaller scale. The acquisition of black-owned companies by white-owned companies affected the racial composition of the ethnic beauty aids industry. For instance, black manufacturers lost sizable shares of the ethnic beauty aids market during the late 1980's, "Once controlling 80% of the total market, their share was estimated by industry analysts to be as low as 48% by the late 1980's."[8]

One of the black manufacturers who was interviewed had been employed by a black-owned company that was taken over by a white-owned conglomerate, and he discussed how the transition took place. He pointed out that there were several negative implications for the former employees of the black-owned company when the acquisition occurred. Many blacks lost jobs when the new parent company took over the black-owned company. In addition, the parent company's marketing and production strategies affected how the black-owned company did business after its acquisition. The black manufacturer described this in detail:

> What they were doing is, they were buying just for, it's what we call cherry-picking the line. And, major conglomerates sometimes, when they buy smaller companies, they cherry-pick the line. You can call up any different, most companies have fifty, seventy-five, one-hundred, one-hundred fifty different items. The major conglomerate, they bought that company based on those two or three different items that were number one sellers. They don't care about all the rest, because as far as they're concerned it really didn't make no numbers.

Cherry-picking allowed a large white-owned conglomerate to use the brand name of the black-owned company it took over. In addition, sales and marketing strategies were focused on highly profitable items from the black-owned company's product line. These products were mass marketed to black consumers. However, the parent company would remove less profitable items from the acquired company's product line, and allocated fewer resources to the development of new products for black consumers. As a result, monies that were once channeled into research and market development in the black community were accumulated as profits by white-owned companies that acquired black-owned companies.

The growing role of white manufacturers in the ethnic beauty aids industry had additional implications. The expanded role of white manufacturers raised the cost of advertising, since larger white-owned companies were able to flood the market with advertisements for their products. Before this, advertising was not as capital intensive in the industry, and black manufacturers found various advertising outlets to introduce new product lines to black customers. However, after white-owned companies expanded their role in the ethnic beauty aids industry, the cost of advertising increased. As a result, a company needed to invest more capital in advertising campaigns. If a manufacturer did not have sufficient capital to invest in advertising, then the only option was to adopt a direct marketing approach.

The disparity in the ability to advertise made it more difficult for black consumers to identify products manufactured by black companies. This was not only due to the capital advantages of white-owned companies. It was also because of the themes that white-owned companies focused on in their advertising campaigns. White-owned companies integrated afrocentric themes into their marketing strategies, since they assumed black consumers wanted to buy ethnic beauty aids from black-owned companies. One black manufacturer discussed how such marketing practices affected his company:

> You take a company like Dark and Lovely. They put a black face on a container, they got billboards up and around, and this and that. They can paint a great image. Like they're some great company that really specializes in the black hair, so forth and so on. I could be a small black company, have a better product, but I can't give the consumer that image that they do.

The use of racial images to attract black consumers was effective, since they implied that a given product was made by a black manufacturer. White manufacturers aggressively pursued this type of advertising, and black manufacturers could not mobilize enough capital to counter it.

In areas of the market where capital is highly influential, such as the retail niche of the ethnic beauty aids industry, aggressive advertising campaigns by large white-owned conglomerates made it difficult for black manufacturers to compete. However, in other parts of the industry, such as the professional niche, the role of such class resources was balanced by ethnic resources. For this reason, black manufacturers were more successful at protecting their markets in the professional niche of the ethnic beauty aids industry since it was based on direct sales and the mobilization of ethnic resources in the black community.

DEMAND CREATORS AND DEMAND SUPPLIERS

Two distinct niches existed in the ethnic beauty aids industry, the retail niche and the professional niche. In each of these niches, networks were formed between manufacturers, distributors and merchants. For instance, in the professional niche black manufacturers often sold products to black distributors, who in turn sold to black merchants and salons. In the retail niche, white manufacturers often sold products to Jewish and Korean distributors, who in turn sold to chain stores and Korean merchants. Although there are exceptions to these general patterns of business networking, they reflect the dominant modes of business interactions in the ethnic beauty aids industry. The emergence of these networks was tied to the relationship between class and ethnic resources.

Although capital constraints made it difficult for black manufacturers to compete in the retail niche of the ethnic beauty aids industry, the ability to mobilize ethnic resources in the black community allowed them to control the professional niche. This was because the mobilization of ethnic resources allowed black manufacturers to establish rapport with other black entrepreneurs in the industry. Developing rapport was essential, since sales in the professional niche of the ethnic beauty aids industry were done on a more informal level than in the retail niche. In fact, black manufacturers distinguish between the roles of the professional and retail niches in the industry. For instance, one black manufacturer referred to black distributors, merchants and salon owners as "demand-creators," since they played and active role in creating demand for new products. While he referred to middleman distributors, chain stores and Korean merchants as "demand-suppliers," since they were passive actors in minority markets, responding to existing consumer demand.

The distinction between demand-creators and demand-suppliers highlighted each group's advantages in mobilizing class and ethnic resources. This is reflected in the following comment made by the black manufacturer cited above:

> A distributor who goes to the salons, he takes a product and he says, "Mrs. Jones why don't you buy this product?" He's the one who will put on the show with you, invite the hairstylists to come in so that you can entice them to buy your product and help you create demand. But the Koreans don't do that, so they are the demand-suppliers, and that has, in the cases where the manufacturers have tried to sell the same product to a demand-creator and a demand-supplier, the demand-supplier always kills the demand-creator, because he

lowers the price, the demand is already there, and he sits in his store and he waits for people to come in.

Other black manufacturers identified these distinctions, and pointed out that black distributors, merchants and salons owners were essential to the success of their companies, since they exposed black customers to new products. In fact, black manufacturers developed a market for their products by mobilizing ethnic resources in the black community and promoting them through word-of-mouth in black salons. This strategy allowed them to bypass mass advertising strategies to promote their products. In fact, one black manufacturer stated that his company did no formal advertising, and relied on contacts with black salons and word-of-mouth to sell his products. He explained that, "what happens is the consumer goes into the salon to get their hair fixed, and they look to see what they're using." If the customer liked the product, they would buy it from the salon. As the product became more popular, black customers would increasingly "go to the Korean shops or some of the other retail outlets," and ask for it. In turn, the retailers would try to order the professional product. If demand was high enough, a manufacturer could stop selling it in the professional niche, and begin selling it in the retail niche. However, there were risks associated with such a move.

One black manufacturer discussed how one of his competitors lost credibility in the professional niche of the ethnic beauty aids industry, since the company had "bastardized" its professional products by moving them into retail stores too rapidly. He described the reaction of black professionals to this black manufacturer:

> They made the same products available to the Koreans as to the demand-creators, and the demand-creator says, "well I'm not going to carry their product, why should I create demand for this guy down the street to make the money," so they stopped pushing (the black manufacturer's products) in the salons.

Other black manufacturers also discussed this issue. One pointed out that some black-owned companies keep their professional and retail products distinct, by manufacturing them under separate labels. One label would be sold exclusively in salons, while the other would be sold in retail outlets. This strategy allowed a black manufacturer to do volume sales on a short-term basis with a few popular products, while maintaining a strong long-term relationship with black distributors and salons.

Despite selling some products in the retail niche of the ethnic beauty aids industry, the professional niche remained the mainstay of all of the black manufacturers who were interviewed. Black manufacturers who neglected it and focused exclusively on the retail niche often saw their profits deteriorate over time. This was because they faced direct competition from larger white-owned companies in the retail niche of the ethnic beauty aids industry. In fact, by the early 1990's, black manufacturers found it increasingly difficult to gain access to the retail niche. This was due to economic stagnation in minority markets, increasing advertising costs, and growing competition from larger white manufacturers. These trends led to a number of changes in the ethnic beauty aids industry.

TIGHT MARKETS AND SHRINKING OPPORTUNITIES IN THE 1990'S

Business Survival and the Need for Further Specialization

The most important factor influencing change in the ethnic beauty aids industry was the stagnation of minority markets that began during the late 1980's and early 1990's. This created a number of repercussions for the black-owned businesses that depended on these markets for their survival. Rising competition in the ethnic beauty aids industry was an outgrowth of a tightening markets in the black community. For instance, earlier chapters described how black distributors and merchants found it more difficult to do business in the retail niche of the ethnic beauty aids industry as minority markets stagnated on the South Side of Chicago, since this market stagnation elevated the importance of mobilizing capital for business success. During this period, black manufacturers experienced similar problems, which caused them to refocus their businesses. As white-owned conglomerates began to take over the retail niche in the ethnic beauty aids industry, black merchants focused on the professional niche. They found the professional niche to be less capital intensive and more stable.

Despite these benefits, the small size of the professional niche limited the growth potential of black-owned companies. In fact, some of the black manufacturers who were interviewed reported that they did not have enough capital to manufacture and market their products simultaneously. Because of this acute undercapitalization, they specialized in either production or marketing. For instance, two of the black manufacturers who were interviewed reported that they contract out the manufacturing of their products to other black-owned companies. One black manufacturer stated, "I have people do the packaging and everything, the products, so I contract manufacture." The other black manufacturer explained why his company adopted this strategy:

> The reason why it's contracted out is that manufacturing itself is another business, and the secret to the industry is not making the products. By selling the products, or marketing the products, my costs would not be that much lower for the trouble that I would have to go through to manufacture. So that's why we don't manufacture.

Some black-owned companies lacked the necessary capital to manufacture their own products, in part, because sales in the professional niche of the ethnic beauty aids industry were limited. As a result, some black manufacturers paid other companies to bottle their products, while they focused their resources on marketing activities.

On the other side of this arrangement, there were black manufacturers who focused on making products for other companies, while selling few products of their own. Many of these black manufacturers began contract manufacturing in the early 1990's, when sales began to stagnate in minority markets. At this time, they were confronted with a dilemma. The market appeared to be saturated, and their manufacturing facilities were not operating at full capacity. In order to keep their companies profitable, they began packaging products for other companies. Over time, their product lines waned, and contract manufacturing became the focus of their business activities. For example, one black manufacturer who began contract manufacturing in 1992, explained how adopting this strategy changed his business:

> What we've done now is we've gotten out of marketing ourselves. In other words, (this company) started off pushing its

own plan, getting out there beating its own drum, what ever the means we had available to the consumer, to get our brand over. I found that I was not a very good marketing person. So, as a result, with the times of large companies scaling back, we decided to go into private packaging. We turned ourselves into a private packaging manufacturer, which was very lucrative and a good move for us, because we found that a lot of companies... For example, they may have a project which is 2 or 3 million dollars, they don't want to erect, or rent, another facility and get equipment in just to do that. They'll look for companies like myself, who have the equipment, who have the quality control already in place, and they'll come to us, and give us those small jobs.

In part, this strategy became feasible since some black manufacturers did not have the capital to build their own manufacturing facilities. However, contract manufacturing also came about since blacks who owned manufacturing facilities could not take advantage of economies of scale by producing their own products. This was the case, since the professional niche of the ethnic beauty aids industry was smaller and they lacked sufficient capital to market their products in the retail niche.

When minority markets stagnated in the early 1990's, blacks began contract manufacturing. This strategy was an outgrowth of a saturated domestic market for ethnic beauty aids. Although it entailed short-term profits for some black manufacturers, it did not create new growth in the industry. In fact, contracting out was a strategy used to save a struggling business, and not a strategy for expansion. During the early 1990's, it was difficult for black manufacturers to expand their businesses. Many faced capital constraints, and they perceived racial barriers to business development. For example, one black manufacturer described how these issues affect his business:

> You're like a marked person. Man, I mean, you're looked at as inferior. If you're a black company, and you produce a product, it doesn't measure up to the white counterpart. You don't have the marketing expertise, nor dollars, so your image is not the same as theirs.

Capital constraints and the perception of racial barriers in the economy created a number of dilemmas for black manufacturers interested in expanding their businesses. Black manufacturers found few opportunities to expand their businesses. In the ethnic beauty aids industry, access to the retail niche was limited due to increasing competition from white-owned conglomerates. Additionally, business expansion in the mainstream economy was considered risky, since whites were thought to be averse to buying products made by blacks. As a result, many black manufacturers focused on mobilizing ethnic resources to overcome these barriers.

Mobilizing Ethnic Resources Abroad

The effects of racial discrimination on the scope of business opportunities available to black manufacturers became clearer when their strategies for business expansion were examined. When discussing business expansion, the black manufacturers identified strategies that focused on the mobilization of ethnic resources. For instance, many of the black manufacturers expressed an interest in exporting products to other countries. However, their interest in exporting was limited to countries with predominantly black populations. The focus on the ethnic characteristics of foreign markets was clearly expressed in the following comments by a black manufacturer:

> The majority of the companies today, since there's no growth here, what they're doing is going overseas. If you open markets like Iran, Iraq, Uganda, Ghana, Nigeria, all that, it's over 400 million people of color, compared to 25 million here. So that's where the growth, that's where the potential is. Everybody's going to South Africa and all these different places where all the masses of people are.

When black manufacturers thought about business expansion, entering the mainstream market was not considered to be a viable option. Racial barriers to participation in the mainstream economy made an economic detour strategy more appealing. This was the case, despite the added risks that exporting entailed.

Exporting was riddled with risks which expansion into the general market did not entail. However, because of racial barriers, black manufacturers perceive few alternatives for business expansion. Like domestic markets, foreign markets were unstable since they were influenced by changes in fashion and general trends. However, they were also unstable because of fluctuations in foreign exchange rates, and because of the political uncertainty that some foreign markets entailed.

In addition, exporting was a cash business which could involve large volumes of merchandise. One black manufacturer commented that, "A lot of companies have gotten burned for hundreds of thousands of dollars, you know, trying to get that big business." Another black manufacturer stressed this point in the following comment:

> Gots to get your money up front. No letters of credit, ut uh. A lot of my potential deals, I have people ring my phone, they're interested in so many, I mean big orders, to go to Africa, and different stuff. Fine. When the white boy over there at my bank tells me the money is there, I'll ship the merchandise.

This was the biggest barrier to foreign trade. Black manufacturers operated with limited capital, and the risk of losing money while conducting overseas businesses was high. Exporting was made more precarious since profit margins in exporting were lower than in the domestic economy. Despite lower profit margins, exporting remained attractive to black manufacturers since they could make volume sales without the encumbrance of marketing and advertising costs. However, as one black manufacturer put it, this attraction fades away when, "your stuff is on this slow boat going over to Africa some damn where, and hell, you can't find anybody to get your money."

Despite the risks associated with exporting, there were few other alternatives available to black manufacturers interested in expanding their businesses. This situation resulted from a number of factors. Initially, capital constraints and racial barriers hinder the growth of black-owned businesses. Then, in the early 1990's, the spending power of black consumers stagnated. At the same time, competition from large white-owned conglomerates squeezed black manufacturers out of the retail niche in the ethnic beauty aids industry. In response to these obstacles, black entrepreneurs mobilized ethnic resources in the black community and developed their businesses in the context of an economic detour. For most black manufacturers, this meant they would focus on doing business in the professional niche of the ethnic beauty aids industry. For some, this also meant they would attempt to export products to countries with large black populations.

INSTITUTIONAL COMPLETENESS IN THE BLACK COMMUNITY?

The adoption of a business strategy based on mobilizing ethnic resources was possible for black entrepreneurs since a dense network of formal and informal institutions existed in the black community. The role of such networks is discussed in the theoretical arguments concerning institutional completeness.[9] These arguments say that dense networks of ethnic institutions create alternative resources for ethnic group members to draw from in society. Such resources were available to black entrepreneurs in the ethnic beauty aids industry since an agglomeration of ethnic institutions was found in the black community. These institutions worked together to transmit messages to blacks which promoted ethnic solidarity and counteracted racism in mainstream society.

In part, formal institutions in the ethnic beauty aids industry articulate such messages to black Americans. For instance, in the mid 1980's, black manufacturers formed the American Health and Beauty Aids Institute (AHBAI) to raise public awareness about growing competition in the ethnic beauty aids industry from white-owned companies. This organization provided technical assistance to black businesses and acted as a clearinghouse for information related to the ethnic beauty aids industry. One of the more visible effects of AHBAI on the industry was its "Proud Lady Symbol" which appears on products of the organization's members. The symbol was designed to alert black consumers to the fact that a particular product was made by a black-owned company. AHBAI provided information and assistance to black businesses, and it also helps to disseminate a unifying message to the black community. This theme was grounded in ethnic resources, which are reflected in this statement of AHBAI's goals:

> Our goal is to pull resources and recycle dollars back into the African-American community, where it counts! Purchasing AHBAI member products featuring the Proud Lady Symbol assures consumers that the product was manufactured by a Black-owned company that reinvests its profits in the community to build a stronger Black America. DON'T BE DECEIVED! Purchase Black haircare and beauty products that feature the Proud Lady Symbol and recycle your Black dollars in the Black community. It's good for Black America![10]

This was a clear articulation of the doctrine of the double duty dollar, which was aimed at slowing the encroachment of mainstream institutions on the black community. In this case, the expansion of large white-owned conglomerates into the ethnic beauty aids industry.

At a more intermediate level, black manufacturers mobilized ethnic resources by using their businesses to help other black Americans. For instance, all of the black manufacturers saw their businesses as catalysts for job creation in the black community. Although scholars such as Wilson have argued that both black and white employers on the South Side of Chicago are reluctant to hire inner-city residents, such conclusions regarding black employers in the ethnic beauty aids industry are inaccurate.[11] In fact, all of the black business owners who were interviewed in this study expressed an interest in hiring inner-city residents. The principal barrier to making such hires was capital. There was no evidence that inner-city residents were systematically removed from the hiring queue by black employers during the course of this study. In fact, the contrary was true. Black employers proactively sought such applicants when they were able to hire new employees.

At an even more informal level, black manufacturers mobilize ethnic resources through acts of charity and community service. One black manufacturer described how his company got involved in going to schools and talking to children, and acting as a "role model" in the black community. Another black manufacturer discussed how his company cultivated similar ties in the black community:

> What we've done is adopted schools. Where we honor the student of the month kind of thing. Tell these guys they did well, they got good grades for that month. They'll have an assembly and we'll come down as a company, we'll have gift bags and different things for them, and we'll award them at the ceremony there. A lot of the less fortunate kids in some of these schools who last year couldn't come up with $50 or $60 per person graduation fee, to get the cap and gown and stuff, we would go to our clients and plead their case. And a lot of these guys would send donations in to us and stuff so that all of the kids could go across the stage and get their diploma with their cap and gown. And last Christmas we did a fund drive for all of the kids in the schools for fund raising, and there again we counted on our clients, they sent in combs,

gloves, caps, all this stuff, and we were able to give these kids stuff like that.

Black manufacturers are important role models in the black community. Filling this role is personally rewarding to them, and it generates a positive image of black-owned companies in the black community.

One black manufacturer described how his company's activities in the black community attracted black customers. Maintaining a presence in the community helped advertise his products, "it's a way for them to know you are there, I like doing it." The desire to generate community ties entailed a combination of idealistic and pragmatic goals. However, the primary motivation for black manufacturers to get involved in the black community grew out of ethnic solidarity with other blacks. One black manufacturer expressed this with clarity:

> I think it should be our responsibility, the black-owned companies ourselves, because these are our kids, it's our future. And we need to stand up and be counted, be recognized, and we need to change the image of ourselves in those kids eyesights, let them know that we care about our own.

This type of agency was linked to ethnic identity. Black entrepreneurs approached the black community as co-ethnics. Because of this, they acted as custodians for the black community, and attempted to shield it from outside exploitation.

Black entrepreneurs mobilize ethnic resources in minority markets to generate a sense of autonomy in the black community. This is illustrated through an examination of the ethnic beauty aids industry, since class resources are less pronounced. It is somewhat surprising that the relationship between ethnic resources and black entrepreneurship is not discussed. However, this discussion has helped to highlight the importance of this relationship to black entrepreneurship in minority markets. In fact, it has been shown that ethnic resources had a substantial influence on black business in the ethnic beauty aids industry, despite the acute capital constraints and discrimination that confront blacks entrepreneurs in American society. The implications of these findings, and issues identified in prior chapters, are discussed in greater detail in the concluding chapter of this study.

NOTES

[1] M.S. Stuart, *An Economic Detour, A History of Insurance in the Lives of American Negroes*, (College Park: McGrath Publishing Company, 1969); John Sibley Butler, *Entrepreneurship and Self-Help Among Black Americans, A Reconsideration of Race and Economics*, (Albany: State University of New York Press, 1991).

[2] M.S. Stuart, *An Economic Detour, A History of Insurance in the Lives of American Negroes*, (College Park: McGrath Publishing Company, 1969).

[3] John Sibley Butler, *Entrepreneurship and Self-Help Among Black Americans, A Reconsideration of Race and Economics*, (Albany: State University of New York Press, 1991).

[4] Ibid, 74-75.

[5] American Health and Beauty Aids Institute, (1991), Newsletter.

[6] Laurie Freeman, "Big Marketers move in on Ethnic Haircare," *Advertising Age*, May 12 (1986): 24; Penelope Wang and Maggie Malone, "Targeting Black Dollars, White-Owned Companies Muscle Minority Firms out of the Hair-Care Market," *Newsweek*, October 13 (1986): 54; Phyllis Furman, "Ethnic Haircare Marketers Battle for Share," *Advertising Age*, March 2 (1987): 52.

[7] *Dudley's Haircare Fact Book*, (Greensboro: Dudley Products, Inc., 1993): 34.

[8] Ibid, 35.

[9] Raymond Breton, "Institutional Completeness of Ethnic Communities and the Personal Relations of Immigrants," *The American Journal of Sociology*, 70 (1964): 193-205.

[10] *Dudley's Haircare Fact Book*, (Greensboro: Dudley Products, Inc., 1993): 42.

[11] William Julius Wilson, *When Work Disappears, The World of the New Urban Poor*, (New York: Alfred J. Knopf, 1996): 111-146.

CHAPTER 9:

Conclusion

INTERNAL COLONIALISM AS A THEORETICAL PARADIGM

This study argues that internal colonial conditions hamper economic development in minority markets. This situation results from several issues surrounding the relationship between mainstream society and minority markets. For instance, the variety of business establishments in minority markets is limited, and undercapitalization stunts the growth of many of them. This is particularly true for black-owned businesses. In addition, large corporations in mainstream society contribute to the underdevelopment of minority markets. Mainstream conglomerates focus on selling goods and services in secure niches of minority markets, and limit their activities in other areas.[1] As a result, minority entrepreneurs are unable to compete directly with these larger companies and end up selling goods and services in less stable niches of minority markets. The relationship between mainstream conglomerates and minority-owned businesses is identified by Marable in his discussion of the effects of corporate American on business development in the black community. From this analysis, he concluded that the activities of mainstream conglomerates in minority markets led to, "the increased marginalization of the Black entrepreneur, the manipulation of Black culture and social habits by white corporations, and a new kind of economic underdevelopment of all Blacks at all income levels."[2]

In addition to limiting the scope of black business, mainstream institutions also influence the behaviors of black consumers. In part, this is the result of the commercialization of minority markets by corporate America, and the saturation of these markets with massive advertising campaigns. However, on a more fundamental level, consumer behavior in minority markets is regulated by the government, through a system based on economic dependence. The government is the source of income for many consumers in minority markets. In some cases, they rely on the public sector for jobs. In others, they depend on a variety of social insurance programs and public assistance programs for income. This relationship was reflected in the comments of the Korean merchants on the South Side of Chicago, who believed that the majority of their black customers received welfare, or some other form of public assistance. This type of economic dependence makes minority markets sensitive to shifts in public policy. In fact, changes in public sector employment and social welfare spending have a concentrated effect on consumer behavior in minority markets. This is because business in minority markets is oriented toward poor consumers, and a large proportion of the consumers in such markets depend on the government to supplement their incomes. As a result, when social welfare programs change, the businesses that sell goods and services to poor consumers in minority markets absorb these effects immediately.

The effects of underdevelopment and economic dependence in minority markets are further complicated by racial discrimination in mainstream society. Minority entrepreneurs and consumers are often stigmatized in mainstream society, and stereotypes are used to rationalize the limited scope of economic opportunities available to them. For example, some of the Korean entrepreneurs who were interviewed on the South Side of Chicago perceived racial barriers to accessing business networks in mainstream society, and they identified similar barriers which caused them to feel alienated from local government. Some of the black entrepreneurs who were interviewed in the South Side of Chicago also discussed how race affected their ability to access business networks and resources in the public sector, particularly when they discussed issues concerning capital. However, these issues are not always focused upon in studies of minority entrepreneurship. As a result, too little attention is paid to the role of mainstream institutions in generating the economic conditions found in minority markets. Instead, conditions in minority markets are often attributed to social pathologies among minority entrepreneurs and consumers. This results in the further stigmatization of minority entrepreneurs and consumers, and the maintenance of the internal colonial conditions that shape minority markets.

The combined effects of undercapitalization, economic dependence, and the stigmatization of minority communities create and maintain internal colonial conditions in minority markets. In this study, the relationship between these factors was discussed in the context of black and Korean entrepreneurship in the ethnic beauty aids industry. However, the observations made about this particular industry, and the minority entrepreneurs in it, can be generalized from to create hypotheses for the analysis of other entrepreneurial groups in minority markets. This is because this analysis has refined the discussion of ethnic entrepreneurship by applying the internal colonial paradigm. The conceptual categories that have emerged from this analysis open new avenues for research and empirical testing. In particular, several theoretical distinctions have been made between middleman and black entrepreneurs through an examination of their business strategies in minority markets. These distinctions are outlined below in order to illustrate how the analysis of middleman and black entrepreneurship is informed by the internal colonial paradigm.

INTERNAL COLONIALISM AND MIDDLEMAN BUSINESS

The discussion of middleman entrepreneurship becomes more focused when placed in the context of the internal colonial paradigm. In particular, two central characteristics of the middleman role are best understood when this paradigm is adopted. The first characteristic is the buffering role that middleman minorities fill between mainstream institutions and subordinate groups in society.[3] The internal colonial paradigm highlights how this role reenforces institutional relationships in society. In particular, it emphasizes that middleman minorities become scapegoats as a result of specific types of social conflicts. The scapegoating of middleman minorities occurs in response to conflicts between mainstream institutions and subordinate minority groups in society. The second characteristic of middleman entrepreneurship that is informed by the internal colonial paradigm is sojourning.[4] The internal colonial paradigm adds context to the discussion of sojourning behavior, since it focuses on how middleman minorities perceive minority markets as separate from the mainstream economy, and somewhat volatile due to tensions that exist between mainstream institutions and subordinated minority groups. As a result, middleman minorities initially view minority markets as places to do businesses temporarily. In fact, sojourning behavior should be viewed as a form of agency adopted by middleman entrepreneurs in response to internal colonial conditions in minority markets and the subsequent potential for scapegoating. By emphasizing the importance of scapegoating and sojourning, the internal colonial paradigm helps to refine middleman minority theory.

When this framework is not adopted, middleman minority theory becomes spurious. One pitfall of ignoring the internal colonial paradigm is that the centrality of scapegoating and sojourning to middleman theory becomes diluted by discussions of the assumed cultural attributes of middleman minorities. For instance, Light based his conclusions about ethnic entrepreneurship on cultural distinctions between Chinese, Japanese, and black entrepreneurs.[5] However, such conclusions are brought into question by this study. In fact, the comparison of black and Korean entrepreneurs on the South Side of Chicago indicates that a number of similarities exist between the two groups. For instance, black and Korean entrepreneurs raised the start-up capital for their businesses by drawing from personal savings and borrowing informally from friends and family members. Both groups also operated small family firms, and employed family members in their businesses. In addition, black and Korean entrepreneurs hold a personal philosophy based on individualism and a strong work ethic. In fact, these characteristics are not distinct to either ethnic group, but appeared to be general attributes of entrepreneurs.

Despite these similarities, there were other areas where some of the Korean entrepreneurs on the South Side of Chicago had distinct advantages. The principal advantage that Korean entrepreneurs had over black entrepreneurs involved their ability to mobilize class resources. In particular, when Korean entrepreneurs started their businesses they held greater amounts of capital than black entrepreneurs. This gave them an advantage when doing business in minority markets. Importantly, the Korean merchants who were interviewed on the South Side of Chicago stressed that this wealth came predominantly from person saving and familial assets, rather than from participation in communal organizations. In fact, the advantage that Korean entrepreneurs found when doing business in minority markets was more the result of selective migration from Korea than communalism. For instance, Kim and Min pointed out that Korean immigrant in the post-1965 period, "generally represented the middle-class strata of the Korean population."[6] In effect, the capital advantages that Korean entrepreneurs have in minority markets stem from their earlier class position in Korea.

These class resources made sojourning in the black community possible, since many Korean immigrants initially found it difficult to access the mainstream economy. In part, Korean immigrants found it difficult to access the mainstream economy, since opening a business in white America was considerably more expensive than opening one in black America. The risks associated with doing business in the mainstream economy were heightened for Korean immigrants by language barriers and the perception of anti-immigrant sentiment in white America. As a result, many Korean immigrants elected to sojourn in the black community while they accumulated additional capital that could be used to improve their future chances of integrating into the mainstream economy. However, the class resources that many Korean immigrants possessed also accented the disparity in wealth between them and many members of the black community. This disparity fueled resentment toward Koreans in the black community, which had the potential to escalate during periods of heightened racial tension in mainstream society. As a result, black-Korean tension at the parochial level insulates mainstream institutions from grievances concerning the exploitation of black America. This state of affairs is a direct result of racial discrimination in mainstream society, since it limits the access Koreans have to the mainstream economy, while it steers them toward business opportunities in minority markets.

INTERNAL COLONIALISM AND BLACK BUSINESS

Racial discrimination in mainstream society had a more profound effect on the economic opportunities available to black entrepreneurs. The persistence of racism in white America affects how black entrepreneurs raise capital for their businesses, the business networks they have access to, and ultimately who they do business with. In part, opportunities in the mainstream economy are limited because many whites hold negative perceptions of black entrepreneurs, and are averse to doing business with them.[7] This creates an ominous barrier to black entrepreneurs, since attracting white customers is imperative to accessing the mainstream economy. This situation is compounded by racial barriers that black entrepreneurs face in the business world. For instance, black entrepreneurs experience difficulty when trying to access business and professional networks in the mainstream economy.[8] In addition, black entrepreneurs experience difficulty when trying to borrow capital from mainstream banks.[9] These obstacles create an environment where black entrepreneurs are denied equal access to the mainstream economy by white consumers and mainstream institutions. Both processes restrict the growth of black businesses and contribute to their undercapitalization. Although black entrepreneurs often have limited capital to start their businesses, their ability to borrow additional capital is further reduced by the effects of racial discrimination on the scope of economic opportunities available to blacks in America.

The dual disadvantages of racial discrimination and undercapitalization have historically hampered black business. For instance, Oliver and Shapiro identify the connection between racial discrimination in mainstream society and black entrepreneurship:

> Severe economic restrictions have historically prevented many African Americans from establishing successful business. These include segregation, legal prohibitions, acts of violence, discrimination, and general access only to so-called black markets.[10]

In the past, when black businesses developed that competed in size and scope with white businesses, "intimidation and ultimately, in some cases, violence were used to curtail their expansion or get rid of them altogether."[11] For example, chapter 2 discussed how a group of white racists, known as the White Citizens' Council, organized a boycott of Fuller Products in the 1960's, since it was a black-owned company. On a larger scale, Butler describes how whites systematically looted and burned black businesses in Tulsa,

Oklahoma in the early 1920's when race relations were strained in that city.[12] Contemporary black entrepreneurship has been imprinted by this legacy of discrimination.

This legacy has contributed to the development of a distinct economic strategy among black entrepreneurs which focuses on the mobilization of ethnic resources in the black community. The concept of an economic detour was used to describe this strategy in the historically oriented studies conducted by Stuart and Butler.[13] This study has further expanded the concept of an economic detour further, through an examination of contemporary black-owned businesses in minority markets. The examination of the concept of an economic detour in the context of the internal colonial paradigm has enhanced this study's findings in two respects. First, it highlights the relationship between the business strategies of black entrepreneurs and racial discrimination in mainstream society. This is because black entrepreneurs embark on an economic detour in response to barriers they face to accessing capital and doing business in the mainstream economy. This should be viewed as a form of agency on the part of blacks, similar to the adoption of sojourning behavior by middleman minorities. Second, the relationship between the capital constraints that black entrepreneurs experience and their focus on ethnic resources is highlighted by the concept of an economic detour. This is because black entrepreneurs are able to substitute ethnic resources for class resources by pursuing entrepreneurship in the black community. The advantage of this strategy is that it allows black entrepreneurs to sustain their businesses because of the insulation afforded to them by a co-ethnic clientele. The disadvantage of this strategy is that the mobilization of ethnic resources is an ineffective method for accumulating wealth in minority markets, since such markets are characterized by acute poverty and underdevelopment. In the long-term, the generation of wealth in minority markets is more heavily dependent on an entrepreneur's ability to mobilize capital.

The experiences of the black entrepreneurs who were interviewed on the South Side of Chicago illustrate these points. All of the black entrepreneurs attempted to mobilize ethnic resources in the black community in response to the market and capital constraint they faced. However, this was not a strategy for business growth. Rather, it was an adaptation to economic scarcity, aimed at maintaining control of their businesses and the economic niche in which they are embedded. Although the economic detour strategy allowed these black entrepreneurs to remain in business, the growth potential of their businesses was truncated by the inability to marshal capital. This was an outgrowth of racial discrimination in mainstream society, which functioned to maintain the internal colonial conditions that produce minority markets.

AN AGENDA INFORMED BY INTERNAL COLONIALISM

The issues that black and Korean entrepreneurs face in the ethnic beauty aids industry highlight the constraints inherent to doing business in minority markets. As a result, this study has identified several characteristics of internal colonialism which should be addressed in public discourse. Three of the mechanisms that produce internal colonial conditions in minority markets stand out. First, racial discrimination and stereotyping in mainstream society stigmatize minority communities. This affects blacks and middleman minorities, and it creates a rationale for the exploitation and scapegoating of those groups. Second, many of the consumers in minority markets are economically dependent on the public sector. This economic dependence limits their ability to accumulate wealth and it makes minority markets highly responsive to shifts in public policy, particularly in the area of social welfare spending. Third, the reluctance of mainstream institutions to loan money to minority entrepreneurs and invest in minority markets results in underdevelopment. To a large extent, this reluctance grows out of various forms of racial discrimination in society.

Because of the link between racial discrimination and underdevelopment, pragmatic steps should be taken to curb racism in mainstream society. Of course, public education is one aspect of an agenda aimed at reducing racism and anti-middleman ideologies in mainstream society. However, more immediate steps are required to address the economic effects of racial discrimination in minority markets. One particular finding of this study should be taken into consideration when formulating an agenda for economic development in minority markets. This involves the relationship between the welfare economy and minority markets. The examination of black and middleman businesses revealed that the economy on the South Side of Chicago was strongly influenced by social welfare spending. Given this relationship, public resources should focus on expanding the role of the social welfare system to promote wealth creation for the poor and economic development in disadvantaged communities. Such an agenda would help remedy the current deficiencies in the social welfare system which promote economic dependence, rather than economic empowerment at the individual and community levels. In addition, focusing on wealth creation and economic development strengthens many current recommendations for welfare reform that call for the creation of jobs, but lack an investment component that targets the poor.

Using the social welfare system to create incentives for the poor to invest has the dual advantage of addressing the issue of undercapitalization in minority markets, which is at the root of cyclical poverty. To accomplish this task, the social welfare system must be linked to economic development in disadvantaged communities. In many respects, policy recommendations for this type of welfare reform are discussed by Oliver and Shapiro.[14] They recommend the development of a welfare system that assists the poor in wealth creation. According to their proposal, welfare recipients would be allowed to deposit money in "broad-based asset accounts" which could be drawn from for specified purposes, such as "education, home ownership, start-up capital for businesses, self-employment, and funds for retirement."[15] Individual deposits in such accounts would be matched by federal grants on a sliding scale for poor individuals.[16] This strategy allows the poor to save while on welfare, and later use those savings to become economically independent.

In order to link such an asset based strategy more closely to minority markets, I would further specify that banks in disadvantaged communities should be targeted for such investments. For instance, banks that are subsidiaries of community development corporations that focus on economic development in poor communities should be certified as depositories for asset accounts which are matched by federal grants. For instance, the South Shore Bank in Chicago would be an example of a bank with such an affiliation.[17] In this way, incentives would be created for the poor to save, and those savings would be held in banks that are the most likely to make capital accessible to borrowers in minority markets. Over time, this type of investment based assistance would reduce the level of economic dependence in minority markets, at both the individual and community levels.

The use of investment based assistance to promote economic empowerment among the poor and economic development in minority markets would give disenfranchised groups a stake in their communities, and fill an important social control function. In part, this is because the investments of the poor would be tied to social and economic stability in minority markets. In addition, the development of a welfare system that assists the poor in wealth creation would be the first step toward accomplishing the goals of a broader agenda aimed at eliminating racial discrimination in society. This would be the case, since economic empowerment would assist the poor in circumventing current racial barriers to capital accumulation. However, in order to address the issue of internal colonialism, further dialogue is needed in mainstream society concerning the effects of racism on minority groups, since ultimately minority group members must have full access to opportunities in the mainstream economy. Unless this obstacle is overcome, minority markets will continue to be separate from the mainstream economy.

NOTES

[1] Manning Marable, *How Capitalism Underdeveloped Black America*, (Boston: South End Press, 1983):158-163.

[2] Ibid, 164.

[3] Hubert Blalock, *Toward a Theory of Minority-Group Relations*, (New York: Capricorn Books, 1967), 79-84; Walter P.Zenner, *Minorities in the Middle, A Cross-Cultural Text*, (Albany: State University of New York Press, 1991).

[4] Paul C. P. Siu, "The Sojourner." *The American Journal of Sociology,* LVIII, 1952: 33-44; Rose Hume Lee, *The Chinese in the United States of America,* (Oxford: Oxford University Press, 1960), 69-85; Edna Bonacich, "A Theory of Middleman Minorities," *American Sociological Review,* 38 (October 1973): 583-594; Light, Ivan. and Edna Bonacich,*Immigrant Entrepreneurs, Koreans in Los Angeles, 1965-1982,* (Berkeley: University of California Press, 1988); Marlene Sway, *Familiar Strangers, Gypsy Life*

in America, (Champaign: University of Illinois Press, 1988), 21-23 and 125-127.

⁵ Ivan Light, *Ethnic Enterprise in America, Business and Welfare Among Chinese, Japanese, and Blacks,* (Berkeley: University of California Press, 1972); Ivan Light, "Asian Enterprise in America, Chinese, Japanese, and Koreans in Small Business," in Scott Cummings, ed. *Self-Help in Urban America, Patterns of Minority Business Enterprise,* (Port Washington: National University Publications, 1980): 33-57.

⁶ Hyun Sook Kim and Pyong Gap Min, "The Post-1965 Korean Immigrants: Their Characteristics and Settlement Patterns," *Korea Journal of Population and Development,* 21.2 (December 1992): 132-143.

⁷ Joe R. Feagin and Melvin P. Sikes, *Living With Racism, The Black Middle-Class Experience,* (Boston: Beacon Press, 1994): 212-219.

⁸ Ibid, 187-222.

⁹ Ibid, 187-222.

¹⁰ Melvin L. Oliver and Thomas M. Shapiro, *Black Wealth / White Wealth, A New Perspective on Racial Inequality,* (New York, Routledge, 1995): 182.

¹¹Ibid, 5.

¹² John Sibley Butler, *Entrepreneurship and Self-Help Among Black Americans, A Reconsideration of Race and Economics,* (Albany: State University of New York Press, 1991): 197-226.

¹³ M.S. Stuart, *An Economic Detour, A History of Insurance in the Lives of American Negroes,* (College Park: McGrath Publishing Company, 1969); John Sibley Butler, *Entrepreneurship and Self-Help Among Black Americans, A Reconsideration of Race and Economics,* (Albany: State University of New York Press, 1991).

¹⁴ Melvin L. Oliver and Thomas M. Shapiro, *Black Wealth/White Wealth, A New Perspective on Racial Inequality,* (New York, Routledge, 1995).

¹⁵ Ibid, 180.

¹⁶ Ibid, 180.

¹⁷ Richard P. Taub, *Community Capitalism, The South Shore Bank's Strategy for Neighborhood Revitalization,* (Boston: Harvard Business School Press, 1994).

APPENDIX A

INTERVIEW GUIDE FOR BEAUTY AIDS MERCHANTS

This interview is part of my research on minority business relations in Chicago. In essence, I study the ties that exist between large and small minority-owned businesses. Your store was identified using the local telephone directory, local business directories, and with the help of local business organizations. Your store was included in a sample of small businesses to be interviewed for this research. Your name and your store's name will be kept confidential. I am legally and professionally obligated to protect your identity and the identity of your business. This interview will last approximately 20 minutes. In it, I will ask you a series of questions about running a business like yours. All of the responses that you give in this interview are voluntary. I will tape record the interview to ensure accuracy, and when this study is complete the tape will be destroyed. You may refuse to answer any question, or stop the interview at any time.

1). There are a lot of reasons that people give for opening there own business. When did you start thinking about opening your own Business?

PROBES:

a. Tell me a little bit about the history of this business.

b. How did you raise money to start this business?

c. How easy was it to purchase this business?

d. How did you find out this building was available for purchase/lease?.

e. Have you always sold the same products?

2).The time and energy that a person puts into a business can be seen as an investment. In what ways do you see this business as a stepping stone to bigger and better things?

PROBES:

a. Do you plan to expand this store?

b. Do you plan to open another store?

c. Do you plan to open another kind of business?

3).One thing I'm very interested in is how small businesses get the products they sell. Tell me about the types of businesses that you deal with to get your supplies.

PROBES:

a. What types of things do you get from distributors?

b. Who are the distributors? Are they Korean, black, white?

c. A number of the companies that distribute the products you sell are Korean-owned. How does doing business with these distributors compare to doing business with others?

d. What types of things do you get from manufacturers?

e. Who are the manufacturers? Are they Korean, black, white?

f. A number of the companies that manufacture the products you sell are black-owned. How does doing business with these manufacturers compare to doing business with others?

g. What proportion of the products you sell are made by black-owned companies?

h. When you buy products how often is it based on credit or strictly for cash? Why? What proportion?

4).There are a lot of other businesses like yours in Chicago. Tell me about the businesses you compete with.

PROBES:

a. How do you compete with other businesses on this street?

b. How does your business compete with the big chains?

c. A lot of Koreans have been successful in this type of business. What are some of the reasons that Koreans have done well in this type of business?

d. There are some/other black-owned businesses like yours. How much do black businesses compete with your store?

e. How has competition changed in the last few years?

5).One ways that people can stay on top of what's going on in the business world is to join a business association. Tell me about some of the organizations you belong to that help you meet people in you line of work.

PROBES:

a. What local trade associations do you belong to?

b. How do you meet people who can connect you with the companies that manufacture the products you sell?

c. What types of things does the city government do for this business?

6). Finding good employees is a challenge that all businesses face. Tell me a little bit about the people who work here.
PROBES:

a. How many people work here?

b. How do you find your employees?

c. Do you have family members working in your business? How many?

7). I'm interested in what your workload is like. What things take up most of your time?

PROBES:

a. How much time do you spend at the store?

8). Tell me about some of the ways you advertise. How do people find out about your   business?

PROBES:

a. How do distributors/manufacturers find out that your business exists?

b. How much of your business comes from word of mouth?

9). Every business has a different mix of customers. Who are your customers?

PROBES:

a. What percent of your customers live in this neighborhood?

b. On average, how would you describe your customers income level? Are they poor, just getting bye, middle class, pretty well off?

10). The way a business handles its customer's complaints can make a big difference. Tell me about some of the things your customers complain about.

>PROBES:
>
>a. Have you ever contacted a distributor or a manufacturer about a customers complaint? Why? What happened?
>
>b. Do you think distributors and manufacturers treat you differently because you are Korean/black? Why or why not?
>
>c. Do you think that your customers treat you differently because you are   Korean/black? Why or why not?

11). How old are you?

12). Tell me about your educational background.

>PROBES:
>a. Did you major in business?
>
>b. Did you attend a college in the United States?
>
>c. Did you attend a college in Illinois?

13). How many years have you lived in Chicago?

14). Were you born in the United States/Illinois?

APPENDIX B

BEAUTY AIDS MERCHANT SURVEY

This survey is part of my research on minority business relations in Chicago. In essence, I study the ties that exist between large and small minority-owned businesses. Your store was identified using the local telephone directory, local business directories, and with the help of local business organizations. Your store was included in a sample of small businesses to be surveyed for this research. In order for this research to be correct scientifically it is necessary for me to attempt to gather information from all of the businesses in the sample. Your name and your store's name will be kept confidential. I am legally and professionally obligated to protect your identity and the identity of your business. There is a series of multiple choice questions in this survey about the business you run, it will take about 5 minutes to complete. All of the responses that you give in this survey are voluntary. You may refuse to answer any question. I have enclosed an envelope for you to return this survey in. If you have any questions about this survey or how any of the information that is gathered will be used contact me at (XXX)XXX-XXXX.

Please answer the following questions in the space provided below.

1) How long has this business been opened?

        a. less than 1 year
        b. 1 - 3 years
        c. 4 - 6 years
        d. 7 or more years

2) Where do you typically get information about what's going on in your line of work? (circle all that apply)

        a. business organizations like the chamber of commerce
        b. high school or college alumni groups
        c. church groups
        d. distributors
        e. manufacturers
        f. sales representatives

g. publications like Beauty Times
h. other (please specify) _____

3) What types of business plans do you have for the future? (circle all that apply)

a. plans to expand this store
b. plans to open another store like this one
c. plans to open some other type of business
d. other (please specify) _____

4) How many hours do you work in a typical week?

a. less than 40 hours
b. 41 - 50 hours
c. 51 - 60 hours
d. 61 - 70 hours
e. more than 70 hours

5) How many people work here?

a. less than 5 people
b. 5 - 10 people
c. 11 - 15 people
d. 16 or more people

6) How many of your relatives work for this business?

a. 1 - 5 relatives
b. 6 - 10 relatives
c. 11 or more relatives
d. I have no relatives working for this business

7) Do your African-American employees live in the same neighborhood that this business is located in?

a. yes
b. no
c. This business has no African-American employees

8) How would you describe the majority of your customers?

    a. poor
    b. just getting by
    c. middle class
    d. pretty well off

9) How do you typically advertise this business to your customers? (circle all that apply)

    a. newspaper
    b. radio
    c. flyers
    d. through the mail
    e. other (please specify) _____

10) Have you ever contacted a distributor or a manufacturer about a customer's complaint?

    a. yes
    b. no

If you did, what happened:

11) Who do you purchase the majority of your supplies from?

    a. directly from a manufacturer
    b. through a distributor
    c. about half from a manufacturer and half from a dis tributor
    d. other (please specify) _____

12) What types of things do you prefer to buy from a distributor, and what types of things do you prefer to buy from a manufacturer?

    prefer to buy from a distributor:

    prefer to buy from a manufacturer:

13) Most of the distributors I deal with are:

      a. African-American
      b. Caucasian
      c. Korean
      d. other (please specify)_____

14) A number of the distributors in the ethnic beauty aids industry are Korean. On the whole, Korean distributors are:

      a. less competitive than other distributors
      b. equally as competitive as other distributors
      c. more competitive than other distributors
      d. other (please specify) _____

15) Most of the manufacturers I deal with are:

      a. African-American
      b. Caucasian
      c. Korean
      d. other (please specify)_____

16) A number of the companies that manufacture the products that this business sells are owned by African-Americans. Doing business with these manufacturers is:

      a. easier than doing business with other manufacturers
      b. about the same as doing business with other manufacturers
      c. more difficult than doing business with other manufacturers
      d. I do not do business directly with African-American manufacturers
      e. other (please specify) _____

17) Has there ever been a time when you felt your business was discriminated against:
(circle all that apply)

      a. by a manufacturer

b. by a distributor
c. by a sales representative
d. by a customer
e. by the media
f. by the police
g. other (please specify)_____
h. this business has never been discriminated against

18)   How old are you?_____

19) What is your Gender?

a. male
b. female

20) Which of the following best describes you educational background:

a. I have not completed high school
b. I have a high school degree, or equivalent
c. I have a two year associates degree
d. I have a bachelors degree
e. I have a masters degree
f. other (please specify)_____

21) How long have you lived in the Chicago area?_____

22) Were you born in the United States?

a. yes
b. no

23) Were you born in Illinois?

a. yes
b. no

APPENDIX C

INTERVIEW GUIDE FOR BEAUTY AIDS DISTRIBUTORS

This interview is part of my research on minority business relations in Chicago. In essence, I study the ties that exist between large and small minority-owned businesses. Your business was identified using the local telephone directory, local business directories, and with the help of local business organizations. Your business was included in a sample of businesses to be interviewed for this research. Your name and the name of your business will be kept confidential. I am legally and professionally obligated to protect your identity and the identity of your business. This interview will last approximately 20 minutes. In it, I will ask you a series of questions about running a business like yours. All of the responses that you give in this interview are voluntary. I will tape record the interview to ensure accuracy, and when this study is complete the tape will be destroyed. You may refuse to answer any question, or stop the interview at any time.

1).There are a lot of reasons that people give for opening there own business. When did you start thinking about opening your own Business?

    PROBES:

      a. Tell me a little about the history of this business.

      b. How did you raise money to start this business?

      c. How easy was it to purchase for this business?

      d. How did you find out this building was available for purchase/lease?

      e. Were you in retailing in the past? What about now?

2). The time and energy that a person puts into a business can be seen as an investment. In what ways do you see this business as a stepping stone to bigger and better things?

PROBES:

a. Do you plan to expand this business?

b. Do you plan to open another business? (in this community or elsewhere)

c. Do you plan to open another kind of business?

3). I'm very interested in learning about the companies you purchase products from. Tell me about the manufacturers you deal with.

PROBES:

a. How did you find the manufacturers?

b. Have you always dealt with the same companies?

c. A number of the companies that manufacture the products you sell are black owned. How does doing business with these manufacturers compare to doing busines with others?

d. What proportion of the products that you sell come from black owned companies?

c. Do you usually buy products on credit or for cash?

4). I'm very interested in learning about the stores you sell products to. Tell me about the retailers you deal with.

PROBES:

a. How did you find retailers?

b. A number of the small businesses that sell beauty supplies are Korean owned. How does doing business with these retailers compare to doing business withother retailers?

c. Some of the small businesses that sell beauty supplies are Black owned. How does doing business with these retailers compare to doing business with other retailers?

d. Do they usually buy products on credit or for cash? Why, what's the breakdown?

e. How do you advertise?

5). There are a lot of other businesses like yours in Chicago. Tell me about the businesses you compete with.

PROBES:

a. A lot of Koreans have been successful in this type of business. What are some of the reasons that Koreans have done well in this type of business?

b. What types of things make it more difficult for Koreans to run a business like this?

c. How has competition in this industry changed over the last few years?

6). One ways that people can stay on top of what's going on in the business world is to join a business association. Tell me about some of the organizations you belong to that help you meet people in you line of work.

PROBES:

a. What local trade associations do you belong to?

b. How do you meet people who can connect you with the companies that manufacture the products you sell?

   c. What types of things does the city government do for
   this business?

7).Finding good employees is a challenge that all businesses face.
Tell me a little bit about the people who work here.

   PROBES:

   a. How many people work here?

   b. How do you find your employees?

   c. Do you have family members working in your business?
   How many?

   d. What is the racial breakdown of you workforce? How
   many Koreans, whites, blacks?

8).I'm interested in what your workload is like. What things take
up the bulk of your time?

   PROBES:

   a. How much time do you spend on the job (hours, days
   a week)?

9).How old are you?

10).Tell me about your educational background.

   PROBES:

   a. Did you major in business, or do you have business
   training?

   b. Did you attend a college in the United States/Illinois?

11).How long have you lived in Chicago?

12).Were you born in the United States/Illinois?

APPENDIX D

BEAUTY AIDS DISTRIBUTOR SURVEY

This survey is part of my research on minority business relations in Chicago. In essence, I study the ties that exist between large and small minority-owned businesses. Your business was identified using the local telephone directory, local business directories, and with the help of local business organizations. Your business was included in a sample of businesses to be surveyed for this research. In order for this research to be correct scientifically it is necessary for me to attempt to gather information from all of the businesses in the sample. Your name and the name of your business will be kept confidential. I am legally and professionally obligated to protect your identity and the identity of your business. There is a series of multiple choice questions in this survey about the business you run, it will take about 5 minutes to complete. All of the responses that you give in this survey are voluntary. You may refuse to answer any question. I have enclosed an envelope for you to return this survey in. If you have any questions about this survey or how any of the information that is gathered will be used contact me at (XXX)XXX-XXXX.

Please answer the following questions in the space provided below.

1) How long has this business been opened?

      a. less than 1 year
      b. 1 - 3 years
      c. 4 - 6 years
      d. 7 or more years

2) Where do you typically get information about what's going on in your line of work? (circle all that apply)

      a. business organizations like the chamber of commerce
      b. high school or college alumni groups
      c. church groups
      d. retailers
      e. manufacturers

f. sales representatives
g. publications like Beauty Times
h. other (please specify) _____

3) What types of business plans do you have for the future? (circle all that apply)

a. plans to expand this business
b. plans to open another business like this one
c. plans to open some other type of business
d. other (please specify) _____

4) How many hours do you work in a typical week?

a. less than 40 hours
b. 41 - 50 hours
c. 51 - 60 hours
d. 61 - 70 hours
e. more than 70 hours

5) How many people work here?

a. less than 5 people
b. 5 - 10 people
c. 11 - 15 people
d. 16 or more people

6) How many of your relatives work for this business?

a. 1 - 5 relatives
b. 6 - 10 relatives
c. 11 or more relatives
d. I have no relatives working for this business

7) Do your African-American employees live in the same neighborhood that this business is located in?

a. yes
b. no
c. This business has no African-American employees

8) The majority of the manufacturers I deal with are:

    a. African-American
    b. Caucasian
    c. Korean
    d. other (please specify)_____

9) The majority of the retailers I deal with are:

    a. African-American
    b. Caucasian
    c. Korean
    d. other (please specify)_____

10) A number of the companies that manufacture the products that this business sells are owned by African-Americans. Doing business with these manufacturers is:

    a. easier than doing business with other manufacturers
    b. about the same as doing business with other manufacturers
    c. more difficult than doing business with other manufacturers
    d. I do not do business directly with African-American manufacturers
    e. other (please specify) _____

11) A number of the retailers that sell beauty supplies are Korean. Doing business with these retailers is:
    a. easier than doing business with other retailers
    b. about the same as doing business with other retailers
    c. more difficult than doing business with other retailers
    d. I do not do business directly with Korean retailers
    e. other (please specify) _____

12) Some of the retailers that sell beauty supplies are black. Doing business with these retailers is:

    a. easier than doing business with other retailers
    b. about the same as doing business with other retailers

c. more difficult than doing business with other retailers
d. I do not do business directly with black retailers
e. other (please specify) _____

13) Has there ever been a time when you felt your business was discriminated against:
    (circle all that apply)

      a. by a manufacturer
      b. by a retailer
      c. by a sales representative
      d. by a customer
      e. by the media
      f. by the police
      g. other (please specify)_____
      h. this business has never been discriminated against

If you feel that your business has been discriminated against, please describe what happened:

14) How old are you?

15) What is your Gender?

      a. male
      b. female

16) Which of the following best describes you educational background:

      a. I have not completed high school
      b. I have a high school degree, or equivalent
      c. I have a two year associates degree
      d. I have a bachelors degree
      e. I have a masters degree
      f. other (please specify)_____

17) How long have you lived in the Chicago area?_____

18) Were you born in the United States?

      a. yes
      b. no

APPENDIX E

INTERVIEW GUIDE FOR BEAUTY AIDS MANUFACTURER

This interview is part of my research on minority-business relations in Chicago. In essence, I study the ties that exist between large and small minority owned businesses. Your company was identified using the local telephone directory, the Chicago Black pages, and information from local business organizations. Your name and your company's name will be kept confidential. This interview will last approximately 20 minutes. In it, I will ask you a series of questions about running a business like yours. All of the responses that you give in this interview are voluntary. I will be tape recording the interview to ensure accuracy, and when this study is complete the tape will be destroyed. You may refuse to answer any question, or stop the interview at any time.

1). There are a lot of reasons that people give for starting their own company. When did you begin to think about starting this company?

   PROBES:

   a. How long have you had this business?

   b. Have you ever operated a distributorship or a retail establishment in this industry?

   c. How did you raise money to start this company?

   d. How easy was it to get a lease or purchase the commercial property for this business?

   e. Have you always sold the same products?

2).The time and energy that a person puts into a business can be seen as an investment. In what ways do you see this company as a stepping stone to bigger and better things?

> PROBES:
>
> a. Do you plan to introduce a new product line?
>
> b. Do you plan to expand this company?
>
> c. Do you plan to relocate this company?
>
> d. Do you plan to open another kind of business?

3).One thing I'm very interested in knowing more about is how a company like yours gets its products from the factory to local retailers. Tell me about the types of businesses you use to distribute your products.

> PROBES:
>
> a. What proportion of your sales come from: in-house accounts?
> b. Tell me about the distributors/wholesalers who handle your products. What proportion of them are black, Korean, white?
>
> c. How has the composition of distributors changed in the last few years?
>
> d. How does your company deal with distributors who are Korean/black?
>
> e. Tell me about the difference between salon and retail products? Who handles the distribution and sales of salon and retail products? Why?
>
> f. When you make sales are they typically on a credit or cash basis. Why?

4). There are a lot of other businesses like yours in Chicago. Tell me about the companies that you compete with in this industry.

   PROBES:

   a. Where does your main competition come from?

   b. A lot of your products are marketed to African-Americans. In what ways are black manufacturers more competitive than white manufacturers in this industry? In what ways are they less competitive?

   c. How has your competition changed over time?

5).There are a few different types of retailers that sell your products. Tell me a little about the stores where your products are sold.

   PROBES:

   a. What proportion of the retailers are big chains, small independent stores?

   b. What proportion of the retailers are black, Korean, white?

   c. There are a lot of Korean distributors and retailers in this industry. Why do you think they've been successful?

   d. There are a some black distributors and retailers in this industry. How competitive do you think they are in this industry?

   e. In what ways are black salons important to this industry?

   f. How has the composition of the retailers changed in the last few years?

6).One way that people can stay on top of what's going on in their industry is to join a business association. Tell me about some of the organizations you belong to.

PROBES:

a. What local trade associations do you belong to?

b. What types of things does the city government do for this business?

c. Where do you get information that can help your company?

7).Tell me a little bit about the people who work here.

PROBES:

a. How many people work here?

b. How do you find your employees?

c. Do you ever hire people who have worked in distribution or retailing in another part of this industry? Why or why not?

d. Do you have family members working in your company?

8).I'm interested in what your workload is like. What things take up the bulk of your time?

PROBES:

a. How much time do you spend at the office?

b. How much of your businesses time is spent dealing with production, distribution, marketing, retailing, personnel issues, customer relations?

    c. In what ways has your customer base changed over time?

9).Tell me about some of the ways you advertise. How do people find out about your business?

    PROBES:

    a. How do distributors find out about your products?

    b. How do retailers find out about your products?

    c. Where do you advertise to consumers?

10). Every business has a different mix of customers. Who are your core customers?

    PROBES:

    a. What kinds of market research do you do to identify your customer base?

    b. Do you have separate product lines that you target at different income and demographic groups?

    c. What percent of your sales do your core customers account for?

    d. On average, what income group would you put your core customers in? Are they poor, just getting bye, middle class, or pretty well off?

11). The quality of the feedback a company gets from consumers can make a big difference. Tell me about some of the ways you get feedback on your products.

    PROBES:

    a. How do you gather information from distributors about your products?

    b. How do you gather information from retailers about your products?

    c. How do you gather information from consumers about your products?

12).Most large companies try to try to establish good relations with the communities they do business in. What types of community work is your company involved in?

    PROBES:

    a. Tell me about a particular instance where your company made a difference in a community you do business in?

    b. When your company gets involved in a community, what types of other businesses and voluntary organizations do you join forces with?

    c. Do you feel that there's more pressure placed on your company to be involved in the black community because it's a black owned company?

13).How old are you?

14).Tell me about you educational background:

    PROBES:

    a. Did you major in business?

    b. Did you attend a historically black university?

    c. Did you attend college in Illinois?

15).How long have you lived in Chicago?

16).Were you born in Illinois?

APPENDIX F

BEAUTY AIDS MANUFACTURER SURVEY

This survey is part of my research on minority business relations in Chicago. In essence, I study the ties that exist between large and small minority-owned businesses. Your company was identified using the local telephone directory, the Chicago Black Pages, and information from local business organizations. Your Company was included in a sample of businesses to be surveyed for this research. In order for this research to be correct scientifically it is necessary for me to attempt to gather information from all of the businesses identified in my sample. Your name and your company's name will be kept confidential. I am legally and professionally obligated to protect your identity and the identity of your business. There is a series of multiple choice questions in this survey about your company, it will take about 5 minutes to complete. All of the responses that you give in this survey are voluntary. You may refuse to answer any question. I have enclosed an envelope for you to return this survey in. If you have any questions about this survey or how any of the information that is gathered will be used contact me at (XXX)XXX-XXXX.

Please answer the following questions in the space provided below.

1) How long has your company been operating?

       a. less than 5 years
       b. 6 - 10 years
       c. 11 - 15 years
       d. 15 or more years

2) Where do you typically get information about what's going on in your industry? (circle all that apply)

       a. business organizations like the chamber of commerce
       b. high school or college alumni groups
       c. church groups
       d. distributors
       e. retailers

    f. sales representatives or brokers
    g. publications like Beauty Times
    h. other (please specify) _____

3) What types of business plans do you have for the future? (circle all that apply)

    a. plans to expand this company
    b. plans to introduce a new product line
    c. plans to open some other type of business
    d. other (please specify) _____

4) How many hours do you work in a typical week?

    a. less than 40 hours
    b. 41 - 50 hours
    c. 51 - 60 hours
    d. 61 - 70 hours
    e. more than 70 hours

5) How many people work for your company?

    a. less than 49 people
    b. 50 - 99 people
    c. 100 - 149 people
    d. 150 or more people

6) How many of your family members work for this company?

    a. 1 - 5 relatives
    b. 6 - 10 relatives
    c. 11 or more relatives
    d. I have no family members working for this business

7) Are the majority of your employees natives of Chicago?

    a. yes
    b. no

8) How would you describe the majority of the consumers who buy the products your company manufactures?

    a. poor
    b. just getting by
    c. middle class
    d. pretty well off

9) How do you typically advertise your company's products to customers?(circle all that apply)

    a. newspaper
    b. radio
    c. magazines
    d. through the mail
    e. other (please specify) _____

10) How do consumers typically contact this company when they have a problem, or question, about a product? (circle all that apply)

    a. through a distributor
    b. through a retailer
    c. by writing a letter
    d. by using an 800 number
    e. other (please specify) _____

11) Who do you sell the majority of your products to?

    a. directly to retailers
    b. to distributors
    c. about half directly to retailers and half to distributors
    d. other (please specify) _____

12) The majority of the distributors I deal with are:

    a. African-American
    b. Caucasian
    c. Korean
    d. other (please specify)_____

13) A number of the distributors that sell the products that this company manufactures are owned by Koreans. Doing business with these distributors is:

    a. easier than doing business with other distributors
    b. about the same as doing business with other distributors
    c. more difficult than doing business with other distributors
    d. This company does not do business directly with Korean distributors
    e. other (please specify) _____

14) A number of the distributors that sell the products that this company manufactures are owned by African-Americans. Doing business with these distributors is:

    a. easier than doing business with other distributors
    b. about the same as doing business with other distributors
    c. more difficult than doing business with other distributors
    d. This company does not do business directly with African-American distributors
    e. other (please specify) _____

15) The majority of the retailers I deal with are:

    a. African-American
    b. Caucasian
    c. Korean
    d. other (please specify)_____

16) A number of the retailers that sell the products that this company manufactures are owned by Koreans. Doing business with these retailers is:

    a. easier than doing business with other retailers
    b. about the same as doing business with other retailers
    c. more difficult than doing business with other retailers
    d. This company does not do business directly with Korean retailers
    e. other (please specify) _____

17) A number of the retailers that sell the products that this company manufactures are owned by African-Americans. Doing business with these retailers is:
  a. easier than doing business with other retailers
  b. about the same as doing business with other retailers
  c. more difficult than doing business with other retailers
  d. This company does not do business directly with African-American retailers
  e. other (please specify) _____

18) A number of the companies that manufacture products like the ones that this business sells are owned by African-Americans. The majority of the black manufacturers in this industry are:

  a. less competitive with this company than other manufacturers
  b. equally as competitive with this company as other manufacturers
  c. more competitive with this company than other manufacturers
  d. I do not compete directly with African-American manufacturers
  e. other (please specify) _____

19) Has there ever been a time when you felt your business was discriminated against: (circle all that apply)

  a. by a retailer
  b. by a distributor
  c. by a marketing representative
  d. by a customer
  e. by the media
  f. by the city
  g. other (please specify)_____
  h. this business has never been discriminated against

20) How old are you?_____

21) What is your gender?

  a. male
  b. female

22) Which of the following best describes you educational background:

        a. I have not completed high school
        b. I have a high school degree, or equivalent
        c. I have a two year associates degree
        d. I have a bachelors degree
        e. I have a masters degree
        f. other (please specify)_____

23) Did you attend a historically black college or university?

        a. yes
        b. no

24) How long have you lived in the Chicago Area?_____

25) Were you born in Illinois?

        a. yes
        b. no

Bibliography

"A Compulsive Buyer or a Master Builder." *Business Week*. (28 June 1993): 38.

"A Negro Businessman Speaks His Mind." *U.S. News & World Reports*. (19 August 1963): 58.

Adams, Russell L. *Great Negroes Past and Present* . Chicago: Afro-Am Publishing Company, 1964.

"Aiming for $100-Million Sales." *Fortune*, (September 1957): 76.

Aldrich, Howard. and Albert J. Reiss, Jr. "The Effect of Civil Disorders on Small Business in the Inner City."*Journal of Social Issues*. 26.1 (1970): 187-206.

"Anthony Overton, Known As the 'Merchant Prince' of His Race, Heads the Overton Hygienic Manufacturing Company, Rated by Bradstreet and Dun At a Million Dollars." *Pittsburgh Courier* . (10 August 1929).

"Anthony Overton, Obit."*Chicago Tribune*. (4 July 1946).

Averitt, Robert T. *The Dual Economy, The Dynamics of American Industry Structure*. New York: Norton, 1968.

Bates, Timothy. *Banking on Black Enterprise, The Potential of Emerging Firms for Revitalizing Urban Economies*. Washington D.C.: Joint Center for Political and Economic Studies, 1993.

_____. "An Analysis of Korean-Immigrant-owned Small-Business Start-ups with   Comparisons to African-American-and-Nonminority-Owned Firms." *Urban Affairs Quarterly* . 30.2 (1994): 227-248.

Berkow, Ira. *Maxwell Street, Survival in a Bazaar*. New York: Doubleday and Company, Inc., 1977.

Blalock, Hubert. *Toward a Theory of Minority-Group Relations.* New York: Capricorn Books, 1967.

Blauner, Robert. *Racial Oppression in America.* New York: Harper and Row, 1972.

Bluestone, Barry and Bennett Harrison. *The Deindustrialization of America, Plant Closing,   Community Abandonment, and the Dismantling of Basic Industry.* New York: Basic Books, 1982.

_____.*The Great U-Turn, Corporate Restructuring and   the Polarizing of America.* New York: Basic Books, 1988.

Bonacich, Edna. "A Theory of Middleman Minorities." *American Sociological Review.* 38 (1973): 583- 594.

Bonacich, Edna and John Modell. *The Economic Basis of Ethnic Solidarity, Small Business in the Japanese American Community.* Berkeley: University of California Press, 1980.

Boyd, Robert L."Inequality in the earnings of Self-Employed African and Asian Americans."*Sociological Perspectives.* 34.4 (1991): 447-472.

"Brawl in the Family at Johnson Products." *Business Week.* (23 March 1992): 34.

Breton, Raymond. "Institutional Completeness of Ethnic Communities and the Personal   Relations of Immigrants." *The American Journal of Sociology.* 70 (1964): 193-205.

"Business in Bronzeville."*Time.* (18 April 1938): 70.

Butler, John Sibley. *Entrepreneurship and Self-Help Among Black Americans, A   Reconsideration of Race and Economics.* Albany: State University of New York Press, 1991.

"C.A. Barnett,77, Founder of Negro Wire Service, Dies." *Chicago Sun-Times.* (3 August 1967): 88.

"Charles D. Murray, Obit." *Chicago Tribune.* (26 July 1955).

Cheng, Lucie and Yen Espiritu. "Korean Businesses in Black and Hispanic Neighborhoods, A Study of Intergroup Relations."*Sociological Perspectives.* 32.4 (1989): 521-534.

"Chicago Claims Supremacy." *Opportunity.* (March 1929): 92-93.

Chin, Ku-Sup, In-Jin Yoon and David Smith, "Immigrant Small Business and International Economic Linkage, A Case of the Korean Wig Business in Los Angeles, 1968-1977." *IMR.* 30.2 (1996): 485-510.

Cohen, Lizabeth. *Making a New Deal, Industrial Workers in Chicago, 1919-1939.* New York: Cambridge University Press, 1990.

Cummings, Scott. *Self-Help in Urban America, Patterns of Minority Business Enterprise.* Port Washington: National University Publications, 1980.

Drake, St. Clair and Horace R. Cayton. *Black Metropolis, A study of Negro Life in a Northern City.* Chicago: University of Chicago Press, 1993.

DuBois, W.E. Burghardt. *Atlanta University Publications, Volume 1.* Octagon Books, Inc.: New York, 1968.

Dudley's Haircare Fact Book. Greensboro: Dudley Products Inc. 1993.

Dunn, Seamus. *Managing Divided Cities.* London: Kent University Press, 1994.

Edwards, R.C., M. Reich and D.M. Gordon. *Labor Market Segmentation.* Lexington: Health, 1975.

Fanon, Frantz. *Black Skin, White Mask.* New York: Grove Weidenfeld, 1968.

Feagin, Joe R. and Melvin P. Sikes. *Living With Racism, The Black Middle-Class Experience.* Boston: Beacon Press, 1994): 212-219.

Flynn, James J. *Negroes of Achievement in Modern America.* New York: Dodd, Mead and Company, 1970.

Foley, Eugine P. "The Negro Businessman, In Search of a Tradition." *Daedalus.* 95 (Winter 1966): 107- 144.

Frazier, E. Franklin. *Black Bourgeoisie, The Rise of a New Middle Class in the United States.* New York: Collier Books, 1962.

Freeman, Laurie. "Big Marketers Move in on Ethnic Haircare." *Advertising Age.* (12 May 1986): 24.

"Fuller Brings It To Your Door, House-To-House Selling Pays Off." *The Chicago Defender.* (26 May 1951): 13.

Furman, Phyllis. "Ethnic Haircare Marketers Battle for Shares." *Advertising Age.* (2 March 1997): 52.

Glaser, Barney G. and Anselm L. Strauss. *The Discovery of Grounded Theory, Strategies for Qualitative Research.* New York: Aldine de Gruyter, 1967.

Harris, Abram L.*The Negro as Capitalist, A Study of Banking and Business Among American Negroes.* New York: Negro University Press, 1969.

Harrison, Bennett. *Education, Training and the Urban Ghetto.* Baltimore: Johns Hopkins   University Press, 1972.

Herrnstein, Richard J. and Charles Murray. *The Bell Curve: Intelligence and Class in American Life.* (New York: Free Press, 1994.

Holli, Melvin G. and Peter d'A. Jones. *Ethnic Chicago, A Multicultural Portrait.* Grand Rapids: William B. Eerdmans Publishing Company, 1995.

Ingham, John N. and Lynne B. Feldman. *African-American Business Leaders, A Bibliographical Dictionary.* Westport: Greenwood Press, 1994.

Jo, Moon H. "Korean Merchants in the Black Community, Prejudice Among the Victims of Prejudice."*Ethnic and Racial Studies.* 15.3 (1992): 395-411.

"Johnson Products Co. Regrouping After Family Row." *Black Enterprise.* (May 1992): 17.

"Johnson Products Tries to Catch a New Wave." *Business Week.* (27 August 1990): 56.

Joravsky, Ben "Koreans Sell, Blacks Buy, A Clash of Cultures at the 63rd Street Mall." *Reader.* February 13 (1987): 3.

Katz, Michael B. *The Undeserving Poor, From the War on Poverty to the War on Welfare.* New York, Pantheon Books, 1989.

Kim, Hyun Sook and Pyong Gap Min. "The Post-1965 Korean Immigrants: Their Characteristics and Settlement Patterns." *Korea Journal of Population and Development.* 21.2 (December 1992): 132-143.

Kim, Kwang Chung and Won Moo Hurh. "Ethnic Resources Utilization of Korean Immigrant Entrepreneurs in the Chicago Minority Area."*International Migration Review.* 19.1 (1985): 82- 109.

Kunjufu, Jawanza. *Black Economics, Solutions for Economic and Community Empowerment.* Chicago: African American Images, 1991.

Lee, Rose Hume. *The Chinese in the United States of America.* Oxford: Oxford University Press, 1960.

Lehrer, Brian. *The Korean Americans.* New York: Chelsea House Publishers, 1988.

Levine, Donald N. *Simmel, On Individuality and Social Forms.* Chicago: The University of Chicago Press, 1971.

Light, Ivan.*Ethnic Enterprise in America, Business and Welfare Among Chinese, Japanese, and Blacks.* Berkeley: University of California Press, 1972.

Light, Ivan and Edna Bonacich. *Immigrant Entrepreneurs, Koreans in Los Angeles,1965-1982.* Berkeley: University of California Press, 1988.

Lofland, John and Lyn H. Lofland. *Analyzing Social Settings, A Guide to Qualitative Observation and Analysis, Second Edition.* Belmont: Wadsworth Publishing Company, 1984.

Longworth, R. C. "One Street, Two Different Paths of Success." *Chicago Tribune.* (17 September 1992): Section 1.

"Making Black Beautiful."*Time.* (7 December 1970): 87.

Marable, Manning. *How Capitalism Underdeveloped Black America.* Boston: South End Press, 1983.

Meister, Richard J. *The Black Ghetto: Promised Land or Colony.* Lexington: D.C. Heath and Company, 1972.

Memmi, Albert. *The Colonizer and The Colonized.* New York: The Orion Press, 1965.

Min, Pyong Gap. *Ethnic Business Enterprise, Korean Small Business in Atlanta.* New York: Center for Migration Studies, 1988.

_____. *Caught in the Middle, Korean Communities in New York and Los Angeles.* Berkeley: University of California Press, 1996.

Min, P.G. and C. Jaret. "Ethnic Business Success: The Case of Korean Small Business in   Atlanta."*Sociology and Social Research.* 69 (1985): 412-435.

Min, Pyong Gap and Andrew Kolodny. "The Middleman Minority Characteristics of Korean Immigrants in the United States," *Korea Journal of Population and Development* . 23.2 (December 1994): 179-202.

Murray, Charles. *Losing Ground, American Social Policy 1950-1980.* New York: Basic Books, 1984.

Myrdal, Gunnar. *An American Dilemma, The Negro Problem and Modern Democracy.* New York: Harper and Row, 1962.

Oliver, Melvin L. and Thomas M. Shapiro, *Black Wealth, White Wealth, A New Perspective on Racial Inequality.* New York: Routledge, 1995.

Olzak, Susan and Joane Nagel, eds, *Competitive Ethnic Relations.* New York: Academic Press, Inc., 1986.

Park, Kyeyong. "The Re-Invention of Affirmative Action, Korean Immigrants' Changing Conceptions of African Americans and Latin Americans."*Urban Anthropology.* 24.1 (1995): 59- 92.

Patton, Michael Quinn. *Qualitative Evaluation and Research Methods, Second Edition.* Newbury Park: Sage Publications, 1990.

Peterson, Paul E. and Mark C. Rom. *Welfare Magnets, A New Case for a National Standard.* Washington D.C.: The Brookings Institute, 1990.

Pierce, Joseph.*Negro Business and Business Education, Their Present and Prospective Development.* Westport: Negro University Press, 1971.

Portes, Alejandro and L. Bach. *Latin Journey, Cuban and Mexican Immigrants in the United States.* Berkeley: University of California Press, 1985.

Rossi, Peter H., James D. Right and Andy B. Anderson. *Handbook of Survey Research*. New York, Academic Press, Inc., 1983.

"S.B. Fuller, A Man and His Products." *Black Enterprise*. 6.1 (August 1975): 46.

"S.B. Fuller, Black Entrepreneurs' Dean, Obit." *Chicago Tribune*. (26 October 1988).

"S.B. Fuller Dead, a Business Legend, Obit." *Chicago Defender*. (25 October 1988).

"Salvation of Negro in America Lies in Controlling Economy." *Pittsburgh Courier Centennial Edition*. (17 August 1963): 4-1.

Shibutani, Tamotsu and Kian M. Kwan. *Ethnic Stratification, A Comparative Approach*. New York: The Macmillan Company, 1965.

Siu, Paul C. P. "The Sojourner."*The American Journal of Sociology*. 58 (1952): 33-44.

Spear, Allan H. *Black Chicago, The Making of a Negro Ghetto, 1890-1920*. Chicago: The   University of Chicago Press, 1967.

Squires, Gregory D., Larry Bennett, Kathleen McCourt and Philip Nyden. *Chicago, Race, Class, and the Response to Urban Decline*. Philadelphia: Temple University Press, 1987.

Stanbeck, Thomas M. and Thierry J. Noyelle. *Cities in Transition: Changing Job Structures in Atlanta, Denver, Buffalo, Phoenix, Columbus (Ohio), Nashville, and Charlotte*. Totowa: Allanheld, Osmun And Co. Publishers, 1982.

Stewart, Ella. "Ethnic Cultural Diversity, An Interpretive Study of Cultural Differences and   Communication Styles Between Korean Merchants/Employees and Black Patrons in South Los Angeles." Masters Thesis. Los Angeles: California State University, Los Angeles, 1989.

Strauss, Anselm L. *Qualitative Analysis for Social Scientists*. New York: Cambridge University Press, 1987.

Strauss, Anselm and Juliet Corbin. *Basics of Qualitative Research, Grounded Theory Procedures and Techniques*. Newbury Park: Sage Publications, 1990.

Stuart, M.S.. *An Economic Detour, A History of Insurance in the Lives of American Negroes*. College Park, McGrath Publishing Company, 1969.

Sway, Marlene. *Familiar Strangers, Gypsy Life in America*. Champaign: University of Illinois Press, 1988.

Tabb, William K. *The Political Economy of the Black Ghetto*. New York: W.W. Norton and Company, 1970.

Taub, Richard P. *Community Capitalism, The South Shore Bank's Strategy for Neighborhood Revitalization.* Boston: Harvard Business School Press, 1994.

"The Dean of Black Entrepreneurs." *Chicago Tribune.* (9 June 1987): 3-1.

Vatter, Harold G. and Thomas Palm. *The Economics of Black America.* New York: Harcourt Brace Jovanovich, Inc., 1972.

Velez-Ibanez, Carlos G. *Bonds of Mutual Trust, The Cultural System of Rotating Credit   Associations Among Urban Mexicans and Chicanos.* New Brunswick: Rutgers University Press, 1983.

Waldinger, Roger. *Still The Promised City.* Cambridge: Harvard University Press, 1996.

Wang, Penelope and Maggie Malone. "Targeting Black Dollars, White-Owned Companies Muscle Minority Firms Out of the Hair-Care Market." *Newsweek.* (13 October 1986): 54.

Washington, Booker T. *The Negro in Business.* New York: AMS Press, 1971.

Weber, Max. *Ancient Judaism.* Glencoe: The Free Press, 1952.

_____.*Economy and Society.* Berkeley: University of California Press, 1978.

Whyte, William Foote. *Street Corner Society, The Social Structure of an Italian Slum, Fourth Edition.* Chicago: University of Chicago Press, 1993.

Wilson, William Julius. *The Truly Disadvantaged, The Inner City, The Underclass, and   Public Policy.* Chicago: University of Chicago Press, 1990.

_____.*When Work Disappears, The World of the New Urban Poor.* New   York: Alfred A. Knopf Publishing, 1996.

Wirth, Louis. *The Ghetto.* Chicago: University of Chicago Press, 1956.

Wong, Charles Choy. "Black and Chinese Grocery Stores in Los Angeles' Black Ghetto." *Urban Life.* 5.4 (January 1977): 460.

Yoon, In-Jin. "Self-Employment in Business, Chinese-, Japanese-, Korean-Americans, Blacks, and Whites." Dissertation. Chicago: University of Chicago, 1991.

_____. "The Changing Significance of Ethnic and Class Resources in Immigrant Businesses: The Case of Korean Immigrant Businesses in Chicago."*IMR.* 25.2 (1991): 303-331.

_____. "The Growth of Korean Immigrant Entrepreneurship in Chicago."*Ethnic and Racial Studies.* 18.2 (1995): 315-335.

Zenner, Walter P. *Minorities in the Middle, A Cross-Cultural Text.* Albany: State University of New York Press, 1991.

Zhou, Min. *Chinatown, The Socioeconomic Potential of an Urban Enclave.* Philadelphia: Temple University Press, 1992.

Index

Printed in the United States
by Baker & Taylor Publisher Services